Seagram's

BARTENDING
GUIDE

Seagram's

BARTENDING GUIDE

VIKING

VIKING
Published by the Penguin Group
Penguin Books USA Inc., 375 Hudson Street,
New York, New York 10014, U.S.A.
Penguin Books Ltd, 27 Wrights Lane,
London W8 5TZ, England
Penguin Books Australia Ltd, Ringwood,
Victoria, Australia
Penguin Books Canada Ltd, 10 Alcorn Avenue,
Toronto, Ontario, Canada M4V 3B2
Penguin Books (N.Z.) Ltd, 182–190 Wairau Road,
Auckland 10, New Zealand

Penguin Books Ltd, Registered Offices:
Harmondsworth, Middlesex, England

First published in 1995 by Viking Penguin,
a division of Penguin Books USA Inc.

3 5 7 9 10 8 6 4

Seagram's and Seagram Crest Design are trademarks of
The Seagram Group of Companies, used under license.

Page 259 constitutes an extension of this copyright page.

Grateful acknowledgment is made to Siebel/Mohr, Beisler & Associates,
Seagram Chateau & Estate Wines Company, Bronner Slosberg Humphrey, and The
House of Seagram for supplying photographs.

Specific acknowledgment is made to:
p.ii, Kan Photography, represented by Watson & Spierman, Inc; p.vi, Amy Reichman/Envision;
p.2, Amy Reichman/Envision; p.4, Kan Photography, represented by Watson & Spierman, Inc.;
p.24, Steven Needham/Envision; p.32, Chuck Kintzing Photography; p.44, Judd Piloss of
Photography, represented by Marge Casey; p.62, Chuck Kintzing Photography; p.88, Colin
Cooke Photography, represented by Robert Bacall; p.92, Mike Wilson Photography; p.123,
David Hecker Photography; p.126, Kan Photography, represented by Watson & Spierman Pro-
ductions, Inc.; p.137, Kan Photography, represented by Watson & Spierman Productions, Inc.;
p.156, Dennis Galante/Envision; p.167, David Hecker Photography; p.172, Ellen Schuster/The
Image Bank; p.185, Dennis Galante/Envision; p.188, Ted Chin Photography, represented by
Sue Miller Represents; p.200, Cuisine Productions/The Image Bank; p.225, Thom DeSanto
Photography, represented by Kevin R. Schochat.; p.222, Mike Wilson Photography; p.228,
David Hecker Photography; p.232, David Hecker Photography; p.235, Kan Photography,
represented by Watson & Spierman Productions, Inc.; p.244, Mike Wilson Photography

LIBRARY OF CONGRESS CATALOGUING-IN-PUBLICATION DATA
Seagram's bartending guide.
p. cm.
Includes index.
ISBN 0–670–86397–1
1. Bartending.
TX951.S426   1995
641.8′74—dc20   95–31023

This book is printed on acid-free paper.

∞

Printed in the United States of America
Set in Columbus   Designed by Amy Hill
Another book by Affinity Communications Corp.

Contents

1. Introduction *1*
2. Responsibilities of the Bartending Host *3*
3. Glossary *5*
4. The Well-Appointed Bar: Tools & Tips of the Trade *9*
   Utensils & Glasses *10–11*
   Stocking the Bar *12*
   Buying Tips *17*
   Insiders' Tips & Techniques *20*
5. Bourbon *25*
6. Brandy & Cognac *33*
7. Cordials & Liqueurs *45*
8. Gin *63*
9. Rum *93*
10. Scotch *117*
11. Tequila *127*
12. Vodka *141*
13. Whiskey *157*
14. Beers & Ales *173*
15. Wine *179*
16. Frozen Drinks *189*
17. Sangria, Eggnog, & Other Hot & Cold Punches *201*
18. Liquored Coffees, Teas, & Other "Hot Toddies" *211*
19. Drinks for Every Occasion, Holiday, and Season *223*
20. Low- and Nonalcohol Drinks *233*
21. Recipes for the Chef *245*

   Index 260

INTRODUCTION

Welcome to the first edition of the *Seagram's Bartending Guide*—an easy-to-use modern bar companion that offers tasty drink recipes and contemporary solutions to the mixologist's most frequently asked questions.

In this volume we cover the essentials of bartending—from selecting utensils to stocking inventory. Boasting more than 1,500 recipes—more than 200 of which are from the Seagram library—this guide is brimming with insider tips for creating the perfect drink, as well as fascinating discussions, beautiful photographs, illuminating anecdotes, bold illustrations, and clever toasts.

Beer lovers, don't worry, we've provided information on international and domestic beer and ale, including a discussion of the emerging popularity of America's microbreweries. In our handy section on pairing food and wine, we demystify the selecting process and help you choose the ideal bottle.

The adventurous bartender/host will appreciate the special section filled with holiday and celebration drink recipes. We've included unique recipes for such occasions as Thanksgiving, Valentine's Day, Mardi Gras, and many more.

And who said that drinks are just for drinking? Complementing our drink recipes is an expansive selection of simple but imaginative recipes for delicious appetizers, soups, entrees, and desserts that are rendered sublime by the inclusion of beverage alcohol and liqueurs.

Last but not least, in consideration of you and your guests, we've also provided advice on being a responsible host and accordingly have included a multitude of recipes for low- and nonalcohol drinks. We know you will enjoy the *Seagram's Bartending Guide,* a comprehensive bartender's reference that will become an indispensable fixture for your bar.

Cheers!

RESPONSIBILITIES OF THE BARTENDING HOST

A party like any form of social entertaining, is not just an event but a process with a beginning, middle, and end. After you choose a guest list, you'll be creating a party theme, selecting appropriate entertainment, decorating the space, and inventing enticing hors d'oeuvres and drink menus.

Of course, your responsibilities as the bartender/host do not end once the guests arrive. Preparing exotic drinks is a fine way to show off your creative mixology skills. But hosts of successful parties must also create the right ambiance for their guests' comfort. Of utmost importance in meeting this goal is being considerate of their requests and concerns. As a gracious host, do not force drinks on a guest or push for refills. Be sure to have a selection of nonalcohol soft drinks and low-alcohol beverages available. Of course, guests who are under the legal drinking age must *not* be served beverage alcohol. For younger guests and anyone preferring softer beverages, offer nonalcohol drinks served in fancy glasses.

As the party winds down and guests begin to depart, see them off safely. Since moderate overindulgence can impair good judgment, make sure that guests who will be driving home are alert enough to do so. Undoubtedly, your guests are responsible for their own actions. However, as a host you can contribute to their well-being by encouraging them to designate a driver who will abstain from drinking during the party. Despite your precautions, a guest may have one drink too many. Here are four options in case this happens. Notice that they all exclude the guest from driving:

   ◆ ask another guest to drive that person home
   ◆ ask the guest to spend the night
   ◆ call a cab and offer to pay the driver
   ◆ drive the person home yourself

By acting as a responsible and caring host, you will ensure that *everyone* has fun. And after all, *fun* is the key ingredient in all memorable parties!

GLOSSARY

The following glossary includes terminology and ingredients that are used for mixing the recipes in this book. After all, the ingredients selected by the mixologist can make the difference between a simple drink and an artistic creation.

akvavit—a clear Danish spirit which closely resembles vodka and whose name means "water of life."

amaretto—a liqueur with a slightly bitter almond flavor, made from apricot pits.

amontillado—a pale, dry sherry from Spain.

anisette—a fragrant liqueur with a sharp licorice flavor, made from anise seeds.

aperitif—a term that once meant a before-dinner liqueur drink is now used almost interchangeably with the word cocktail.

applejack—a very sweet apple-flavored brandy.

bitters (Angostura, orange)—a concentrated extract made from roots, herbs, or fruits that is used sparingly to flavor cocktails.

blended whiskey—whiskey produced from a combination of whiskeys and/or neutral spirits containing at least 20% straight whiskey.

Bourbon—a whiskey mash of not less than 51% corn, rye, wheat, malted barley, or malted grain and stored in charred new oak containers.

brandy—a spirit produced primarily from the juice of grapes but also made from the juice of apples, peaches, plums, and other fruits.

Canadian whisky—distilled in Canada usually from rye grains.

cassis—a purple liqueur made from currants.

cherry brandy—a colorless spirit produced from the distillation of cherries, often called by its German name, Kirschwasser.

cobbler—an iced drink combining wine or liqueur with fruit juice and sugar.

coffee brandy—a spirit made from distilled coffee beans.

Cognac—the world's best-known and most highly regarded brandy. Distilled from grapes, true Cognac originates only in the Cognac region of west-central France.

cooler—a mixture with a base of either wine, malt, or a spirit, combined with ingredients such as fruit flavors or popular cocktail flavors.

cream of coconut—a canned preparation made from coconut milk, sugar, and other nonalcohol ingredients useful in making tropical drinks.

crème de—this French term usually denotes a liqueur of a rather thick consistency.

crème de banana—a sweet, banana-flavored liqueur.

crème de cacao—a sweet, chocolate-flavored liqueur. White crème de cacao contains no coloring; dark does.

crème de cassis—a sweet, black currant-flavored liqueur.

crème de menthe—a sweet, mint-flavored liqueur. White crème de menthe contains no coloring; green does.

crème de noya—an almond-flavored liqueur made from fruit pits.

crème de violette—a sweet liqueur flavored with violet oil and vanilla.

curaçao—a cordial flavored with the peel of the sour orange, used frequently in preparing cocktails and tropical drinks. White curaçao contains no added color; the colored varieties such as blue and orange, of course, do.

Falernum—a tasty West Indian syrup made from almonds and spices

fino sherry—a pale, very dry Spanish sherry.

grappa—an Italian brandy made from distilling grape skins that remain after wine production.

grenadine—a thick, red syrup used in cocktails, traditionally made from pomegranate juice.

Irish whiskey—whiskey made in Ireland, often produced using barley.

liqueur—a class of spirit that is usually sweet and often served after dinner. It is produced by either mixing or redistilling spirit with natural ingredients such as fruits, plants, flowers, or chocolate. Sugar must be at least 2½% of the contents by weight.

madeira—a wine resembling sherry traditionally produced in the Madeira Islands, a chain of eight islands off the northwest coast of Africa.

maraschino liqueur—a cordial distilled from a bitter wild cherry called the marasca.

orange-flower water—a particularly fragrant distillation of orange petals that is used sparingly to accent mixed drinks.

port—a dark dessert wine from Portugal.

pousse-café—an after-dinner drink made with liqueurs of varying weights and colors. The liqueurs must be delicately poured into the glass so that several separate layers of liquid are the result.

praline liqueur—a cordial flavored to taste like buttery pecan pralines.

raspberry liqueur—a raspberry-flavored cordial, sometimes called crème de framboise.

rock and rye—an amber-colored American liqueur originally made from rye whiskey and rock candy.

rum—a spirit produced from the fermented juices of sugar cane, sugar cane syrup, sugar cane molasses or other sugar cane by-products. It is traditionally produced in the Caribbean.

rye—a whiskey distilled from a mash containing not less than 51 percent rye grain, traditionally produced in the United States and Canada.

sake—wine produced from rice.

sambuca—an Italian licorice-flavored liqueur made from elderberries.

schnapps—dry European spirit. Popular flavors include apple, peppermint, peach, black cherry, cinnamon, and wild berry.

Scotch—whisky distilled in Scotland, usually from malted barley, broadly divided into two types: blended and single-malt.

sherry—a dessert wine from southern Spain.

simple syrup—a combination of water and granulated sugar that, when boiled, condenses into a clear, sweet syrup—often used in cocktail recipes.

sloe gin—a cordial or liqueur whose characteristic flavor is derived from sloe berries.

sour mash—a blended grain mash used to make whiskeys.

tequila—a spirit distilled from the agave plant, produced in Mexico.

tonic water—a carbonated beverage containing lemon, lime, and quinine, an alkaloid obtained from cinchona bark.

triple sec—a type of curaçao liqueur.

vermouth—an aperitif wine derived from grapes.

vodka—a clear spirit that is generally made from grain, but can be distilled from other starches such as potatoes, corn and beets. Vodkas are commonly flavored with essences of citrus or other fruits, or spices such as pepper.

whiskey—a spirit distilled from fermented grain mash, stored in oak containers.

By understanding the rich vocabulary of wines, the bartender/host will be better prepared to serve guests a rare vintage bottle or an elegant Champagne cocktail. The following is a basic guide to vinification and its terminology that will be helpful in navigating your way through the expansive offerings of the vine.

acidity—the backbone of a wine; too much creates a tart, unpleasing taste and too little detracts from the character.

aerate—the exposing of wine to oxygen to bring out the bouquet.

aroma, bouquet, nose—all refer to the scent of a wine. Aroma and bouquet are similar terms alluding to the strength and type of scent in a wine (a spicy bouquet or a peachy aroma), while nose is a specific term meaning a strong and intense scent.

balance—when all the components of a wine (primarily the acidity, aroma, color, fruit, sugar, and tannin) are in harmony, none being stronger than another.

body—the weight of a wine in the mouth, and the depth or substance of the taste. Wine ranges from light-bodied to medium-bodied to full-bodied, a full-bodied wine being the heaviest.

bottled by or cellared by—term on a bottle indicating that the winery did not necessarily make the wine, but definitely bottled it. (see estate bottled)

character—the nature of a wine; also, the blend of fine qualities in a wine.

dry—the lack of sweetness and sugar.

estate bottled—term on a bottle indicating that the wine was produced completely by one vineyard (cultivation of grapes, fermentation, aging, bottling).

fermentation—the conversion of ripe grapes to alcohol and carbon dioxide gas through a yeast agent.

herbaceous—a term for wine with a grassy flavor.

herbal—a wine that contains an aroma of vegetables.

noble—a wine having exceptional balance and character.

oenology (or enology)—the science of winemaking.

residual sugar—the unfermented sugar left in a wine following fermentation that provides the sweetness.

sweet—containing sugar from the grapes.

tannin—an acid found in grape stems and skins, as well as oak fermentation casks, that assigns a bitterness to the wine.

varietal—refers to a wine produced solely from one type of grape.

vinification—the process of winemaking.

vintage—the year in which a wine was bottled, often displayed on the label. (May also refer to a "good" year.)

THE
WELL-APPOINTED BAR
Tools & Tips of the Trade

Having the right tools makes it easier for you to create fine cocktails. Although substitution is allowable, the enterprising bartender/host should set up shop with the following:

UTENSILS & GLASSES

A jigger measure in ¼ oz., ½ oz., ¾ oz. (½ jigger), 1 oz. (pony), and 1½ oz. (1 jigger) measures. Jigger measures also come with pouring spouts that can be attached to each bottle.

A long bar spoon that can be used as a stirrer and a measuring spoon

A muddler, a round-based wooden stick, or mortar and pestle for grinding bitters or herbs, or smashing fruit

Glass or plastic stirring rod for use with carbonated beverages

Combination can and bottle opener

Waiter's corkscrew

Paring knife for preparing garnishes

Bar strainer for pouring mixed drinks

Hand juicer to squeeze fresh ingredients such as lemon and lime juice

Cocktail shaker with a good, solid lid

Sturdy bag and mallet for crushing ice

Ice bucket and tongs

Electric blender for mixing frozen drinks

Pitcher for mixing drinks such as martinis. Make sure the pitcher has a molded lip that prevents the ice from pouring out with the drink.

Tray for serving drinks to delighted guests

Jigger

Bar Spoon

Muddler

Can and
Bottle
Opener

Waiter's
Corkscrew

Paring Knife

Ice Bag and Mallet

Cocktail Shaker

Juicer

Bar Strainer

Pitcher

Ice Bucket

Blender

Tray

Shot   Cocktail   Collins   Highball   Old-Fashioned

Cordial   Sour   Hurricane   Pousse-Café   Brandy   Irish Coffee
or
Pony

White Wine   Red Wine   Sherry   Flute   Saucer   Tulip

Champagne

Pilsner   Beer Goblet   Beer Mug   Parfait   Margarita

Raise a Glass

In the same way that clothes go a long way in making the man or woman, the right glasses can add a dash of character or elegance to cocktails. Although the lure of colorful glasses can be tempting on a shelf, they obscure your creations, so use clear ones.

Your minimum glassware inventory:

- cocktail glasses—which can double as sour glasses
- goblets—for wine, sours, and brandy
- highball glasses—which can be used for Collinses and juleps
- old-fashioned glasses—can be substituted for highball and shot glasses
- sherry glasses—which can double for liqueurs, wine, and sours
- specialty glasses—for hurricanes, blended margaritas, and piña coladas

The full repertoire would include:

- shot or jigger glasses
- cocktail glasses
- Collins glasses
- highball glasses
- old-fashioned glasses
- pony glasses
- sour glasses
- Hurricane glasses
- pousse-café glasses
- brandy snifters
- white-wine glasses
- red-wine glasses
- sherry glasses
- flute glasses
- pilsner glasses
- beer mugs
- margarita glasses

STOCKING THE BAR

Whether hosting an intimate party for six or a Super Bowl party for fifty, you must have the proper bar to mix your guests' requests. Depending on your entertaining needs, the following bar-stocking variations are recommended: the Starter Bar, the Standard Bar, and the Complete Bar.

The Starter Bar

For the occasional entertainer, the Starter Bar allows for the mixing of many simple, common drink recipes such as the Vodka Tonic, Screwdriver, and 7&7. This bar also allows for the creation of fancier drinks such as the Daiquiri, Bloody Mary, or Vermouth Spritzer.

Spirits
- 1 liter Bourbon
- 1 liter Canadian blended whisky
- 1 liter Irish whiskey
- 1 liter rum
- 1 liter Scotch whisky
- 1 liter vodka
- 1 bottle dry vermouth
- 1 bottle white wine
- 1 bottle red wine
- 12 bottles beer

Mixers
- beef bouillon
- 1 bottle grenadine
- 1 bottle lime juice

Juices
- orange juice
- grapefruit juice
- spicy tomato juice

Soft Drinks and Waters
- cola (regular & diet)
- ginger ale
- lemon-lime soda (regular & diet)
- club soda
- tonic water

Creams and Eggs
- Half-and-Half

Garnishes
- stuffed green olives
- maraschino cherries
- 1 lemon
- 1 lime

The Standard Bar

Bartenders and hosts with a flair for the exotic can create a multitude of delicious drinks from the well-stocked Standard Bar. From Margaritas to White Russians, the following inventory will allow for over 75 percent of the recipes listed in this book.

Spirits
- 1 liter Bourbon
- 1 liter Canadian blended whisky
- 1 liter gin
- 1 liter Irish whiskey
- 1 liter vodka
- 1 liter rum
- 1 liter Scotch whisky
- 1 liter tequila
- 1 liter brandy
- 1 bottle Irish cream
- 1 bottle crème de menthe
- 1 bottle Chartreuse
- 1 bottle Kahlua

- ◆ 1 bottle triple sec
- ◆ 2 bottles red wine
- ◆ 2 bottles white wine
- ◆ 1 bottle sparkling wine or Champagne
- ◆ 1 bottle dry vermouth
- ◆ 1 bottle Campari
- ◆ 12 bottles beer

Mixers

- ◆ 1 bottle grenadine
- ◆ 1 bottle Worcestershire sauce
- ◆ 1 bottle Tabasco sauce
- ◆ 1 bottle lime juice
- ◆ 1 bottle sour mix
- ◆ 1 bottle sweet and sour mix
- ◆ coffee
- ◆ beef bouillon
- ◆ bar sugar

Juices

- ◆ orange juice
- ◆ tomato juice
- ◆ cranberry juice
- ◆ grapefruit juice

Soft Drinks and Waters

- ◆ cola (regular & diet)
- ◆ ginger ale
- ◆ lemon-lime soda (regular & diet)
- ◆ sparkling water, club soda, and tonic water

Creams and Eggs

- ◆ cream
- ◆ whole milk
- ◆ 6 eggs (refrigerated)

Garnishes

- ◆ lemon and lime slices
- ◆ stuffed green olives
- ◆ celery stalks
- ◆ mint sprigs
- ◆ maraschino cherries

The Complete Bar

For those who consider their bartending more than just a hobby or occasional party stint, the Complete Bar stocks the ingredients necessary to take on just about any concoction. From exotic Egg Creams to Blue Bayous, the following repertoire will allow the bartender/host's imagination to run wild!

BORDERS
BOOKS AND MUSIC
290 COMMONS WAY
BRIDGEWATER TOWNSHIP NJ
(908) 231-0111

STORE: 0094   REG: 03/78   TRAN#: 3967
SALE   08/20/2001   EMP: 00108

EMP #:00118   Blakeslee   ,Richar
SEAGRAMS BARTENDING GD
        1013665   CL T   10.02
    14.95 33%EMPLOYEE
METAL BKMARK HARRY POTTER
        6403505   SL T   3.34
     4.99 33%EMPLOYEE

            Subtotal   13.36
            NJ 6%   .80
2 Items   Total   14.16
            CASH   15.16
            CASH   1.00-

        08/20/2001 06:19PM

  THANK YOU FOR SHOPPING AT BORDERS
PLEASE ASK ABOUT OUR SPECIAL EVENTS

Visit our website @ www.borders.com!

Spirits

- 1 liter Bourbon
- 1 liter blended whiskey
- 1 liter premium gin
- 1 liter Irish whiskey
- 1 liter single-malt Scotch whisky
- 1 liter spiced rum
- 1 liter dark rum
- 1 liter gold tequila
- 1 liter vodka
- 1 liter flavored vodka
- 1 liter brandy
- 1 bottle akvavit
- 1 bottle Cognac
- 1 bottle Kirschwasser
- 1 bottle Godiva Liqueur
- 1 bottle Grand Marnier
- 1 bottle Southern Comfort
- 1 bottle Cointreau
- 1 bottle Drambuie
- 1 bottle coffee liqueur
- 1 bottle triple sec
- 1 bottle anisette
- 1 bottle green Chartreuse
- 1 bottle yellow Chartreuse
- 1 bottle blue curaçao
- 1 bottle crème de cacao
- 1 bottle light crème de cacao
- 1 bottle green crème de menthe
- 1 bottle white crème de menthe
- 1 bottle crème de banana
- 1 bottle melon liqueur
- 1 bottle dry vermouth
- 1 bottle sweet vermouth
- 1 bottle Campari
- 3 bottles red wine
- 3 bottles white wine
- 2 bottles sparkling wine or Champagne
- 1 case premium quality beer
- 12 bottles nonalcohol beer

Mixers

- almond syrup (such as Orgeat or Orzata)
- apple cider
- beef bouillon
- bitters (Angostura and orange)
- cassis
- cream of coconut
- coffee
- currant syrup
- ginger beer
- grenadine
- honey
- lime juice
- orange-flower water
- raspberry syrup
- passion-fruit syrup or nectar
- peach nectar
- salt
- simple syrup
- sour mix
- superfine sugar
- sweet and sour mix
- tea
- Tabasco
- Worcestershire sauce

Juices

- apple juice
- Clamato juice
- cranberry juice
- grape juice
- grapefruit juice
- lemon juice
- pineapple juice
- tomato juice
- vegetable or V-8 juice

Soft Drinks and Waters

- bitter-lemon soda
- club soda
- cola (regular & diet)
- ginger ale
- lemon-lime soda (regular & diet)
- mineral water
- seltzer water
- tonic water

Creams and Eggs

- butter
- cream
- 6 eggs (refrigerated)
- Half-and-Half
- milk

Garnishes

- allspice, freshly ground
- almonds
- bananas
- cherries
- cinnamon sticks
- cloves
- lemons
- limes
- mint sprigs
- nutmeg, freshly ground
- olives, stuffed
- onions, cocktail or pearl
- oranges
- pineapple
- strawberries

Note: In drinks that call for raw eggs, make sure that the eggs are fresh and have been properly refrigerated. Raw eggs can carry the *Salmonella* virus, which can cause illness.

BUYING TIPS

Buying for a Crowd: A Party Planning Sample

Stocking a bar for a party or gathering can be a hit-or-miss experience. But it doesn't have to be. Here is an easy guide for stocking a bar for ten to forty guests.

Liquor	QUANTITY 10–20 guests	21–40 guests
Vodka	2–3 liters	4 liters
Gin	1–2 liters	3 liters
Scotch	1–2 liters	3 liters
Dry Vermouth	½ liter	1 liter
Tequila	1–2 liters	2 liters
Bourbon	1 liter	1 liter
Whisk(e)y	1 liter	2 liters
Wine	1 case	2 cases
Beer	1–2 cases	3 cases
Brandy	1 liter	1 liter
Rum	1–2 liters	2 liters

If you find it easier to think about how many drinks you are likely to serve at a party, the following guide shows how many drinks per bottle you can expect to make.

For mixed drinks, you will use approximately 1.25 ounces or 37 milliliters per serving.

Number of Bottles	1	2	4	6	12
750 ml	20	40	81	121	243
Liter	27	54	108	162	324
1.5 Liter	40	81	162	243	486

For wine and Champagne, the serving size is 5 ounces or 118 milliliters.

Number of Bottles	1	2	4	6	12
750 ml	6	12	25	38	76
Liter	8	16	33	50	101
1.5 Liter	12	25	50	76	152
3 Liter	25	50	101	152	305

When buying wine, note that a case contains 12 bottles. You may want to purchase larger sizes such as jeroboams or magnums, which will certainly impress your guests!

BOTTLE VOLUME

Liquor	Wine	U.S. Measure	Metric Measure
Split		6.3 oz.	187 ml.
Tenth	Half bottle	12.7 oz.	375 ml.
Fifth	Standard bottle	25.4 oz.	750 ml.
Quart	Liter bottle	33.8 oz.	1 liter
Magnum	Magnum	50.7 oz.	1.5 liters
Double magnum	Jeroboam	101.4 oz.	3 liters

Brand Buying Guide

There are varying degrees of fineness for every type of beverage alcohol, which is often reflected in the price. The differences between standard and premium brands can be attributed to distillation, aging, and the cost of superior ingredients. The following is a representative list of liqueurs as well as comparative guide to standard and premium brands of popular spirits.

BRAND BUYING GUIDE

Liqueur		
	Capucello	Frangelico
	Drambuie	Galliano
	Godiva Liqueur	Goldschlager
	Amer Picon	Jägermeister
	Bailey's Irish Cream	Kahlua
	Cherry Heering	Pernod
	Cointreau	Southern Comfort
	Campari	Tia Maria

Spirit	Standard	Premium
Bourbon	Jim Beam	Baker's
	Ancient Age	Wild Turkey
	Hiram Walker	
	Evan Williams	Jack Daniels (sour
	Old Grand-Dad	mash)
Brandy and Cognac	Pedro Domecq	Martell VS
	Raynal	Martell VSOP
	The Christian	Martell Cordon Bleu
	Brothers	Martell L'Or
	E & J	Blantons
	Korbel	Germain-Robin

Spirit	Standard	Premium
Gin	Boodles British Gin	Seagram's Extra Dry
	Gilbeys	Bombay
	Gordons	Tanqueray
	Popov	
Rum	Captain Morgan	Myers's Jamaican
	Original Spiced Rum	Original Dark Rum
	Baccardi	
	Ronrico	
Scotch whisky	Johnnie Walker Red	The Glenlivet (single malt)
	J & B	Chivas Regal
	Dewars	Macallan
	Ballantine	Glenfiddich
	Passport	Johnny Walker
	Scoresby	Black
Tequila	Sauza Special	Patrón Añejo,
	Sauza Tequila	Gold, Silver
	Jose Cuervo	Cuervo Gold
Vodka	Skyy Vodka	Absolut
	Smirnoff	Finlandia
	Fleischmann's	Vikin Fjord
	Gilbey's	Stolichnaya

Whisk(e)y	**Blended**	
	Fleischmann's	Seagram's 7 Crown
	Preferred	
	Kessler	
	Canadian	
	Seagram's Canadian	Seagram's V.O
	Hunter	Crown Royal
	Canadian Mist	Crown Royal
	Black Velvet	Special Reserve
		Canadian Club
		Canadian Club
		Classic
	Tennessee	
	George Dickel	Jack Daniels
	Old #12	Gentleman Black
	Irish	
	Jameson Premium	Jameson 1780 Special
	Old Bushmill's	Reserve 12-year-old
		Black Bush Irish

INSIDERS' TIPS & TECHNIQUES

To Shake or to Stir?

Filling the shaker: Never add ice to the ingredients in a shaker. Always place the ice first so it can cool the ingredients as they are added. Although the order of the ingredients is not important, once they've been added they'll need room to shuttle back and forth inside the shaker, so don't fill the shaker to the brim. Leave some room. In time the shaker will feel icy cold, indicating that the drink is ready. Pour the drink at once to prevent it from becoming diluted.

Stirring: To keep their icy clarity, cocktails such as Manhattans, Rob Roys, and gimlets should be stirred, not shaken. To ensure that the drinks are well mixed, stir a minimum of twenty times. One exception: When carbonated water is added to tall drinks, stir as briefly as possible to prevent the spirit from rising to the top.

When in doubt whether to shake or stir, a general rule is that drinks made with sugars, creams, or juices should be shaken (or blended).

The Mission: Mixing vs. Pouring

Mixing: Mixing is the act of measuring ingredients into a jigger or spoon before shaking or pouring into a glass. The host should trust the jigger rather than the eye, like a professional bartender does.

Pouring: A poured drink is one that is created right in the glass. Never pour drinks higher than ¼ inch from the rim of the glass. In the case of wine, a large glass should never be more than ⅓ to ½ full to permit swirling of the wine and liberation of its aromas. In large brandy snifters, a 1½-oz. drink is the maximum. When garnishes such as orange slices and pineapple sticks are being used, allow sufficient room to add them without causing the drink to overflow. When pouring more than one mixed drink, line up the glasses rim-to-rim, fill them halfway, then pour again to the same height in each glass.

It's Always the Ice Age

It's usually best to buy packaged ice—frozen at an outside plant—as all too often the ice processed in your refrigerator absorbs odors from other items in the freezer and can affect the drink quality.

- ◆ Drinks poured into pre-chilled glasses will stay cold longer
- ◆ For an instant chill, fill the glass with ice and swirl for a couple of minutes, then discard the ice.
- ◆ Use ice cubes for long drinks and stirred cocktails, and cracked ice for shaken cocktails.

Chilling glasses: The astute bartender will seek to provide a chilled glass when appropriate. Chilling glasses can be accomplished in several ways: by storing glassware in the refrigerator or freezer until cold; by immersing the glasses in crushed ice prior to use; and by filling the glass with cracked ice and swirling until the glass is cold, after which the ice is poured out.

Frosting glasses: For frozen drinks, frosted glasses create a magical appearance and also help to keep the beverage from melting. For the best frosting, dip the glasses in tap water and place them in the freezer for two to four hours.

Sure-fire blender techniques:

♦ Use crushed ice. Buy it already crushed if available or, to make it at home, place a few cubes at a time into your blender with a little water. Prepare the crushed ice before you need it and store it in plastic bags in the freezer.

♦ For blender drinks with a sherbetlike consistency, figure about 1 cup crushed ice per drink. Pour all the drink ingredients into a blender, then add the crushed ice and blend. If the drink gets too watery, switch off the blender and add more ice. If a solid mass forms, switch off the blender and break it up with a spatula.

How to Salt or Sugar Glasses

Moisten the inside and outside rim of the glass about ¼″ down by using a lemon or orange wedge, liqueur, grenadine, or water, then dip it into a platter of sugar or salt.

Floating and Layering

The most colorful way to serve liqueurs is the pousse-café or "rainbow cordial": a combination of liqueurs "floated" on top of each other to create layers. The pousse-café is made by pouring the heaviest of the liqueurs first and finishing with the lightest.

This multilayered drink is easier to create than you would imagine. Ingredients for multilayered drinks are always written in the order of weight, so that the heaviest liqueur would be poured first, and so forth; gravities are often listed on liqueur bottles. To keep the layers separate, be sure to use liqueurs with at least a point in weight difference. The higher the gravity, the heavier it is. A crème de cacao is heavier than a sloe gin, for example, so the crème de cacao would be floated first.

The most popular way to create a multilayered drink is by pouring over the back side of a teaspoon held at the top of the glass. Many bartenders also swear that pouring down a glass mixing rod is as efficient—and more impressive to guests. An easier way (though not as impressive to guests) is to pour liqueurs slowly into the glass, in any order, and place the glass in the refrigerator. The cold will separate the liqueurs by weight and create a multilayered effect. However, a pousse-café may only last an hour before blending.

WEIGHTS OF BRANDIES AND LIQUEURS

sloe gin	4.7	blackberry liqueur	11.5
kümmel	4.8	blue curaçao	11.9
peppermint liqueur	5.4	cherry liqueur	12.0
peach liqueur	5.7	apricot liqueur	12.7
rock-and-rye liqueur	6.6	coffee liqueur	13.9
triple sec	7.9	maraschino liqueur	14.3
ginger brandy	8.0	white crème de cacao	15.1
apricot brandy	8.1	brown crème de cacao	15.2
cherry brandy	8.4	crème de menthe	16.2
blackberry brandy	8.5	crème de noya	17.0
peach brandy	8.7	anisette	17.2
orange curaçao	10.4	crème de banana	18.2

A Note on Ingredients

◆ Simple syrup is essentially liquefied sugar. Easier to mix in drinks than granulated sugar, simple syrup will be a useful addition to your bar.

To make, slowly pour a one-pound bag of granulated sugar into 12 ounces of hot water. Simmer slowly, stirring frequently. Do not allow the mixture to come to a boil. Once the mixture is cooled, it can be used to mix a variety of drinks.

Pairing Wine and Food

The marriage of wine and food is something to celebrate. By following simple rules, the pairing can be a palatably pleasing union. There is never only one "right" wine for a given meal, but often a dozen that may be equally agreeable. Like all marriages, the union of wine and food is both tenuous and exciting. No two combinations will ever be exactly the same, making each venture truly inspiring. The following chart provides some initial guidelines for selecting an appropriate bottle.

Wines	Serving Temperature	Serve with:
Appetizer Wines Dry Sherry, Vermouth Flavored Wines such as Dubonnet or Lillet	chilled: 50°F room temperature: 65°F	Appetizers, hors d'oeuvres, soups, and salads
White Dinner Wines Chablis, Chardonnay, Chenin Blanc, White Riesling, French Columbard, Sauvignon Blanc	chilled: 50°F	Light foods and meats, poultry, fish, and shellfish
Red Dinner Wines Burgundy, Cabernet Sauvignon, Chianti, Pinot Noir, Zinfandel, Merlot	room temperature: 65°F	Heavier foods such as beef, pork, game, heavy pastas
Dessert Wines Port, Muscatel, Sauternes, Sherry, Riesling	room temperature: 65°F	Desserts, fruits, cheese, nuts, sweet breads
Sparkling Wines Champagnes	chilled: 45°F	All foods

BOURBON

In 1964, Congress passed a resolution naming Bourbon whiskey the "distinctive product of the United States." Scotch runs through the Highlands of Scotland, and rum sweetens the water of the

Caribbean; Bourbon is, and always will be, the spirit of America.

Bourbon has played a great role in this country's heritage. Mark Twain navigated readers down the Mississippi River while imbibing this special whiskey. And after the Union army's victorious Civil War Battle of Vicksburg, President Lincoln sent General Ulysses Grant a congratulatory message—accompanied by an entire case of fine Bourbon. Today, sipping a mint julep as race horses thunder down the homestretch of the Kentucky Derby has become as much an American pastime as the seventh-inning stretch.

Although eighty percent of the world's Bourbon is produced by fourteen distilleries sequestered in the lush hills of Kentucky, there is no law limiting its production to the Bluegrass state, where it was first distilled. However, restrictions concerning the production of Bourbon are written into Kentucky law.

According to this law, whiskey can be labeled Bourbon if it is a whiskey mash of at least 51 percent corn, rye, wheat, malted barley, or malted grain. In addition, it must be distilled not exceeding 180 proof (most is distilled at between 125 and 145) and bottled at no less than 80 proof. The singular aging process must utilize new charred oak barrels.

Bourbon is as old as America itself. Three centuries ago, European settlers landing on American shores were looking for ways to simulate the rye- and barley-based whiskeys of their native lands. Almost as soon as the indigenous North Americans taught the settlers how to grow corn, the newcomers started to distill it. Whiskey made entirely from corn, however, was too sweet, so they experimented by combining the corn with wheat, rye, and barley.

The question of who invented Bourbon is a matter of dispute. Some attribute the feat to Colonel Matt T. Winn, who also created the first Kentucky Derby. The *Collins' History of Kentucky* claims that the first Bourbon was distilled in Georgetown, Kentucky, in 1798. But according to the Bourbon Information Bureau, the whiskey was first distilled in 1789 by Baptist minister Elijah Craig in an area of western Virginia that is now part of Kentucky.

Reverend Craig's remarkable recipe for success—robust corn, select grain, clear limestone spring water, and masterful distilling—endured, and by 1811 there were over 2,000 distilleries in Kentucky. As recently as thirty years ago, private individuals could even buy Bourbon futures by purchasing warehouse receipts that represented a claim on their aging Bourbon. Commercial banks in whiskey-distilling areas of the South used this practice to redeem the capital on their loans to small distillers by selling it to a secondary market. However, the practice ended when a few large corporations became responsible for the majority of Bourbon distilling.

Blended Comfort

¾ oz. Bourbon
⅜ oz. Southern Comfort
⅛ oz. dry vermouth
1 oz. lemon juice
½ tsp. bar sugar

Carefully combine all ingredients in a blender with cracked ice and blend at low speed until smooth. Pour into chilled Collins glass over ice cubes. Garnish with peach slices.

Bourbon and Branch

1¼ oz. Bourbon
1 oz. bottled water

Pour the Bourbon and water over ice cubes in a highball glass. Do not chill the glass. This drink may also be served straight up at room temperature.

Bourbon Cobbler

¾ oz. Bourbon
½ oz. Southern Comfort
1 tsp. peach brandy
2 tsp. lemon juice
½ tsp. simple syrup
sparkling water

Combine all ingredients except water with cracked ice in a cocktail shaker. Shake well. Strain into chilled highball glass over ice cubes and top off with sparkling water. Stir and garnish with peach slice.

Bourbon Collins

1¼ oz. Bourbon
½ oz. lime juice
½ tsp. bar sugar
sparkling water

Combine all ingredients except water in a cocktail shaker. Shake well. Strain into chilled Collins glass over ice cubes and fill with sparkling water. Garnish with a lime twist.

Bourbon Sidecar

¾ oz. Bourbon
½ oz. triple sec
½ oz. lemon juice

Combine all ingredients with crushed ice in a cocktail shaker. Shake well. Strain into chilled cocktail glass.

Bourbon Sloe Gin Fizz

¾ oz. Bourbon
½ oz. sloe gin
1 tsp. lemon juice
1 tsp. simple syrup
sparkling water

Pour all except water into a chilled Collins glass. Add some cracked ice and stir. Add three ice cubes, fill with sparkling water, and garnish with fruit.

Bourbon Sour

1¼ oz. Bourbon
1 oz. lemon juice
½ tsp. bar sugar

Combine all ingredients with cracked ice in a cocktail shaker. Shake well. Strain into chilled sour glass. Garnish with orange slice.

Frozen Mint Julep

1¼ oz. Bourbon
1 oz. lemon juice
1 oz. simple syrup
6 fresh mint leaves

Muddle all ingredients in a glass. Pour into a blender with ½ cup of cracked ice and blend at low speed until slushy. Pour into chilled highball glass and garnish with mint sprig.

Golden Glow

¾ oz. Bourbon
½ oz. dark rum
2 oz. orange juice
1 tbsp. lemon juice
½ tsp. simple syrup
1 dash grenadine

Combine all ingredients except grenadine with cracked ice in a cocktail shaker. Shake well. Strain into chilled cocktail glass. Float grenadine on top.

Jamaican Shakin'

¾ oz. Bourbon
½ oz. dark rum
1½ oz. Half-and-Half

Combine all ingredients with cracked ice in a cocktail shaker. Shake well. Strain into chilled cocktail glass.

Jolly Julep

¾ oz. Bourbon
½ oz. green crème de menthe
1½ oz. lime juice
1 tsp. bar sugar
5 fresh mint leaves
sparkling water

Combine all ingredients except water with cracked ice in a blender. Blend until smooth. Pour into chilled Collins glass over ice cubes. Fill with sparkling water and garnish with mint sprig. Stir gently.

Kentucky Colonel Cocktail

¾ oz. Bourbon
½ oz. Benedictine

Stir ingredients with ice cubes in a mixing glass. Strain into chilled cocktail glass and garnish with lemon twist.

Kentucky Orange Blossom

1 oz. Bourbon
¼ oz. Cointreau
1 oz. orange juice

Combine all ingredients with cracked ice in a cocktail shaker. Shake well. Pour into chilled old-fashioned glass. Garnish with lemon twist.

Lafayette

¾ oz. Bourbon
¼ oz. dry vermouth
⅛ oz. Lillet rouge
½ tsp. bar sugar
½ egg white

Combine all ingredients with cracked ice in a cocktail shaker. Shake vigorously. Pour into chilled old-fashioned glass.

Man o' War

¾ oz. Bourbon
¼ oz. triple sec
⅛ oz. sweet vermouth
1 oz. lime juice

Combine all ingredients with cracked ice in a cocktail shaker. Shake well. Strain into chilled cocktail glass.

Mint Julep

1¼ oz. Bourbon
1 tbsp. simple syrup
10–15 large fresh mint
   leaves

Muddle mint leaves with simple syrup in the bottom of a chilled highball glass. Fill glass with shaved or crushed ice and add bourbon. Garnish with mint sprig.

Narragansett

¾ oz. Bourbon
½ oz. sweet vermouth
1 dash Pernod

Stir ingredients in a chilled old-fashioned glass with ice cubes. Top with lemon twist.

New Orleans Cocktail

1 oz. Bourbon
¼ oz. Pernod
½ oz. simple syrup
1 dash anisette
1 dash Angostura bitters
1 dash orange bitters

Combine all ingredients with cracked ice in a cocktail shaker. Shake well. Strain into chilled old-fashioned glass. Garnish with lemon twist.

Polo Dream

1¼ oz. Bourbon
1 oz. orange juice
½ oz. almond syrup

Combine all ingredients with cracked ice in a cocktail shaker. Shake well. Strain into chilled cocktail glass.

Sadie Song

1¼ oz. Bourbon
4 fresh mint sprigs
1 tsp. bar sugar
1 oz. sparkling water

Muddle the mint sprigs with sugar and sparkling water in the bottom of a chilled old-fashioned glass. Fill the glass with ice cubes and add bourbon. Stir and garnish with orange slice and maraschino cherry.

Soul Kiss

¾ oz. Bourbon
¼ oz. dry vermouth
⅛ oz. Lillet rouge
½ oz. orange juice

Combine all ingredients with cracked ice in a cocktail shaker. Shake well. Strain into chilled cocktail glass.

Southern Ginger

1 oz. Bourbon
¼ oz. ginger brandy
½ oz. lemon juice
ginger ale

Combine all ingredients except ginger ale with cracked ice in a cocktail shaker and shake well. Pour into chilled highball glass. Fill with ginger ale and stir gently. Garnish with lemon twist.

Sweet & Sour Bourbon

1¼ oz. Bourbon
3 oz. orange juice
1 oz. lemon juice
¼ tsp. bar sugar
1 dash salt

Combine all ingredients with cracked ice in a cocktail shaker. Shake well. Strain into chilled sour glass. Garnish with maraschino cherry.

Trilby Cocktail

¾ oz. Bourbon
½ oz. sweet vermouth
3 dashes Angostura bitters

Combine all ingredients with cracked ice in a cocktail shaker. Shake well. Strain into chilled cocktail glass.

Waldorf Cocktail

¾ oz. Bourbon
¼ oz. Pernod
⅛ oz. sweet vermouth
1 dash Angostura bitters

Combine all ingredients with cracked ice in a cocktail shaker. Shake well. Strain into chilled cocktail glass.

Bar Game

◆ *The Game:* Ask someone to balance a quarter on a dollar bill folded lengthwise.

◆ *The Solution:* Fold the dollar bill lengthwise, then bend the short ends together to form a "V." Place the quarter on top of the V fold in the center of the dollar bill. Grasp both ends of the dollar bill without lifting it off the table. Slowly pull the ends in opposite directions, straightening the bill. The quarter will remain balanced.

BRANDY & COGNAC

BRANDY

According to one story, a sixteenth-century Dutch ship captain stumbled upon the process of making brandy while trying to conserve space on his boat. He heated his cargo of wine and vaporated the water, intending to restore it after he arrived at his destination. At the end of the journey, however, the captain's load became even lighter—his friends sampled the tasty distilled wine and loved it.

Originally named *brandewijn* (Dutch for "burnt wine"), this delicious discovery is produced by distilling fermented mashed fruit or wine. Once distilled, the liquid is moved to wooden casks for aging, where the brandy will receive its nuances of flavor and color, and lose some of its proof, allowing the spirit to mellow.

Italian lore on how brandy came to be aged in wood is as rich as the spirit itself. According to legend, an alchemist in the Middle Ages stored his *aqua vitae* in cedar barrels. One day, in an attempt to save the young brandy from unscrupulous soldiers who were pillaging his town, he buried the barrels, but died before he could retrieve the precious spirit. Years later someone unearthed the half-evaporated barrels, and presto, the young brandy was infused with a lovely amber color and a distinctive mature flavor.

Another story about brandy, though not legend, is that it is made exclusively from grapes. Fruit brandies—most commonly based on apples, cherries, and plums—are made all over the world. However, these "white" spirits (named for their clear color), are often expensive because they require larger quantites of fruit. But when served cold, they are worth every penny as a refreshing after-dinner drink.

When serving brandy solely as a drink, pour it into a snifter, a type of glass known for holding brandy's bouquet. Also, a snifter's balloonlike shape allows for the hand to warm its contents to the proper temperature.

COGNAC

Cognac is the result of a patient quest for perfection.

—Anonymous

While all Cognac is brandy, all brandy is not Cognac. In order to be called Cognac, the skillful metamorphosis of grape into wine and wine into eau-de-vie must be done in the Cognac region of France.

Established by decree in 1909, the Region of Cognac is unique for its maritime climate—not completely littoral nor entirely continental—and its varied, chalky soil. This combination allows for the growing of a special white grape whose quality cannot be easily replicated in other regions.

Further distinguishing Cognac from other fruit or grain spirits is the distillation process. Using the Charente method, a process virtually unchanged since the sixteenth century, two distillations are achieved. The first yields a product of weak alcoholic strength known as the *brouillis* which is then redistilled to produce the *bonne chauffe,* of which only the heart will become Cognac. The heart of the *bonne chauffe* is then aged in Limousin or Troncais oak, which imparts its tannin. The combined action of wood and time matures the limpid spirit, filling it out with mellowness, bouquet, and a rich golden amber color. This process, however, is not without sacrifice—evaporation occurs causing the Cognac to lose not only alcoholic strength but also volume. At Martell, this represents the equivalent loss of two million bottles each year and is poetically known as "the angels' share."

No single Cognac, however, possesses all the necessary fineness. Perfection is achieved through blending. Thus, a Cognac's quality ultimately rests with the blender's skill. The blending of *eaux-de-vie* of different ages and different growths—a skillful art handed down through the centuries—is the responsibility of the cellar master. Cellar masters are renowned for their extraordinary memory for smells, a perfect palate, and a highly developed sense of proportion.

The quality of Cognac is described with initials: E for "extra aging" of at least 6½ years, F for "fine" grapes grown in the Cognac region, O for "old," S for "superior," P for "pale," and V for "very." Thus, a Martell VSOP is a splendid Very Superior Old Pale Cognac.

Alexander Martell

¾ oz. Martell VS
½ oz. crème de cacao
1 oz. heavy cream

Vigorously shake with crushed ice and strain into cocktail glass.

Alexander's Sister

¾ oz. Cognac
½ oz. white crème de menthe
1 oz. heavy cream

Shake well with ice, strain into chilled cocktail glass.

Almond Frost

½ oz. Cognac
¾ oz. amaretto
1 oz. orange juice
½ oz. cream of coconut
1 oz. heavy cream
8 oz. crushed ice

Mix ingredients in blender till smooth and creamy. Serve in an 8-oz. specialty glass. Sprinkle with crushed almonds, or three almond slivers.

American Beauty Cocktail

¾ oz. Cognac
¼ oz. dry vermouth
1 oz. orange juice
1 dash grenadine
1 dash white crème de menthe
¼ oz. port

Shake all ingredients except the port with ice. Strain into an old-fashioned glass. Float the port on top.

Applecar

¾ oz. apple brandy
½ oz. triple sec
1 oz. lemon juice

Shake ingredients with ice and strain into a chilled cocktail glass.

Apricocious

1¼ oz. apricot brandy
2 oz. orange juice
2 oz. pineapple juice

Combine ingredients and shake well. Pour into ice cube–filled highball glass. Garnish with fruit flag.

Apricot Blush

½ oz. apricot brandy
¾ oz. vodka

Combine ingredients and shake well. Pour into ice cube-filled highball glass. Garnish with maraschino cherry.

Apricot Cocktail

1 oz. apricot brandy
¼ oz. gin
⅔ oz. orange juice
⅔ oz. lemon juice

Shake ingredients with ice and strain into a chilled cocktail glass.

Apricot Colada

¾ oz. dark rum
½ oz. apricot-flavored brandy
4 oz. pineapple juice
1 oz. cream of coconut
12 oz. crushed ice

Blend all ingredients until slushy. Serve in specialty glass.

Apricot Cooler

1¼ oz. apricot brandy
juice of ½ lemon
juice of ½ lime
1 dash grenadine
½ tsp. bar sugar
6 oz. club soda

Shake ingredients except soda with ice. Strain into a highball glass over ice cubes. Top with soda and garnish with lemon peel.

Apricot Fizz

1¼ oz. apricot brandy
juice of ½ lime
½ tsp. bar sugar
4 oz. club soda

Shake brandy, lime, and sugar with ice. Strain into highball glass over ice cubes. Top with club soda and stir gently.

Apricot Jerk

¾ oz. apricot brandy
½ oz. dark rum
1 oz. cream of coconut
1 oz. Half-and-Half
1 cup crushed ice

Blend at low speed. Pour into a wine-glass. Garnish with grated coconut.

Apricot Stone Sour

1¼ oz. apricot brandy
2½ oz. sour mix
1½ oz. orange juice

Blend with a small amount of crushed ice. Serve strained in a sour glass. Garnish with a cherry and an orange slice.

Apricot Sweetie

½ oz. apricot brandy
½ oz. dark rum
¼ oz. gin
½ oz. lemon juice
3 dashes grenadine
½ cup crushed ice

Blend at low speed. Pour into wineglass. Garnish with twist of lemon peel.

Betsy Ross Cocktail

¾ oz. Cognac
½ oz. port
1 dash triple sec
1 dash bitters

Stir ingredients with ice and strain into a chilled cocktail glass.

Bombay Cocktail

¾ oz. Cognac
¼ oz. sweet vermouth
¼ oz. dry vermouth
1 dash Pernod
2 dashes orange curaçao

Stir ingredients with ice and strain into a prechilled cocktail glass.

Bossa Nova

¾ oz. apricot brandy
¼ oz. dark rum
¼ oz. Godiva Liqueur
4 oz. pineapple juice
¼ oz. lime juice

Stir ingredients well with crushed ice and strain into a chilled cocktail glass.

Brandy Branch

½ oz. Cognac
½ oz. dark rum
¼ oz. apple brandy
1–2 dashes almond syrup

Shake ingredients with crushed ice and strain into a chilled cocktail glass.

Brandy Fizz

¾ oz. cherry-flavored brandy
½ oz. dark rum
½ oz. sweet & sour mix
soda water

Shake ingredients and pour into ice-filled 12-oz. Collins glass. Top with soda water. Garnish with lime.

Brandy Rim

½ oz. blackberry brandy
¼ oz. rum
¼ oz. crème de banana
¾ oz. grenadine
6 oz. orange juice

Blend and serve on the rocks. Garnish with orange slice and cherry.

Brandy Sour

1¼ oz. brandy
juice of ½ lemon
½ tsp. bar sugar

Shake with ice and strain into sour glass. Garnish with lemon slice and maraschino cherry.

Brown Bear

¾ oz. Cognac
½ oz. coffee brandy

Combine and serve in an old-fashioned glass.

Caribbean Shooter

½ oz. apricot brandy
¾ oz. Myers's Original Dark Rum
1 oz. cranberry juice

Shake over rocks. Strain. Serve in an old-fashioned glass.

Cherry Blossom

¾ oz. cherry brandy
½ oz. dark rum
1 oz. cranberry juice
1 tsp. grenadine
1 tsp. lemon juice

Shake well with crushed ice. Strain into chilled cocktail glass. Garnish with one or two maraschino cherries.

Cherry Snap

¾ oz. cherry-flavored
  brandy
½ oz. dark rum
4 oz. eggnog
1 ginger snap

Whirl ingredients in blender. If desired, garnish with additional ginger snap for dunking.

Crème de Cacao Nightcap

¾ oz. Cognac
½ oz. dark crème de
  cacao
6 oz. milk
1 tsp. sugar
1 tbsp. whipped cream

Heat first four ingredients, pour over a metal spoon into a tempered 6-oz. stemmed glass. Top with a dollop of whipped cream. Garnish with powdered cocoa or nutmeg.

Crisp Apple Cocktail

¾ oz. apple brandy
½ oz. tequila
½ oz. lemon juice
¾ tsp. almond syrup
3 dashes triple sec

Shake all ingredients with cracked ice. Shake well. Strain into chilled old-fashioned glass and garnish with lemon slice.

Deauville Cocktail

½ oz. triple sec
½ oz. apple brandy
¼ oz. Cognac
½ oz. lemon juice

Shake ingredients with ice. Strain into a chilled cocktail glass.

Dream Cocktail

1 oz. Cognac
½ oz. triple sec
1 dash Pernod
1 oz. club soda

Shake Cognac, triple sec, and Pernod with shaved or crushed ice. Strain into a chilled cocktail glass, top with club soda.

East India Cocktail

¾ oz. Cognac
½ oz. curaçao
½ oz. pineapple juice
1 dash bitters

Shake ingredients with ice. Strain into a chilled cocktail glass. Garnish with a twist of lemon peel and a maraschino cherry.

39

España Cocktail

¾ oz. dark rum
½ oz. apple brandy
2 dashes sweet vermouth
1 dash orange bitters

Stir ingredients well with crushed ice and strain into a chilled cocktail glass.

Foreign Affair

¾ oz. Cognac
½ oz. anisette

Stir with ice, strain into chilled cocktail glass.

French 75

1 oz. Cognac
½ oz. lemon juice
1 tsp. bar sugar
3 oz. chilled champagne

Shake Cognac, lemon juice, and sugar with crushed ice. Strain into fluted Champagne glass. Top with Champagne. Garnish with lemon twist, if desired.

French Collection

¾ oz. Cognac
½ oz. Grand Marnier

Pour ingredients into ice cube–filled rocks glass and stir.

Flying Horse

¾ oz. vodka
½ oz. cherry brandy
2 oz. heavy cream

Shake well with crushed ice. Strain into chilled cocktail glass or serve on the rocks. Garnish with maraschino cherry.

Hearts

1 ¼ oz. cherry brandy
5 oz. lemon-lime soda

Combine in an ice cube–filled highball glass. Garnish with lime wedge and maraschino cherry.

Ice Breaker

½ oz. Cognac
½ oz. dark rum
¼ oz. gin
2 oz. lime juice
1 oz. orange juice

Shake ingredients. Strain into crushed ice–filled old-fashioned glass. Garnish with lime wedge.

Italian Stinger

¾ oz. Cognac
½ oz. Galliano

Pour ingredients over ice in an old-fashioned glass and stir.

Jellybean

½ oz. blackberry brandy
½ oz. whiskey
¼ oz. anisette

Shake well with crushed ice. Strain into a chilled cocktail glass or serve on the rocks.

Lady Be Good

¾ oz. Cognac
¼ oz. white crème de menthe
¼ oz. sweet vermouth

Shake ingredients with crushed or shaved ice. Strain into a chilled cocktail glass.

Ladybug

¾ oz. Cognac
½ oz. dark rum
1½ oz. orange juice
1½ oz. lime juice
¼ oz. almond syrup
½ cup crushed ice

Blend ingredients with crushed ice in blender for 15 seconds. Pour into an old-fashioned glass over ice cubes. Garnish with orange slice.

Martell Chanteloupe

1¼ oz. Martell VS
¼ oz. crème de cassis

Shake well with ice cubes, strain into a chilled cocktail glass, or serve on the rocks. Garnish with lemon twist.

Martell Chic

1¼ oz. Martell VS
½ oz. strawberry syrup
½ oz. lemon juice
5 oz. cola

Combine in an ice cube–filled highball glass. Garnish with maraschino cherry.

Martell Daisy

1¼ oz. Martell VS
1 oz. lemon juice
1 tsp. grenadine

Combine in an ice cube–filled cocktail glass. Stir. Garnish with maraschino cherry.

Martell Emeraude or

1 oz. Martell VS
¼ oz. blue curaçao
2 oz. tonic

Combine Martell and blue curaçao in ice cube–filled wineglass. Top with tonic. Garnish with fruit flag.

Martell Highball

1¼ oz. Martell VS
5 oz. club soda

Combine in highball glass with ice cubes. Stir once. Garnish with lemon twist, if desired.

Martell President

1¼ oz. Martell VS
2 oz. orange juice
1 splash grenadine

Serve in a cocktail glass with ice cubes. Garnish with orange slice and serve with stirrer.

Martell Shake

1¼ oz. Martell VS
3 oz. milk
1 tbsp. honey
8 oz. crushed ice

Shake well in cocktail shaker. Pour into highball glass.

Martell Swing

1 oz. Martell VS
2 oz. exotic fruit juice
1 splash grenadine
3 oz. lemon-lime soda

Combine Cognac, juice, and grenadine in an ice cube–filled highball glass. Top with soda. Garnish with fruit flag.

Metro Cocktail

¾ oz. Cognac
½ oz. dry vermouth
2 dashes orange bitters
1 tbsp. simple syrup

Shake well with crushed ice. Strain into chilled cocktail glass. Garnish with orange twist.

Mon Cherie

⅔ oz. cherry brandy
⅔ oz. light crème de cacao
1½ oz. heavy cream

Shake well with crushed ice. Strain into chilled cocktail glass. Garnish with thin chocolate shavings.

Muddy River

1¼ oz. coffee brandy
3 oz. Half-and-Half
4 oz. crushed ice

Shake all ingredients well. Pour into rocks glass.

Root Beer

¾ oz. coffee brandy
¼ oz. vodka
¼ oz. Galliano
4 oz. cola

Pour liquors into ice cube–filled beer mug. Fill with cola. Garnish with two soda straws.

Stinger

¾ oz. brandy
½ oz. white crème de cacao

Serve chilled up or on the rocks. Garnish with a twist.

Sunset

1¼ oz. cherry brandy
4 oz. orange juice

Shake well and serve in an ice cube–filled highball glass. Garnish with fruit flag.

Super Sidecar

¾ oz. Cognac
½ oz. triple sec
¾ oz. lemon juice

Shake ingredients with ice. Strain into chilled cocktail glass. Garnish with a twist of lemon peel.

Valencia II

¾ oz. apricot brandy
½ oz. whiskey
¾ oz. orange juice
1 dash bitters

Shake with ice. Strain over ice cubes in an old-fashioned glass.

Vanderbilt Cocktail

1 oz. Cognac
¼ oz. cherry brandy
2 dashes bitters
2 dashes simple syrup

Shake ingredients with crushed ice. Strain into a chilled cocktail glass.

Yellow Parrot Cocktail

½ oz. apricot brandy
½ oz. Chartreuse, yellow
¼ oz. Pernod

Shake ingredients well with crushed or shaved ice. Strain into a chilled cocktail glass.

CORDIALS &
LIQUEURS

In medieval times, cordials and liqueurs were thought of as love potions or aphrodisiacs. Perhaps this philosophy came from their respective root words: *cor,* which in Latin means "heart," and *lique-facere,* also Latin, means "to melt."

Technically, cordials and liqueurs refer to spirits redistilled with fruit juice, plants, or herbs. Cordials and liqueurs are generally the sweetest distilled spirits.

The foundation of a liqueur is always a spirit, such as whiskey, brandy, rum, or gin. The spirit is then redistilled with different substances—herbs, sweeteners, flowers, seeds, juices, and bark—to impart unique flavors to the finished drink. For example, a "rock and rye" has a whiskey base but is accented with rock candy syrup, lemons, oranges, cherries, and grain-neutral spirits.

There are two types of processes that are used to extract the flavors from the fruits and plants: the hot method, which is fast and economical but may sometimes damage the essence of a fruit; and the cold method, which takes at least a year and is labor intensive, but will maintain delicate fruit flavors. After the flavor of the ingredient is imparted to the beverage, sugars and color are added, and a sweet cordial is born.

As charming as many liqueurs are by themselves, they are known for their versatility. They may be mixed with other liqueurs such as in an All-White Frappé, which combines white crème de menthe, anisette, peppermint schnapps, and lemon juice.

In coffee, liqueur may be a cozy and delicious after-dinner drink. Topped with whipped cream, hot coffee with a splash of Capucello will knock the chill out of the coldest of winter nights. But for those hot summer nights, nothing can be more refreshing than a cordial frappé: a stream of cordial cascading over crushed ice into an old-fashioned glass.

Developed in 1975, cream liqueurs have become extremely popular as well and are wonderful served cold, straight, or on the rocks. Bailey's Irish Cream, consisting of fresh cream and whiskey and not requiring refrigeration, was the first to hit the market. It was such a success that cream liqueurs have become an indispensable bar ingredient worldwide.

Today, the popularity of such liqueurs as Kahlua, Sambuca, Godiva, Midori, Jagermeister, and others has made brand-name liqueurs household words. In fact, many of these liqueurs have begun to rival their companion spirits in popularity, encouraging the distilleries to expand their repertoire of exotic flavors.

A Few Sample Tips
from Professional Tasters

◆ Observe the bottle (which can signal the character of the contents, color, and viscosity).

◆ First use the nose to perceive the many flavors as a harmonious blend. Then try to identify them individually to determine whether they seem real or artificial.

◆ Use the palate to confirm the impressions of the nose, to sense the liqueur's feel on the tongue and, after swallowing, to discover its aftertaste.

Absinthe Cocktail

1 oz. Pernod
¼ oz. anisette
1 oz. water

Shake ingredients with ice. Garnish with twist of lemon peel.

Adam & Eve

1¼ oz. cranberry-apple schnapps
3 oz. club soda
1 splash lemon-lime soda

Pour ingredients over ice in a white-wine glass. Garnish with lime wedge.

À la Mode

1¼ oz. amaretto
2 oz. apple cider
3 scoops vanilla ice cream
2 dashes cinnamon

Blend all ingredients in a blender until smooth.

Almond Delight

¾ oz. amaretto
½ oz. dark crème de
  cacao
2 oz. heavy cream

Shake well with crushed ice. Strain into chilled cocktail glass or serve on the rocks.

Amaretto Sour

1¼ oz. amaretto
4 oz. sweet & sour mix
4 oz. crushed ice

Shake all ingredients well and serve in old-fashioned glass.

Amaretto Spritzer

1¼ oz. amaretto
4 oz. club soda

Pour amaretto and soda over ice in a glass. Stir gently.

Amaretto Supreme

1 oz. Cognac
¼ oz. amaretto
2 oz. heavy cream

Shake well. Strain into chilled cocktail glass or serve on the rocks. Garnish with orange slice.

Amorous Duo

1 oz. raspberry schnapps
¼ oz. amaretto
1 scoop vanilla ice cream
1 scoop crushed ice

Blend ingredients together in a blender. Pour into brandy snifter.

Angel Face

½ oz. apricot brandy
½ oz. apple brandy
¼ oz. gin

Shake ingredients with shaved ice and strain into a chilled cocktail glass.

Angel's Tip

1¼ oz. dark crème de
  cacao
2 oz. Half-and-Half

Pour crème de cacao into a chilled cordial or pony glass. Float Half-and-Half on top.

Apple Calabash

¾ oz. cranberry-apple
schnapps
½ oz. Captain Morgan
Original Spiced Rum
2 oz. pineapple juice
1 oz. heavy cream
½ oz. cream of coconut
1 scoop crushed ice

Blend all ingredients in blender. Pour into margarita glass. Garnish with fresh mint.

Apple Smile

1¼ oz. apple country
schnapps
1½ oz. sweet & sour mix
1 dash grenadine

Shake well with crushed ice. Strain into chilled cocktail glass. Garnish with apple slice or lime wheel.

Banana Mamba

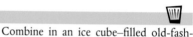

1¼ oz. crème de banana
1 oz. pineapple juice
1 oz. orange juice
1 tsp. lime juice

Combine in an ice cube–filled old-fashioned glass. Garnish with maraschino cherry.

Beach Berry

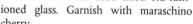

1¼ oz. raspberry
schnapps
3 oz. orange juice
1 splash lemon juice
1 splash grenadine

Pour schnapps and orange juice over ice cubes in an old-fashioned glass. Splash with lemon juice and grenadine. Garnish with lemon wheel.

Berrissimio

¾ oz. blackberry liqueur
½ oz. strawberry liqueur
2 oz. orange juice
1 oz. pineapple juice
1 oz. club soda

Pour liqueurs, orange juice, and pineapple juice over ice in an old-fashioned glass. Stir. Top with club soda and stir gently.

Black Cat

1¼ oz. black-cherry
liqueur
3 oz. cranberry juice
3 oz. cola

Combine ingredients in an ice cube–filled black-stemmed goblet. Garnish with orange quarter and maraschino cherry.

Black Cherry Margarita

¾ oz. black-cherry
    schnapps
½ oz. gold tequila
2 oz. sweet & sour mix
2 oz. orange juice
1 oz. lime juice
8 oz. crushed ice

Combine ingredients in blender. Blend well. Serve in stemmed margarita glass. Garnish with lime wheel.

Blackberries & Cream

¾ oz. blackberry liqueur
½ oz. crème de banana
2 oz. pineapple juice
2 oz. cream of coconut
12 oz. crushed ice

Mix well in blender until smooth. Serve in specialty or wine glass. Garnish with pineapple fruit flag.

Blackthorn

¾ oz. sloe gin
½ oz. sweet vermouth
2 dashes orange bitters

Stir ingredients with ice and strain into a chilled cocktail glass. Garnish with lemon peel.

Blue Lady

1¼ oz. blue curaçao
3 oz. lemon-lime soda
½ oz. lime juice

Stir well with ice. Strain into cocktail glass or serve on the rocks. Garnish with lime slice.

Blue Lagoon

1¼ oz. blue curaçao
5 oz. lemon-lime soda

Combine in an ice cube–filled highball glass. Garnish with lemon slice.

Blue Monday

¼ oz. blue curaçao
1 oz. vodka

Stir well with crushed ice. Strain into chilled cocktail glass or serve on the rocks. Garnish with lemon twist.

Burnt Almond

1¼ oz. amaretto
2 oz. Half-and-Half

Shake well and serve over crushed ice in an old-fashioned glass.

Buttoned Lip

¾ oz. piña colada
    schnapps
½ oz. Captain Morgan
    Original Spiced Rum
3 oz. diet cola
1 oz. orange juice

Pour ingredients over crushed ice in a small brandy snifter. Garnish with orange wedge.

Captain's Cap

1½ oz. Capucello
¼ oz. Captain Morgan
    Original Spiced Rum
1 scoop vanilla frozen
    yogurt/ice cream
8 oz. crushed ice

Mix ingredients in blender until smooth and creamy. Serve in specialty glass.

Capucello Cream Soda

1½ oz. cream soda
1¼ oz. Capucello

Pour over ice into a cocktail glass and stir gently.

Capucello Dreamsicle

1¼ oz. Capucello
3 oz. Tropicana orange
    juice
1 scoop vanilla frozen
    yogurt/ice cream
4 oz. crushed ice

Place ingredients in blender until smooth and creamy. Serve in specialty glass.

Capucello Raspberry Creme

1 oz. Capucello
¼ oz. Chambord
2 scoops vanilla frozen
    yogurt/ice cream
4 oz. crushed ice

Mix ingredients in blender until smooth and creamy. Serve in specialty glass.

Capucello Solo

1¼ oz. Capucello

Pour into a snifter to fully savor the fine taste and aroma.

Capucello Tropico

1¼ oz. Capucello
½ ripe banana
5 oz. scoop crushed ice

Mix ingredients in blender until smooth and creamy. Serve in specialty glass.

Caribbean Grasshopper

¾ oz. white crème de cacao
½ oz. green crème de menthe
1 oz. cream of coconut
2 oz. heavy cream

Shake well with cubed ice. Strain into chilled cocktail glass or serve on the rocks. Garnish with maraschino cherry.

Cheap Sunglasses

¾ oz. melon liqueur
½ oz. peach schnapps
2 oz. orange juice
2 oz. pineapple juice
1 oz. sweet & sour mix
1 splash lemon-lime soda

Shake well and pour over crushed ice into specialty or Collins glass. Top with a splash of lemon-lime soda. Garnish with a pair of sunglasses.

Cherry Hound

1¼ oz. black-cherry schnapps
6 oz. grapefruit juice

Pour ingredients into ice cube–filled highball glass. Garnish with grapefruit section or fresh cherry.

Chocolate Almond

¾ oz. amaretto
½ oz. chocolate syrup
½ oz. cream of coconut
1 oz. Half-and-Half

Blend all ingredients in a blender with a scoop of crushed ice.

Chuck Razzberry

1 oz. raspberry schnapps
¼ oz. amaretto
1 oz. pineapple juice
1 splash grenadine

Pour schnapps, amaretto, and juice over ice. Shake well. Add a splash of grenadine. Serve in Hurricane glass.

Coconut Cap

4 oz. Capucello
2 scoops coconut sorbet
4 oz. crushed ice

Mix ingredients in blender until smooth and creamy. Serve in 8-oz. specialty glass.

Colada Fizz

¾ oz. piña colada schnapps
½ oz. rum cream
3 oz. club soda

Pour ingredients over crushed ice in a red-wine glass. Garnish with pineapple wedge.

Cookie-Cello

1 ¼ oz. Capucello
1 scoop cookies & cream
  frozen yogurt/ice
  cream
1 scoop crushed ice

Mix ingredients in blender until smooth and creamy. Serve in specialty glass.

Copper Penny

¾ oz. amaretto
½ oz. white crème de
  cacao
3 oz. Half-and-Half

Combine and serve in an ice cube–filled old-fashioned glass.

Cranberry Cooler

1 ¼ oz. amaretto
2 oz. cranberry juice
4 oz. orange juice

Pour amaretto and cranberry juice into ice cube–filled highball glass. Fill with orange juice. Garnish with lime wedge or cranberry pick.

Déjà Vu

1 ¼ oz. orange curaçao
3 oz. orange juice
1 oz. cream of coconut
¼ oz. almond syrup
8 oz. crushed ice

Mix well in blender until smooth. Serve in a specialty glass. Garnish with orange flag.

Diana Cocktail

1 oz. white crème de
  menthe
¼ oz. Cognac

Fill a cocktail glass with crushed ice and crème de menthe. Float Cognac on top.

Electric Banana

¾ oz. crème de banana
½ oz. melon liqueur
2 oz. Half-and-Half
1 oz. pineapple juice
1 oz. orange juice
1 oz. cream of coconut

Shake ingredients well. Pour into ice cube–filled glass. Garnish with banana wedge, maraschino cherry and lime wheel.

Frazzled Strawberry

1 ¼ oz. strawberry
  schnapps
4 oz. ginger ale

Pour over ice in highball glass. Garnish with strawberry.

Fuzzy Navel

1¼ oz. peach schnapps
6 oz. orange juice

Combine in ice cube–filled highball glass.

Godiva Cocoa Latte

1¼ oz. Godiva Liqueur
steamed milk

Serve in mug and garnish with cinnamon.

Godiva Cream Soda

1¼ oz. Godiva Liqueur
4 oz. soda
1 oz. milk

Combine all ingredients over ice in a Collins glass. Stir.

Godiva Ice Cream Soda

1¼ oz. Godiva Liqueur
4 oz. cola
1 scoop vanilla ice cream

Pour Godiva into tall glass. Add cola. Top with ice cream.

Godiva Irish Coffee

1 oz. Godiva Liqueur
¾ oz. Irish cream liqueur
4 oz. hot coffee

Pour into mug. Stir. Garnish with whipped cream.

Godiva Irish Freeze

1¼ oz. Godiva Liqueur
¾ oz. Irish cream liqueur

Combine over crushed ice in a snifter. Stir.

Godiva Italiano

1¼ oz. Godiva Liqueur
½ oz. amaretto

Combine over ice and strain into a cocktail glass with a sugar-coated rim. Garnish with a squeeze of orange.

Godiva Martini Noir

1 oz. Godiva Liqueur
½ oz. Absolut Vodka

Shake with ice and strain into martini glass. Garnish with lemon twist.

Godiva Mocha Almond

1 oz. Godiva Liqueur
¼ oz. amaretto
2 oz. milk
2 oz. espresso

Combine all ingredients over ice in a old-fashioned glass. Stir.

Godiva Originale

1¼ oz. Godiva Liqueur

Pour two ounces of Godiva into a cordial glass. Also delicious over ice in a cocktail glass with a twist of lemon. Or, add two ounces of Godiva to six ounces of your favorite coffee, stir, and top with whipped cream.

Godiva Peppermint Kiss

1 oz. Godiva Liqueur
¼ oz. peppermint schnapps

Pour into old-fashioned glass over ice. Stir. Garnish with sprig of mint.

Godiva Whisper

¾ oz. Godiva Liqueur
½ oz. Cognac
3 scoops vanilla ice cream

Combine ingredients in a blender until smooth. Serve in a snifter or cocktail glass.

Godiva White Russian

¾ oz. Absolut Vodka
½ oz. Godiva Liqueur
1 oz. milk

Pour into old-fashioned glass over ice. For a Godiva Black Russian, omit the milk.

Grand Finale

¾ oz. amaretto
½ oz. hazelnut-flavored liqueur
2 oz. cream of coconut
1 oz. heavy cream
6 oz. crushed ice

Mix in blender until smooth. Serve in wineglass. Sprinkle with nutmeg.

Grasshopper

¾ oz. green crème de menthe
½ oz. white crème de cacao
2½ scoops vanilla ice cream or 4 oz. Half-and-Half

Mix in blender until smooth. Serve in appropriate frosted cocktail glass. Garnish with chocolate shavings.

Grasshopper II

¾ oz. green crème de
  menthe
½ oz. white crème de
  cacao
¾ oz. light cream

Shake with ice. Strain into prechilled
cocktail glass.

Hazel Nut

½ oz. dark crème de
  cacao
¾ oz. Frangelico
2 oz. Half-and-Half

Shake ingredients and serve over ice in a
rocks glass or strain into cocktail glass.

Jujube

1¼ oz. banana-strawberry
  schnapps
2 oz. orange juice
1 splash lime juice
1 scoop ice

Blend ingredients in blender. Pour into a
brandy snifter. Garnish with lime wedge.

Lady Luck

1 oz. raspberry schnapps
¼ oz. crème de banana
1 oz. cream of coconut
1 scoop ice

Blend ingredients together in a blender.
Pour into a brandy snifter. Garnish with a
mint leaf.

Liberty Cocktail

¾ oz. applejack
½ oz. dark rum
1 dash simple syrup
1 oz. ice water

Shake ingredients with crushed or shaved
ice. Strain into a chilled cocktail glass.

Lovebird

1¼ oz. amaretto
1 oz. Half-and-Half

Blend all ingredients in a blender with a
scoop of crushed ice.

Mint Whisper

½ oz. crème de cafe
¾ oz. white crème de
  menthe
2 oz. milk
1½ oz. Half-and-Half

Pour over ice in a glass. Stir.

Monk's Secret

1¼ oz. amaretto
¼ oz. lime juice
5 oz. lemon-lime soda

Pour the amaretto and lime juice over ice in a glass. Stir. Add the lemon-lime soda and stir gently.

Muscle Beach
3/4 oz. triple sec
½ oz. vodka
8 oz. pink lemonade

Combine ingredients in an ice cube–filled specialty glass. Garnish with lemon wedge and green maraschino cherry.

The New Wave

1¼ oz. peach schnapps
4 oz. orange juice
1 splash soda

Pour over ice.

Night Cap

3/4 oz. Capucello
½ oz. Godiva Liqueur
1 oz. milk

Pour over ice into a old-fashioned glass and stir gently.

Nutty Banana
1 oz. amaretto
¼ oz. crème de banana
1½ oz. orange juice
1 oz. heavy cream

Blend all ingredients in a blender with a scoop of crushed ice.

Nutty Tropic

1¼ oz. amaretto
3 oz. piña colada mix
3 oz. milk or Half-and-Half

Blend with crushed ice. Garnish with fresh pineapple.

Peach Fuzz

1¼ oz. peach schnapps
2 oz. pureed peaches
½ oz. sour mix
1 dash grenadine

Blend with crushed ice to desired consistency.

Peach Schnapps Splash
1¼ oz. peach schnapps
4 oz. lemon-lime soda
1 splash grenadine

Pour schnapps and soda over ice cubes in highball glass. Top with grenadine. Garnish with lemon twist.

Peachee Keen

¾ oz. peach schnapps
½ oz. triple sec
3–4 oz. club soda

Serve over old-fashioned. Garnish with orange and sprig of mint.

Peachie Keen

¾ oz. peach schnapps
½ oz. triple sec
3 oz. club soda
1 splash grenadine

Pour schnapps and triple sec over crushed ice in a wineglass. Add soda if desired. Splash with grenadine. Garnish with a cherry.

Peppermint Treat

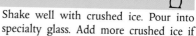

½ oz. peppermint schnapps
¾ oz. green crème de menthe
1 oz. heavy cream

Shake well with crushed ice. Strain into chilled cocktail glass or serve on the rocks. Garnish with maraschino cherry.

Pink Flamingo

1¼ oz. sloe gin
5 oz. orange juice
2 oz. pineapple juice
½ oz. sweet & sour mix
8 oz. crushed ice

Shake well with crushed ice. Pour into specialty glass. Add more crushed ice if necessary.

Pink Squirrel

1 oz. crème de noya
1 tbsp. white crème de cacao
1 tbsp. light cream

Shake with ice. Strain into prechilled cocktail glass.

Rainbow

½ oz. grenadine
1 oz. vodka
5 oz. Collins mix
½ oz. blue curaçao

Pour grenadine into an empty margarita glass. Fill with crushed ice. Combine vodka and Collins mix in shaker. Pour gently into glass. Top with blue curaçao. Garnish with orange fruit flag.

Raspberry Reef

¾ oz. raspberry schnapps
½ oz. piña colada schnapps
3 oz. pineapple juice
1 splash grenadine

Pour ingredients over ice in old-fashioned glass. Garnish with a cherry.

Razzaretto

¾ oz. raspberry schnapps
½ oz. amaretto
3 oz. club soda

Pour ingredients over ice cubes in old-fashioned glass.

Razzle Dazzle

1¼ oz. piña colada
   schnapps
4 oz. lemon-lime soda
2 oz. pineapple juice
1 oz. orange juice
1 splash grenadine

Pour first four ingredients over crushed ice in fluted white-wine glass. Add grenadine. Garnish with pineapple wedge and cherry.

Red Ruby

1¼ oz. amaretto
3 oz. ginger ale
1 oz. orange juice
1 oz. cranberry juice
2 tsp. grenadine

Combine in an ice cube–filled highball glass. Garnish with fruit flag.

Rootarama Bananarama

1¼ oz. root-beer schnapps
1 oz. cream of coconut
½ banana
1 splash club soda

Blend all ingredients in a blender with a scoop of crushed ice. Pour into Champagne flute. Garnish with a cherry.

Rootie Frootie

1¼ oz. root-beer
   schnapps
1 oz. orange juice
1 oz. pineapple juice
1 oz. cream of coconut

Blend all ingredients in blender with scoop of crushed ice.

Ruby Tuesday

1¼ oz. raspberry schnapps
4 oz. diet lemon-lime soda
1 splash grenadine

Pour schnapps and diet soda over ice in double old-fashioned glass. Splash with grenadine. Garnish with lemon wheel.

Ruby Tuesday II

1 oz. raspberry schnapps
¼ oz. crème de banana
2 oz. pineapple juice
1 oz. cream of coconut
1 scoop ice

Blend ingredients together. Pour into a fluted wineglass. Garnish with a pineapple stick.

Schnappin' Strawberries

1¼ oz. strawberry
schnapps
1 oz. pineapple juice
1 oz. cream of coconut
¼ cup strawberries, sliced

Blend all ingredients in blender with scoop of crushed ice. Pour into margarita glass.

Schnappy Dresser

1¼ oz. raspberry
schnapps
4 oz. apple juice

Pour ingredients over ice in double old-fashioned glass. Garnish with lemon wedge.

"Sex on the Beach"

½ oz. melon liqueur
½ oz. raspberry liqueur
¼ oz. vodka
4 oz. pineapple juice
6 oz. crushed ice

Shake ingredients well with crushed ice. Pour into highball glass. Garnish with pineapple wedge.

Sidecar

¾ oz. triple sec
½ oz. Cognac
¾ oz. lemon juice

Shake ingredients with ice. Strain into chilled cocktail glass. Garnish with a twist of lemon peel.

Silver Fox

¾ oz. dark crème de
cacao
½ oz. triple sec
1 oz. coffee, chilled
1 oz. heavy cream

Shake well with crushed ice and strain into chilled cocktail glass.

Sloe Gin Fizz

1¼ oz. sloe gin
½ tsp. bar sugar
1 oz. lemon juice
6 oz. club soda

Shake sloe gin, sugar, and lemon juice with ice and strain into a highball glass over ice cubes. Top with soda and stir.

Sneaky Peach

1¼ oz. peach schnapps
2 oz. cream of coconut
2 oz. orange juice
1 oz. grenadine
1 oz. sweet & sour mix
6 oz. crushed ice

Blend thoroughly. Pour into specialty glass. Garnish with an orange flag.

Summer Sunrise

¾ oz. raspberry liqueur
½ oz. apricot liqueur
4 oz. orange juice
1 oz. cranberry juice

Combine liqueurs with orange juice in an ice cube–filled pint-sized Mason jar. Top with cranberry juice. Garnish with an orange flag stirrer.

Super Tart

1¼ oz. wild-berry schnapps
2 oz. sweet & sour mix
4 oz. lemon-lime soda

Pour schnapps and sweet & sour mix into ice cube–filled Collins glass. Top with lemon-lime soda. Garnish with lemon wedge and cherry.

Sweetheart Sip

1¼ oz. amaretto
2 oz. pineapple juice

Shake well with crushed ice. Strain into cocktail glass or serve on the rocks. Garnish with orange slice.

Toasted Almond

¾ oz. coffee liqueur
½ oz. amaretto
1 oz. heavy cream

Shake in tumbler and pour over ice in an old-fashioned glass.

Tropic Colada

1¼ oz. banana-strawberry schnapps
3 oz. pineapple juice
1 tbsp. cream of coconut
1 scoop ice

Blend ingredients with crushed ice. Garnish with pineapple stick.

Tropical Treasure

¾ oz. melon liqueur
½ oz. crème de banana
2 oz. cream of coconut
2 oz. pineapple juice
2–8 oz. crushed ice

Blend thoroughly. Pour into specialty glass. Garnish with pineapple flag.

Wedding Cake I

¾ oz. amaretto
½ oz. white crème de cacao
3 oz. milk

Shake well with crushed ice. Strain into a chilled Champagne glass or serve on the rocks.

Wedding Cake II

¾ oz. amaretto
½ oz. crème de cacao
3 oz. milk

Shake well with crushed ice. Strain into a chilled Champagne glass, or serve on the rocks.

Witches Tail

1 oz. wild-berry schnapps
¼ oz. blue curaçao
3 oz. sweet & sour mix
3 oz. club soda

Combine ingredients in an ice cube–filled Collins glass. Stir. Garnish with orange wheel and witch's hat.

Write-Off

1 oz. banana-strawberry
   schnapps
¼ oz. dark rum
3 oz. pineapple juice

Pour ingredients over ice in a Collins glass. Garnish with pineapple wedge.

GIN

Hepburn and Tracy, Gable and Lombard, gin and vermouth. Martini. Whether on screen or in the glass, chemistry is everything. And when it happens, it can be magic. When San Francisco bartender Jerry Thomas first combined gin and vermouth in the 1860s, his combination was spellbinding. He published the first recipe for the martini in *The Bon Vivant's Companion* in 1862, but could he have known that he would change the face of business—and drinking habits—forever?

Gin, like many other spirits including brandy, was first conceived with a curative intent. It was first distilled in seventeenth-century Holland by Franciscus de la Boe, a University of Leyden chemist known as Dr. Sylvius. By extracting oil from juniper berries and then redistilling it with pure alcohol, he attempted to invent an inexpensive medicine. The diuretic power of the drink was never really proven, however.

The spirit's original name, *genièvre* (the French word for juniper), was later shortened to *genever* by the Dutch. And the British, desperate to find a cheaper alternative to the heavily taxed French wines and brandies, immediately took to this clear, crisp, refreshing liquid. Nicknaming it "gin," they exported it back to England and it soon became the beverage of fashion. Most gins in eighteenth-century England were sweetened to disguise their harsh taste; and in an attempt to smooth out the spirit's taste, distillers began to produce and perfect unsweetened gin.

The popularity of Thomas's concoction—the classy, elegant martini—gave gin its due, and the world embraced the drink and the spirit.

Today's martini is a far cry from Thomas's first recipe. Present-day versions, often accented with an olive or pearl onion, are fifteen-to-

Jerry Thomas's famous martini formula contained four parts gin to one part vermouth.

one mixes (i.e., just a dash of vermouth). Regardless of its gin-to-vermouth ratio, the key to a martini's success has transcended the permutations of time: It has always depended on the quality of the gin.

Today, gin is made from neutral spirits distilled from juniper berries culled from evergreen trees. The blend is then redistilled in a pot still, over which flavorists often hang spices, herbs, or fruit. Ranging from coriander and licorice to lime and lemon, these botanicals mix with the vapors rising through the still's screen to lend the spirit its subtle flavor. Although it is not a requirement to age gin, some distillers do so to give the liquid added color or smoothness.

The two primary types of gin, Dutch and London Dry, are comprised of a two-step process. First distilled at a low proof—around 100—from equal parts of rye, barley, and corn, the elixir is then redistilled with the essential juniper in pot stills at around 94 to 98 proof.

London Dry gin, the more popular kind, is known for a dry, tangy but fresh juniper flavor and unsweetened taste. Considered the world's finest gin, it is distilled in a column still and is usually comprised of 75 percent corn, 15 percent barley malt, and 10 percent other grains.

Abbey Cocktail

1¼ oz. gin
1 oz. orange juice
1 dash orange bitters

Shake with ice and strain into a chilled cocktail glass. Garnish with a cherry.

Adios Mother

¼ oz. gin
¼ oz. vodka
¼ oz. Captain Morgan
   Original Spiced Rum
¼ oz. blue curaçao
2 oz. sweet & sour mix
6 oz. crushed ice

Shake with crushed ice. Pour into old-fashioned glass.

Alabama Fizz

1¼ oz. gin
juice of ½ lemon
1 tsp. sugar
6 oz. club soda

Shake gin, lemon juice, and sugar with ice and strain into a Collins glass over ice cubes. Top with soda and garnish with mint.

Alaska Cocktail

1 oz. gin
¼ oz. Chartreuse, yellow
1 oz. ice water or soda
2 dashes bitters

Stir ingredients with crushed ice and strain into a chilled cocktail glass.

Alexander

¾ oz. gin
½ oz. crème de cacao
1 oz. Half-and-Half

Combine all ingredients with crushed ice in a cocktail shaker and mix well. Strain into a chilled cocktail glass and sprinkle with nutmeg.

Alfonso Special

½ oz. Grand Marnier
¼ oz. gin
¼ oz. dry vermouth
2 dashes sweet vermouth
1 dash bitters

Shake or stir ingredients with ice and strain into chilled cocktail glass.

All-American Fizz

¾ oz. gin
½ oz. Cognac
juice of ½ lemon
2 dashes grenadine
8 oz. club soda

Shake gin, Cognac, lemon juice, and grenadine with ice and strain into a Collins glass over ice cubes. Fill with soda and stir.

Angler's Cocktail

1¼ oz. gin
3 dashes Angostura bitters
3 dashes orange bitters
3 dashes grenadine

Shake all ingredients in cocktail shaker with cracked ice. Strain over ice cubes into chilled old-fashioned glass.

Apricot Anise Collins

¾ oz. gin
¼ oz. apricot brandy
¼ oz. anisette
½ oz. lemon juice
3 oz. club soda

Shake gin, brandy, anisette, and lemon juice with ice. Strain into a Collins glass over ice cubes. Top with soda and garnish with a slice of lemon.

Aruba

1 oz. gin
¼ oz. white curaçao
1 oz. lemon juice
1 tsp. almond syrup
½ egg white

Combine ingredients with cracked ice in a shaker. Shake well. Strain into chilled cocktail glass.

Barnum

¾ oz. gin
½ oz. apricot brandy
2 dashes bitters

Shake with ice. Strain over ice cubes in old-fashioned glass.

Bayard Fizz

1¼ oz. gin
1 tbsp. maraschino liqueur
1 tbsp. lemon juice
1 tsp. raspberry syrup
sparkling water
fresh raspberries

Combine all except water and raspberries in a cocktail shaker with ice cubes. Shake well. Strain over ice cubes into chilled highball glass. Top off with sparkling water and drop in a few fresh raspberries.

Belmont

1¼ oz. gin
¾ oz. Half-and-Half
½ oz. raspberry syrup

Stir all ingredients with cracked ice in a mixing glass. Strain into chilled cocktail glass.

Bennett Cocktail

1¼ oz. gin
½ oz. lime juice
½ tsp. sugar
2 dashes bitters

Shake ingredients with ice and strain into a chilled cocktail glass.

Bermuda Highball

½ oz. gin
¼ oz. brandy
¼ oz. dry vermouth
sparkling water

Pour liquors into chilled highball glass over ice cubes. Stir well. Fill with water. Add twist of lemon peel and stir again gently.

Bermuda Rose Cocktail

1 oz. gin
¼ oz. apricot brandy
1¼ oz. club soda
¼ oz. lime juice
1 dash grenadine

Shake ingredients with ice and strain into a chilled cocktail glass.

Bijou Cocktail

½ oz. gin
½ oz. sweet vermouth
¼ oz. Chartreuse, green
1 dash orange bitters

Stir ingredients thoroughly with crushed or shaved ice and strain into a chilled cocktail glass. Garnish with a maraschino cherry.

Bird of Paradise Cooler

1¼ oz. gin
1 oz. lemon juice
1 tsp. grenadine
1 tsp. bar sugar
1 egg white
sparkling water

Combine all except water in a cocktail shaker with cracked ice. Shake vigorously. Strain over ice cubes into chilled highball glass. Fill with sparkling water and stir gently.

Blood & Sand Cocktail

½ oz. gin
¼ oz. dry vermouth
¼ oz. sweet vermouth
¼ oz. strawberry liqueur

Shake ingredients with ice and strain into a chilled cocktail glass. Garnish with a fresh strawberry.

Blue Devil

1 oz. gin
¼ oz. blue curaçao
½ oz. lemon juice

Shake with ice. Strain into a chilled cocktail glass. Garnish with a lemon slice.

Blue Moon Cocktail

¾ oz. gin
½ oz. blue curaçao

Shake ingredients with ice and strain over crushed ice in a cocktail glass. Garnish with lemon peel.

Boomerang

1 oz. gin
¼ oz. dry vermouth
½ oz. lime juice

Shake with ice. Strain into a chilled cocktail glass. Garnish with a lime slice.

Boxcar

¾ oz. gin
½ oz. triple sec
1 tsp. lemon juice
1–2 dashes grenadine
1 egg white

Shake well with ice. Strain into a prechilled cocktail glass that has been rimmed with sugar.

Brittany

1 oz. gin
¼ oz. Amer Picon
½ oz. lemon juice
½ oz. orange juice
½ tsp. bar sugar

Combine all with cracked ice in a cocktail shaker. Shake well and strain into chilled cocktail glass. Garnish with orange twist.

Bronx Cocktail

1 oz. gin
⅛ oz. dry vermouth
⅛ oz. sweet vermouth
¼ oz. orange juice

Shake all ingredients with ice and strain into chilled cocktail glass. Garnish with orange slice.

Bronx River

1 oz. gin
¼ oz. sweet vermouth
juice of ½ lemon
½ tsp. bar sugar

Stir ingredients with ice. Strain into a chilled cocktail glass.

Cabaret Cocktail

1 oz. gin
¼ oz. dry vermouth
2 dashes Benedictine
1 dash bitters

Stir ingredients with crushed or shaved ice. Strain into a chilled cocktail glass. Garnish with a maraschino cherry.

Café de Paris Cocktail

1¼ oz. gin
1 tsp. Pernod
1 tsp. Half-and-Half
1 egg white

Combine all with cracked ice in a cocktail shaker. Shake well and strain into chilled cocktail glass.

Campari, Gin, and Soda

¾ oz. Campari
½ oz. gin
6 oz. club soda

Fill highball glass with ice cubes. Add Campari and gin. Top with soda and stir. Garnish with twist of lemon.

Caruso

¾ oz. gin
¼ oz. dry vermouth
¼ oz. green crème de menthe

Combine all with cracked ice in a cocktail shaker. Shake well and strain into chilled cocktail glass.

Casino

1¼ oz. gin
1 tsp. maraschino liqueur
½ oz. lemon juice
2 dashes orange bitters

Combine all with cracked ice in a cocktail shaker. Shake well and strain into chilled cocktail glass.

Chanticleer

1¼ oz. gin
1 oz. lemon juice
1 tbsp. raspberry syrup
1 egg white

Combine all with cracked ice in a cocktail shaker. Shake well and strain into chilled old-fashioned glass.

Chelsea Sidecar

1 oz. gin
¼ oz. triple sec
½ oz. lemon juice

Combine all with cracked ice in a cocktail shaker. Shake well and strain into chilled cocktail glass.

Cherry Cobbler

¾ oz. gin
¼ oz. Cherry Heering
¼ oz. crème de cassis
½ oz. lemon juice
1 tbsp. simple syrup

Combine all with cracked ice in a cocktail shaker. Shake well and strain into chilled old-fashioned glass. Garnish with maraschino cherry and lemon slice.

Clover Club Cocktail

1¼ oz. gin
1 oz. lemon juice
2 tsp. grenadine
1 egg white

Combine all with cracked ice in a cocktail shaker. Shake well and strain into chilled cocktail glass.

Colonial Cocktail

1¼ oz. gin
1 tsp. maraschino liqueur
½ oz. grapefruit juice

Combine all with cracked ice in a cocktail shaker. Shake well and strain into chilled cocktail glass. Garnish with olive.

Colony Club

1 oz. gin
1 tsp. Pernod
3–5 dashes orange bitters

Combine all with cracked ice in a cocktail shaker. Shake well and strain into chilled cocktail glass.

Cooperstown Cocktail

1 oz. gin
⅛ oz. dry vermouth
⅛ oz. sweet vermouth

Combine all with cracked ice in a cocktail shaker. Shake well and strain into chilled cocktail glass. Garnish with mint sprig.

Coronado

1 oz. gin
¼ oz. white curaçao
3–5 dashes Kirschwasser
2 oz. pineapple juice

Combine all with cracked ice in a cocktail shaker. Shake well and strain into chilled old-fashioned glass. Garnish with cherry.

Crimson

1 oz. gin
2 tsp. lime juice
1 tsp. grenadine
¼ oz. ruby port

Combine all except port with cracked ice in a cocktail shaker. Shake well, strain into chilled cocktail glass, and float port on top.

Danish Gin Fizz

1 oz. gin
¼ oz. Cherry Heering
1 tsp. Kirschwasser
½ oz. lime juice
½ tsp. bar sugar
sparkling water

Combine all except water with cracked ice in a cocktail shaker. Shake well and strain into chilled highball glass. Fill with sparkling water and stir gently. Garnish with lime slice and cherry.

Deep Sea

¾ oz. gin
½ oz. dry vermouth
½ tsp. Pernod
1 dash orange bitters

Combine all with cracked ice in a mixing glass. Strain into chilled cocktail glass.

Delmonico Cocktail

¾ oz. gin
¼ oz. brandy
⅛ oz. dry vermouth
⅛ oz. sweet vermouth
2 dashes Angostura bitters

Combine all with cubed ice in a mixing glass. Stir well, strain into cocktail glass, and garnish with lemon twist.

Derby

1 oz. gin
¼ oz. peach brandy

Shake with ice. Strain over crushed ice in a wineglass. Garnish with a mint sprig.

Diamond Fizz

1¼ oz. gin
½ oz. lemon juice
1 tsp. bar sugar
Champagne or sparkling
    wine

Combine all except Champagne with cracked ice in a cocktail shaker. Shake well and strain over ice cubes into chilled highball glass and fill with Champagne. Stir gently.

Diamond Head

1 oz. gin
¼ oz. apricot brandy
1 oz. lemon juice
½ tsp. bar sugar
½ egg white

Combine all with cracked ice in a cocktail shaker. Shake well and strain into chilled cocktail glass.

Dixie Cocktail

¾ oz. gin
¼ oz. dry vermouth
¼ oz. Pernod
juice of ¼ orange
2 dashes grenadine

Shake ingredients with ice. Strain into a chilled cocktail glass.

Dry Martini

1⅛ oz. gin
⅛ oz. dry vermouth

Stir with ice. Strain into prechilled cocktail glass. Garnish with an olive.

Dubarry Cocktail

1 oz. gin
¼ oz. dry vermouth
4 dashes Pernod
1 oz. orange juice
1 dash bitters

Stir ingredients with shaved or crushed ice. Strain into a chilled cocktail glass. Garnish with an orange slice.

Emerald Cooler

¾ oz. gin
½ oz. green crème de menthe
¼ oz. lemon juice
6 oz. club soda

Pour gin, crème de menthe, and lemon juice over ice in a highball glass. Fill with club soda. Stir. Garnish with a lemon twist.

Emerald Isle Cocktail

1 oz. gin
2 tsp. crème de menthe
3 dashes Angostura bitters

Combine all with cracked ice in a mixing glass. Strain into chilled cocktail glass and garnish with green cherry.

Fallen Angel Cocktail

1 oz. gin
¼ oz. white crème de menthe
½ oz. lemon juice
1 dash Angostura bitters

Shake ingredients with shaved or crushed ice. Strain into a chilled cocktail glass. Garnish with a maraschino cherry.

Fare Thee Well

1 oz. gin
¼ oz. dry vermouth
1 dash sweet vermouth
1 dash Cointreau

Combine all with cracked ice in a cocktail shaker. Shake well and strain into chilled old-fashioned glass.

Farmer's Cocktail

¾ oz. gin
½ oz. dry vermouth
1 oz. sweet vermouth
3 dashes Angostura bitters

Combine all with cracked ice in a cocktail shaker. Shake well and strain into chilled cocktail glass.

Fifty-Fifty

½ oz. gin
½ oz. dry vermouth

Combine all with cracked ice in a mixing glass. Strain into chilled cocktail glass and garnish with Spanish olive.

Fino Martini

1¼ oz. gin
1 tsp. fino sherry

Stir ingredients in a mixing glass with ice cubes. Strain into chilled cocktail glass and garnish with lemon twist.

Flamingo Cocktail

¾ oz. gin
½ oz. apricot brandy
½ oz. lime juice
1 dash grenadine

Shake ingredients with crushed or shaved ice. Strain into a chilled cocktail glass.

14-Carat Rock

¾ oz. gin
½ oz. anisette
8 oz. orange juice
1¼ tsp. butter

Heat gin, anisette, and orange juice. Pour into a heated mug. Add butter. Garnish with a cinnamon stick.

Free Silver

¾ oz. gin
½ oz. dark rum
1 oz. lemon juice
1 tbsp. milk
½ tsp. bar sugar
sparkling water

Combine all but water with cracked ice in a cocktail shaker. Shake well and strain over ice cubes into chilled Collins glass. Fill with sparkling water and stir gently.

French Rose

½ oz. gin
½ oz. cherry brandy
¼ oz. cherry liqueur

Shake with crushed or shaved ice. Strain into a chilled cocktail glass.

Genoa

¾ oz. gin
¼ oz. grappa
⅛ oz. white sambuca
2 tsp. dry vermouth

Stir all with cracked ice in a mixing glass. Strain into chilled cocktail glass and garnish with an olive.

Gibson Martini

1 oz. gin
¼ oz. dry vermouth

Stir with ice. Strain into a prechilled cocktail glass. Garnish with a twist of lemon peel and serve with one to three pearl onions.

Gilroy

½ oz. gin
¼ oz. cherry brandy
¼ oz. dry vermouth
¼ oz. lemon juice
3–5 dashes orange bitters

Combine all ingredients with cracked ice in a cocktail shaker and shake well. Pour into chilled old-fashioned glass.

Gimlet

1¼ oz. gin
¼ oz. lime juice

Shake with ice. Strain into a prechilled cocktail glass.

Gin Aloha

¾ oz. gin
½ oz. triple sec
½ oz. pineapple juice
1 dash orange bitters

Combine all ingredients with cracked ice in a cocktail shaker. Shake well and strain into chilled cocktail glass.

Gin and Berries

1 oz. gin
¼ oz. strawberry liqueur
2 oz. frozen strawberries, with juice
4 dashes lemon juice
¼ cup crushed ice
1 oz. club soda

Blend gin, liqueur, strawberries, lemon juice, and crushed ice in a blender at low speed. Pour into wineglass. Top with club soda. Garnish with a fresh strawberry.

Gin and Bitters (Pink Gin)

1¼ oz. gin
1 tsp. Angostura bitters

Pour bitters into cocktail glass and swirl around until it is entirely coated with bitters. Fill with gin. This drink should be served at room temperature.

Gin and Ginger

1¼ oz. gin
ginger ale

Pour gin into chilled highball glass filled with ice cubes. Twist lemon over glass and drop in. Fill with ginger ale and stir gently.

Gin and Tonic

1¼ oz. gin
6 oz. tonic water

Pour gin over ice in a highball glass. Fill with tonic water. Squeeze lime wedge over drink and drop into glass. Stir.

Gin Buck

1¼ oz. gin
⅙ oz. lime juice
6 oz. ginger ale

Pour gin and lime juice over ice cubes in a highball glass. Fill with ginger ale. Stir. Garnish with a lime twist.

Gin Cobbler

1¼ oz. gin
1 tsp. simple syrup
sparkling water

Stir gin and simple syrup with cracked ice in a chilled highball glass. Fill with sparkling water and garnish with orange slice.

Gin Cooler

1¼ oz. gin
½ tsp. bar sugar
sparkling water

Mix gin with sugar in the bottom of a chilled Collins glass. Add ice cubes and fill with sparkling water. Stir gently and garnish with lemon peel.

Gin Daisy

1¼ oz. gin
½ oz. lemon juice
¼ oz. grenadine
4 oz. club soda

Shake gin, lemon juice, and grenadine with ice. Strain into highball glass half-filled with ice. Top with soda. Garnish with lemon slice.

Gin Fix

1¼ oz. gin
1 tsp. bar sugar
1 oz. lemon juice
1 tsp. water

Dissolve sugar in lemon juice and water in the bottom of a chilled highball glass. Add gin and stir. Fill glass with ice cubes and garnish with lemon slice.

Gin Fizz

1¼ oz. gin
juice of ½ lemon
juice of ½ lime
2 tsp. bar sugar
6 oz. club soda

Shake gin, lemon juice, lime juice, and sugar with ice. Strain over ice cubes in a tall glass. Fill with club soda. Stir. Garnish with lemon slice.

Gin Frozen Margarita

1 oz. gin
¼ oz. triple sec
4 oz. sweet & sour mix
1 orange slice
12 oz. crushed ice

Blend all ingredients until slushy. Serve in a prechilled margarita glass rimmed with salt.

Gin Margarita

1 oz. gin
¼ oz triple sec
juice of ½ lime

Shake ingredients with ice. Serve in old-fashion glass rimmed with salt.

Gin Rickey

1¼ oz. gin
juice of ½ lime
6 oz. club soda

Pour gin and lime juice over ice in a highball glass. Add soda. Stir. Garnish with a lime wedge.

Gin Sangaree

1¼ oz. gin
½ tsp. bar sugar
1 tsp. water
sparkling water
1 tbsp. ruby port

Dissolve sugar in water in the bottom of a chilled highball glass. Add gin and stir. Add ice cubes and fill glass with sparkling water. Stir gently and float port on top.

Gin Sidecar

¾ oz. gin
½ oz. triple sec
1 oz. lemon juice

Combine ingredients with cracked ice in a cocktail shaker and shake well. Pour into chilled old-fashioned glass.

Gin Sling

1¼ oz. gin
1 tsp. bar sugar
1 tsp. water
juice of ½ lemon

In an old-fashioned glass dissolve sugar in water and lemon juice. Add ice cubes and gin. Stir. Garnish with lemon twist.

Gin Sour

1¼ oz. gin
juice of ½ lemon
½ tsp. bar sugar

Shake with ice. Strain into prechilled sour glass. Garnish with lemon slice and maraschino cherry.

Gin Swizzle

1¼ oz. gin
1½ oz. lime juice
2 dashes Angostura bitters
1 tsp. bar sugar
sparkling water

Combine all ingredients except water with cracked ice in a cocktail shaker and shake well. Strain over ice cubes and pour into chilled Collins glass. Fill with water and stir gently. Serve with a swizzle stick.

Golden Daze

¾ oz. gin
½ oz. peach brandy
1 oz. orange juice

Combine all ingredients with cracked ice in a cocktail shaker. Shake well and strain into chilled cocktail glass.

Golden Fizz

1¼ oz. gin
1 oz. lime juice
½ tsp. bar sugar
1 egg yolk
sparkling water

Combine all except water with cracked ice in a cocktail shaker and shake well. Pour into chilled Collins glass. Fill with sparkling water and stir gently. Garnish with lemon slice.

Golf Cocktail

1 oz. gin
¼ oz. dry vermouth
3 dashes Angostura bitters

Combine all ingredients with cracked ice in a mixing glass. Strain into chilled cocktail glass.

Grand Passion

¾ oz. gin
½ oz. dry vermouth
1 oz. passion-fruit syrup
½ oz. lemon juice

Combine all ingredients with cracked ice in a cocktail shaker and shake well. Strain into chilled cocktail glass and garnish with orange twist.

Grand Royal Fizz

1¼ oz. gin
1 tsp. maraschino liqueur
1½ oz. orange juice
1 oz. lemon juice
2 tsp. Half-and-Half
½ tsp. bar sugar
sparkling water

Combine all except water with cracked ice in a cocktail shaker and shake well. Strain into chilled highball glass over ice cubes. Fill with sparkling water and stir gently.

Grapefruit Cocktail

1¼ oz. gin
¾ oz. grapefruit juice

Shake ingredients with ice. Strain into a chilled cocktail glass.

Great Dane

½ oz. gin
¼ oz. Cherry Heering
⅛ oz. dry vermouth
1 tsp. Kirschwasser

Combine all ingredients with cracked ice in a cocktail shaker and shake well. Strain into chilled cocktail glass. Garnish with lemon twist.

Great Secret

¾ oz. gin
½ oz. Lillet blanc
3–5 dashes Angostura
  bitters

Combine all ingredients with cracked ice in a cocktail shaker and shake well. Strain into chilled cocktail glass and garnish with orange twist.

Greenback

¾ oz. gin
½ oz. green crème de
  menthe
1 oz. lemon juice

Combine all ingredients with cracked ice in a cocktail shaker and shake well. Strain into chilled old-fashioned glass over ice cubes.

Green Dragon

¾ oz. gin
¼ oz. green crème de
  menthe
⅛ oz. Jägermeister
½ oz. lime juice
3–5 dashes orange bitters

Combine all ingredients with cracked ice in a cocktail shaker and shake well. Strain into chilled cocktail glass.

Hasty Cocktail

1 oz. gin
¼ oz. dry vermouth
2 dashes Pernod
3 dashes grenadine

Shake ingredients with crushed or shaved ice. Strain into a chilled cocktail glass.

Hawaiian Cocktail

1 oz. gin
¼ oz. triple sec
½ oz. pineapple juice

Shake ingredients with crushed or shaved ice. Strain into a chilled cocktail glass.

Homestead Cocktail

¾ oz. gin
½ oz. sweet vermouth

Stir ingredients with crushed or shaved ice. Strain into a chilled cocktail glass. Garnish with a slice of orange.

Honolulu Cocktail

1¼ oz. gin
4 dashes orange juice
4 dashes pineapple juice
4 dashes lemon juice
1 dash bitters
½ tsp. bar sugar

Shake ingredients with crushed or shaved ice. Strain into a chilled cocktail glass and garnish with a slice of pineapple.

Hula-Hula

1¼ oz. gin
1 oz. orange juice
1 tbsp. triple sec

Combine all ingredients with cracked ice in a cocktail shaker and shake well. Strain into chilled cocktail glass.

Ideal Cocktail

¾ oz. gin
½ oz. dry vermouth
½ tsp. maraschino liqueur
1 tsp. lemon juice

Combine all ingredients with cracked ice in a cocktail shaker and shake well. Pour into chilled cocktail glass. Garnish with maraschino cherry.

Imperial Cocktail

1 oz. gin
¼ oz. dry vermouth
½ tsp. maraschino liqueur
2 dashes Angostura bitters

Combine all ingredients in a mixing glass with ice cubes and stir well. Strain into chilled cocktail glass.

Income Tax Cocktail

1 oz. gin
1 tbsp. dry vermouth
1 tbsp. sweet vermouth
1½ oz. orange juice
3 dashes Angostura bitters

Combine all ingredients with cracked ice in a cocktail shaker and shake well. Strain into chilled cocktail glass.

Journalist

1 oz. gin
1 tsp. dry vermouth
1 tsp. sweet vermouth
1 tsp. triple sec
1 tsp. lime juice
1 dash Angostura bitters

Combine all ingredients with cracked ice in a cocktail shaker and shake well. Strain into chilled cocktail glass.

Judgette Cocktail

½ oz. gin
½ oz. peach brandy
¼ oz. dry vermouth
½ tsp. lime juice

Combine all ingredients with cracked ice in a cocktail shaker and shake well. Strain into chilled cocktail glass.

Jupiter Cocktail

¾ oz. gin
½ oz. dry vermouth
2 tsp. crème de violette
2 tsp. orange juice

Combine all ingredients with cracked ice in a cocktail shaker and shake well. Strain into chilled cocktail glass.

Key Club Cocktail

¾ oz. gin
¼ oz. rum
¼ oz. Falernum
½ oz. lime juice

Combine all ingredients with cracked ice in a cocktail shaker and shake well. Strain into chilled cocktail glass. Garnish with pineapple spear.

Kir Gin Cocktail

1 oz. gin
¼ oz. crème de cassis
4 oz. club soda

Pour gin and cassis over ice cubes in a wineglass. Fill with club soda. Stir. Garnish with a lemon twist.

Knickerbocker

1 oz. gin
⅛ oz. dry vermouth
⅛ oz. sweet vermouth

Stir all ingredients with crushed or shaved ice and strain into a chilled cocktail glass. Garnish with lemon peel.

Kyoto Cocktail

¾ oz. gin
¼ oz. melon liqueur
⅛ oz. dry vermouth
¼ tsp. lemon juice

Combine all ingredients with cracked ice in a cocktail shaker and shake well. Strain into chilled cocktail glass.

Lady Finger

¾ oz. gin
¼ oz. Kirschwasser
¼ oz. cherry brandy

Shake ingredients with ice. Strain over crushed ice in a chilled cocktail glass.

Leap Frog Highball

1¼ oz. gin
1½ oz. lemon juice
ginger ale

Pour gin and juice into a chilled highball glass over ice cubes. Fill with ginger ale and stir gently.

Leap Year Cocktail

¾ oz. gin
¼ oz. sweet vermouth
¼ oz. Grand Marnier
½ tsp. lemon juice

Combine all ingredients with cracked ice in a cocktail shaker and shake well. Strain into chilled cocktail glass.

London Cocktail

1 oz. gin
⅛ oz. maraschino liqueur
5 dashes orange bitters
½ tsp. bar sugar

Combine all ingredients with cracked ice in a cocktail shaker and shake well. Strain into chilled cocktail glass. Garnish with lemon twist.

Long Beach Iced Tea

½ oz. triple sec
¼ oz. gin
¼ oz. vodka
¼ oz. dark rum
2 oz. sweet & sour mix
4 oz. cranberry juice

Shake first five ingredients and pour into an ice cube–filled Collins or specialty glass. Top with cranberry juice. Garnish with lemon wedge.

Long Island Iced Tea

¼ oz. gin
¼ oz. vodka
¼ oz. white rum
¼ oz. tequila
¼ oz. triple sec
1 oz. sweet & sour mix
6 oz. cola

Fill Collins glass with ice. Add all except cola. Stir. Add cola to fill. Garnish with lemon wedge.

Maiden's Blush Cocktail

1 oz. gin
¼ oz. triple sec
⅙ oz. grenadine
2 dashes lemon juice

Shake ingredients with crushed or shaved ice. Strain into a chilled cocktail glass.

Martini

¾ oz. gin
½ oz. dry vermouth

Stir with ice. Strain into prechilled cocktail glass. Garnish with an olive.

Matinee

¾ oz. gin
¼ oz. sweet vermouth
⅛ oz. Chartreuse, green
½ oz. orange juice
1 dash orange bitters

Combine all ingredients with cracked ice in a cocktail shaker and shake well. Strain into chilled cocktail glass.

Maurice

¾ oz. gin
¼ oz. dry vermouth
¼ oz. sweet vermouth
1 oz. orange juice
1 dash Angostura bitters

Combine all ingredients with cracked ice in a cocktail shaker and shake well. Strain into chilled cocktail glass.

Melon Cocktail

1 oz. gin
¼ oz. maraschino liqueur
½ oz. lemon juice

Combine all ingredients with cracked ice in a cocktail shaker and shake well. Strain into chilled cocktail glass. Garnish with maraschino cherry and lemon twist.

Merry Widow

¾ oz. gin
¼ oz. dry vermouth
⅛ oz. Pernod
3–5 dashes Peychaud's
  bitters

Combine ingredients with cracked ice in a cocktail shaker and shake well. Strain into chilled cocktail glass. Garnish with lemon twist.

Million Dollar Cocktail

¾ oz. gin
½ oz. sweet vermouth
½ oz. pineapple juice
⅙ oz. grenadine
1 egg white

Shake ingredients vigorously with ice. Strain into a chilled cocktail glass.

Mint Collins

1¼ oz. gin
4 mint leaves
juice of ½ lemon
1 tsp. sugar
6 oz. club soda

In Collins glass, muddle four mint leaves in the gin, lemon, and sugar. Add ½ cup crushed ice. Top with club soda. Garnish with a sprig of mint.

Mississippi Mule

1 oz. gin
¼ oz. crème de cassis
½ oz. lemon juice

Combine all ingredients with cracked ice in a cocktail shaker and shake well. Strain into chilled old-fashioned glass.

Moldau

¾ oz. gin
½ oz. slivovitz
½ oz. orange juice
½ oz. lemon juice

Combine all ingredients with cracked ice in a cocktail shaker and shake well. Strain into chilled cocktail glass.

Montmartre

1 oz. gin
¼ oz. sweet vermouth
¼ oz. white curaçao

Combine all ingredients with cracked ice in a cocktail shaker and shake well. Strain into chilled cocktail glass.

Moonshot

1¼ oz. gin
3 oz. clam juice
1 dash Tabasco sauce

Combine all in a mixing glass with ice cubes and stir. Pour into chilled old-fashioned glass.

Morro

¾ oz. gin
½ oz. dark rum
½ oz. lime juice
½ oz. pineapple juice
½ tsp. bar sugar

Combine all ingredients with cracked ice in a cocktail shaker and shake well. Strain into sugar-rimmed old-fashioned glass over ice cubes.

Napoleon

1 oz. gin
¼ oz. white curaçao
1 tsp. Lillet rouge
1 tsp. Amer Picon

Combine ingredients with cracked ice in a mixing glass and stir. Strain into chilled cocktail glass.

New Orleans Fizz

1 oz. gin
4 oz. milk
½ oz. simple syrup
1 oz. orange flower water

Shake well. Serve in a small ice cube–filled Hurricane glass. Top with nutmeg.

Newbury

¾ oz. gin
½ oz. sweet vermouth
½ tsp. triple sec

Combine all ingredients with cracked ice in a cocktail shaker and shake well. Strain into chilled cocktail glass. Garnish with lemon twist.

Newport Cooler

1 oz. gin
⅛ oz. brandy
⅛ oz. peach liqueur
¼ tsp. lime juice
ginger ale

Pour ingredients except ginger ale into a chilled Collins glass over ice cubes. Fill with ginger ale and stir gently.

Normandy Cocktail

¾ oz. gin
¼ oz. applejack
⅛ oz. apricot brandy
¼ oz. lemon juice

Combine all ingredients with cracked ice in a cocktail shaker and shake well. Strain into chilled cocktail glass.

Opera

¾ oz. gin
¼ oz. Lillet rouge
⅛ oz. maraschino liqueur

Stir ingredients with cracked ice in a mixing glass. Strain into chilled cocktail glass.

Orange Blossom

1¼ oz. gin
1 oz. orange juice

Shake with ice. Strain into a prechilled cocktail glass rimmed with sugar. Garnish with an orange slice.

Orange Oasis

¾ oz. gin
½ oz. cherry brandy
½ cup orange juice
ginger ale

Combine all ingredients except ginger ale with cracked ice in a cocktail shaker. Strain over ice cubes into chilled highball glass. Fill with ginger ale and stir gently.

Paisley Martini

1 oz. gin
½ tsp. dry vermouth
½ tsp. scotch

Combine all with ice cubes in a mixing glass. Stir well and strain into a chilled cocktail glass.

Park Avenue

1 oz. gin
¼ oz. sweet vermouth
½ oz. pineapple juice

Stir ingredients with cracked ice in a mixing glass. Strain into chilled cocktail glass.

Parisian

½ oz. gin
½ oz. dry vermouth
¼ oz. crème de cassis

Shake with ice. Strain into chilled cocktail glass.

Pegu Club Cocktail

¾ oz. gin
½ oz. white curaçao
1 tbsp. lime juice
1 dash Angostura bitters
1 dash orange bitters

Combine all ingredients with cracked ice in a cocktail shaker and shake well. Strain into chilled cocktail glass.

Perfect Martini

1⅛ oz. gin
½ tsp. dry vermouth
½ tsp. sweet vermouth

Combine all ingredients with ice cubes in a mixing glass and stir well. Strain into chilled cocktail glass. Garnish with one olive.

Piccadilly Cocktail

¾ oz. gin
½ oz. dry vermouth
¼ tsp. Pernod
1 dash grenadine

Stir ingredients with ice in a mixing glass. Strain into chilled cocktail glass.

Pink Lady

1¼ oz. gin
¾ oz. lemon juice
½ oz. grenadine
1 egg white

Shake very well with ice. Strain into a chilled cocktail glass.

Pink Pussycat

1¼ oz. gin
pineapple juice
1 dash grenadine

Pour gin into a chilled highball glass over ice cubes. Fill with pineapple juice and add a dash of grenadine. Stir gently and garnish with pineapple spear.

Pink Rose

1¼ oz. gin
1 tbsp. lemon juice
1 tsp. Half-and-Half
¼ tsp. grenadine
1 egg white

Combine all ingredients with cracked ice in a cocktail shaker and shake well. Strain into chilled cocktail glass.

Prince's Smile

¾ oz. gin
¼ oz. apple brandy
¼ oz. apricot brandy
1 tsp. lemon juice

Combine all ingredients with cracked ice in a cocktail shaker and shake well. Strain into chilled cocktail glass.

Ramos Fizz

1¼ oz. gin
juice of ½ lemon
juice of ½ lime
½ oz. heavy cream
2 dashes orange flower water
1 egg white
1 cup crushed ice
2 oz. club soda

Blend all ingredients except soda at high speed for 5 seconds. Pour into a tall glass and fill with club soda. Stir gently.

Racquet Club Cocktail

1 oz. gin
¼ oz. dry vermouth
1 dash orange bitters

Combine all in a mixing glass with ice cubes. Stir well and strain into a chilled cocktail glass.

Red Cloud

¾ oz. gin
½ oz. apricot liqueur
1 oz. lemon juice
1 tsp. grenadine
1 dash Angostura bitters

Combine all ingredients with cracked ice in a cocktail shaker and shake well. Strain into chilled cocktail glass.

Red Lion

¾ oz. gin
½ oz. orange liqueur
½ oz. lemon juice
½ oz. orange juice
½ tsp. grenadine

Combine all ingredients with cracked ice in a cocktail shaker and shake well. Strain into chilled cocktail glass.

Renaissance

1 oz. gin
¼ oz. fino sherry
½ oz. Half-and-Half

Combine all ingredients with cracked ice in a cocktail shaker and shake well. Strain into chilled old-fashioned glass over ice cubes. Sprinkle nutmeg on top.

Rendezvous

¾ oz. gin
½ oz. Kirschwasser
½ oz. Campari

Combine all ingredients with cracked ice in a cocktail shaker and shake well. Strain into chilled cocktail glass. Garnish with lemon twist.

Resolute Cocktail

¾ oz. gin
½ oz. apricot brandy
½ oz. lemon juice

Combine all ingredients with cracked ice in a cocktail shaker and shake well. Strain into chilled cocktail glass.

Rocky Green Dragon

¾ oz. gin
¼ oz. Chartreuse, green
⅛ oz. cognac

Combine all ingredients with cracked ice in a cocktail shaker and shake well. Strain into chilled cocktail glass.

Roman Cooler

¾ oz. gin
½ oz. Punt e Mes
½ oz. lemon juice
½ tsp. sweet vermouth
1 tsp. simple syrup
sparkling water

Combine all ingredients except water with cracked ice in a cocktail shaker and shake well. Strain into chilled highball glass over ice cubes. Fill with water and stir gently. Garnish with orange twist.

Royal Gin Fizz

1¼ oz. gin
1 oz. lemon juice
1 tsp. bar sugar
1 whole egg
sparkling water

Combine all ingredients except water with cracked ice in a cocktail shaker and shake vigorously. Strain into chilled highball glass over ice cubes. Fill with water and stir gently.

Saketini

1 oz. gin
¼ oz. sake

Combine all ingredients with cracked ice in a cocktail shaker and shake well. Strain into chilled cocktail glass. Garnish with lemon twist.

Seagram's Gin Frisco Collins

1¼ oz. Seagram's Extra
    Dry Gin
1 oz. grenadine
1 oz. lemon juice
1 oz. powdered sugar
tonic water

In a cocktail shaker, combine all ingredients except tonic water. Shake well. Fill a Collins glass with ice. Strain gin mixture into glass. Fill with tonic water. Stir. Garnish with a maraschino cherry and lemon or lime twist.

Seagram's Gin Gimlet

1¼ oz. Seagram's Extra
    Dry Gin
¾ oz. lime juice

Fill a cocktail glass with ice. Add gin and lime juice. Stir. Garnish with a slice of lime.

Seagram's Gin Lemonade

1¼ oz. Seagram's Extra
    Dry Gin
6 oz. lemonade

Pour gin over ice in a highball glass. Fill with lemonade. Stir. Garnish with a maraschino cherry and a lemon slice.

Seagram's Gin Salty Dog

1¼ oz. Seagram's Extra
    Dry Gin
6 oz. grapefruit juice

Pour gin over ice in a tall glass rimmed with coarse salt. Fill with grapefruit juice and stir.

Seagram's High Tea

1 oz. Seagram's Extra Dry
    Gin
¼ oz. triple sec
⅙ oz. lemon juice
½ tsp. bar sugar
6 oz. iced tea

Shake gin, triple sec, lemon juice, and sugar with ice. Strain over ice cubes in a highball glass. Fill with iced tea. Garnish with lemon wedge.

Seagram's Pink Lemonade

1¼ oz. gin
6 oz. pink lemonade

Pour gin over ice cubes in a highball glass. Fill with pink lemonade. Garnish with lemon slice.

Seagram's Sunburn

1¼ oz. Seagram's Extra
    Dry Gin
5 oz. lemon-lime soda
cranberry juice

Fill a highball glass with ice. Add gin and lemon-lime soda. Fill with cranberry juice. Stir. Garnish with an orange slice.

Seville

1 oz. gin
¼ oz. fino sherry
½ oz. lemon juice
½ oz. orange juice
1 tbsp. simple syrup

Combine all ingredients with cracked ice in a cocktail shaker and shake well. Strain into chilled old-fashioned glass.

Silver Fizz

1¼ oz. gin
1½ oz. lemon juice
1 tsp. bar sugar
1 egg white
sparkling water

Combine all ingredients except water with cracked ice in a cocktail shaker and shake well. Strain into chilled highball glass over ice cubes. Fill with sparkling water and stir gently.

Silver Shell

¾ oz. gin
½ oz. Jägermeister
⅛ oz. lemon juice

Combine all ingredients with cracked ice in a cocktail shaker and shake well. Strain into chilled cocktail glass.

Silver King Cocktail

1¼ oz. gin
1 oz. lemon juice
1 tsp. simple syrup
1 dash Angostura bitters
1 egg white

Combine all ingredients with cracked ice in a cocktail shaker and shake vigorously. Strain into chilled cocktail glass.

Singapore Sling

¾ oz. gin
½ oz. wild cherry brandy
2 oz. orange juice
2 oz. sour mix
1 splash grenadine for color

Blend with crushed ice. Serve in Hurricane glass. Garnish with lime wheel and a cherry.

Singapore Sling II

1 oz. gin
juice of ½ lemon
1 tsp. grenadine
6 oz. club soda
¼ oz. cherry brandy

Mix gin, lemon juice, and grenadine in a Collins glass. Add crushed ice, top with soda, stir. Float brandy on top. Garnish with a slice of lemon and a maraschino cherry.

Snowball

¾ oz. gin
½ oz. Pernod
½ oz. Half-and-Half

Combine all ingredients with cracked ice in a cocktail shaker and shake well. Strain into chilled cocktail glass.

Star Daisy

¾ oz. gin
½ oz. apple brandy
½ tsp. triple sec
1½ oz. lemon juice
1 tsp. simple syrup

Combine all ingredients with cracked ice in a cocktail shaker and shake well. Strain into chilled wineglass.

Sweet Martini

¾ oz. gin
½ oz. sweet vermouth

Stir with ice. Strain into prechilled cocktail glass. Garnish with an olive.

Tango Cocktail

¾ oz. gin
¼ oz. dry vermouth
¼ oz. sweet vermouth
2 dashes curaçao
½ oz. orange juice

Shake ingredients with ice. Strain into prechilled cocktail glass.

Tom Collins

1¼ oz. gin
1 tsp. bar sugar
juice of ½ lemon
6 oz. club soda

Shake gin, sugar, and lemon juice. Strain over crushed ice in a tall 14-oz. glass. Fill with soda. Stir. Garnish with lemon slice.

Twin Six Cocktail

1 oz. gin
¼ oz. sweet vermouth
½ oz. orange juice
⅙ oz. grenadine
1 egg white

Shake ingredients vigorously with ice. Strain into a chilled cocktail glass.

Wedding Belle Cocktail

½ oz. gin
½ oz. Lillet
¼ oz. cherry brandy
¼ oz. orange juice

Combine ingredients with cracked ice in a cocktail shaker. Shake well and strain into chilled cocktail glass.

Western Rose

¾ oz. gin
¼ oz. apricot brandy
¼ oz. dry vermouth
1 dash lemon juice

Shake ingredients with crushed or shaved ice. Strain into a chilled cocktail glass.

White Alexander

¾ oz. gin
½ oz. white crème de cacao
1 oz. heavy cream

Shake with ice. Strain into prechilled cocktail glass.

White Rose Cocktail

1¼ oz. gin
½ oz. orange juice
½ oz. lime juice
1 tsp. bar sugar
1 egg white

Shake ingredients vigorously with ice. Strain into a chilled cocktail glass.

Xanthia Cocktail

½ oz. gin
½ oz. cherry brandy
¼ oz. Chartreuse, yellow

Stir ingredients with crushed ice. Strain into a chilled cocktail glass.

ZuZu's Petals

¾ oz. gin
½ oz. Lillet
1 tsp. crème de violette
1 dash orange bitters

Stir ingredients well with crushed or shaved ice. Strain into a chilled cocktail glass.

Bar Game

◆ **The Game:** Ask someone to fold a small sheet of paper into three sections and to write one person's name on each section, with his or her own in the middle. Have him or her tear the pieces on the creases, fold each in half, and toss into a hat or a large glass. The object is to pick the person's name out of the hat.

◆ **The Solution:** The piece of paper in the middle will be torn on both sides.

RUM

A *Beachcomber* spent a *Day at the Beach* in Miami not far from the *Bermuda Triangle*. He found *Boston Cooler*, but he decided to wait for the *Midnight Express*, when he would have a *Night Cap*.

The sentence above is made up almost entirely from the names of rum drinks, but the versatility of this spirit is not limited to word games.

Consider this anecdote:

A persnickety lady of high standing attended a dinner party where, at night's end, she declared loudly that she was happy that no rum was present in the room. Ironically, she and the other guests had devoured a sumptuous dinner consisting of flaming cocktail sausages (rum-grilled), a spiced rum ham (basted with a rum-raisin sauce), and Bananas Foster (a dessert fried in rum).

Quite simply, as the story suggests, the strength of rum is in its multifareous uses.

The origins of rum can be traced back to 1493, when Columbus carried sugar cane cuttings from the Canary Islands to the West Indies. The indigenous Carib and Arawak Indians treasured the new-found sweet sticks. And as the sugar plantations grew, the rum industry began to evolve, with the English being the first to adopt the drink. In the 17th century, distilleries in New York and New England began producing rum made from West Indies molasses.

The process, while varied, is simple: sugar cane is boiled into molasses, then distilled and fermented. It is distilled at less than 190 proof and bottled at a proof of at least 80.

Rum, much like wine, reflects its country of origin in flavor, body, and bouquet. In fact rum is often named simply by its birthplace, such as Jamaican rum and Puerto Rican rum.

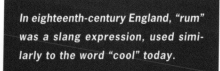

In eighteenth-century England, "rum" was a slang expression, used similarly to the word "cool" today.

The dry, light rums of the Caribbean, made in locales such as Puerto Rico, Trinidad, and Barbados, are always produced in continuous stills. Distilling them at very high proofs and limiting the aging, sometimes for only six months in oak casks, produces their fair complexion. In fact, some brands of Puerto Rican rum are as light as gin.

The dark rums of Jamaica, Haiti, and Martinique are distilled in pot stills at very low proofs and aged for up to twelve years. It is a heavier and richer spirit, and often sipped like a fine brandy. Caramel is sometimes added to further intensify the color, which often results in some Jamaican rums being as thick as black syrup.

The East Indian Batavia *arak,* a specialty rum from Java, is both light-bodied and pungently aromatic. Its offbeat flavor, combined with the fact that few bottles seem to make it to stores where wine and spirits are sold, make this a virtually unknown rum, except by connoisseurs.

American history is steeped in rum. Before 1775 the average North American is said to have consumed four gallons of rum annually. George Washington used to pass out rum during his electoral campaign. Paul Revere, it is said, celebrated after his legendary Midnight Ride with a glass of rum. And the Boston Tea Party was not only in response to the British government's taxation on tea but also an outcry against the new taxes on molasses.

The modern popularity of rum can be attributed to the emergence of two West Coast restaurants in the 1930s, Hollywood's Don the Beachcomber and the Bay Area's Trader Vic. While the Rum-and-Coke has long been on the top-ten list of favorite American cocktails, it was amid the bamboo and palm fronds of these two South Pacific–themed restaurants that the Mai Tai, Daiquiri, Zombie, and Piña Colada were introduced. Soon paper parasols floating in rum were fixtures in virtually every American city.

So, the next time you take a Boston Sidecar with your Bahama Mama to a Pink Paradise, throw up a toast to Trader Vic's, Don the Beachcomber, or Paul Revere.

Acapulco

¾ oz. dark rum	Shake with ice. Strain into chilled cocktail glass.
½ oz. gold tequila	
1½ oz. pineapple juice	
⅓ oz. grapefruit juice	

Aloha

½ oz. dark rum
¼ oz. dry vermouth
¼ oz. Cognac
¼ oz. gin
½ oz. lime juice
1 oz. soda water

Shake with ice cubes and strain into large cocktail glass. Garnish with lime wheel.

Ambrosia

¾ oz. dark rum
½ oz. curaçao
2 oz. orange juice
2 oz. heavy cream
1 oz. cream of coconut
8 oz. crushed ice

Mix ingredients in blender until smooth and creamy. Serve in a specialty glass. Rim glass with crushed toasted coconut and orange slice.

Anna's Wish

¾ oz. dark rum
½ oz. triple sec
6 oz. pineapple juice

Pour all ingredients over ice in a glass. Stir.

Antoine's Lullaby

1 oz. dark rum
⅛ oz. port
⅛ oz. orange curaçao
¾ oz. lemon juice

Stir ingredients with crushed ice. Strain into sugar-rimmed cocktail glass. Garnish with lemon twist.

Apple Pie à la Mode

¾ oz. Captain Morgan
   Original Spiced Rum
½ oz. apple schnapps
2 oz. apple juice
1 oz. cream of coconut
1 oz. heavy cream
2 tbsp. apple pie filling
8 oz. crushed ice

Mix ingredients in blender until smooth and creamy. Serve in specialty glass. Garnish with apple wedge or cinnamon stick.

Apple Pie Cocktail

¾ oz. dark rum
½ oz. sweet vermouth
1 tsp. apple brandy
3 dashes grenadine
1 tsp. lemon juice

Shake ingredients with ice. Strain into a chilled cocktail glass.

Bahama Mama

½ oz. dark rum
3 oz. orange juice
3 oz. piña colada mix
¾ oz. Captain Morgan
   Original Spiced Rum
½ oz. grenadine

Combine dark rum, orange juice, and piña colada mix in ice cube–filled specialty glass. Float Captain Morgan and grenadine on top. Garnish with a pineapple flag.

Bahia Cooler

¾ oz. dark rum
½ oz. white rum
2½ oz. pineapple juice
1 oz. coconut cream

Shake ingredients vigorously. Pour into Collins glass filled with crushed ice. Garnish with pineapple wedge.

Banana Colada

¾ oz. dark rum
½ oz. crème de banana
2 oz. cream of coconut
¼ oz. lemon juice
8 oz. crushed ice

Mix well in blender until smooth. Serve in specialty glass. Garnish with banana round and maraschino cherry on pick.

Banana Daiquiri

1 oz. dark rum
¼ oz. triple sec
juice of ½ lime
½ medium ripe banana
1 tsp. bar sugar
8 oz. crushed ice

Whirl all in a blender until smooth. Pour into wineglass.

Banana Daiquiri II

¾ oz. Captain Morgan
   Original Spiced Rum
½ oz. crème de banana
1¾ oz. sweet & sour mix
½ ripe banana

Blend all ingredients in a blender with a scoop of crushed ice.

Banana Slushee

¾ oz. dark rum
½ oz. crème de banana
4 oz. orange juice
½ oz. simple syrup
8 oz. crushed ice

Blend until slushy.

Barbados Punch

1 oz. Captain Morgan
  Original Spiced Rum
¼ oz. triple sec
1 oz. lime juice
2 oz. pineapple juice

Blend with crushed ice. Garnish with lime and pineapple.

Bat Bite

1¼ oz. dark rum
4 oz. cranberry juice

Combine in an ice cube–filled highball glass. Drop lime wedge into drink.

Beachcomber

1 oz. dark rum
¼ oz. triple sec
½ oz. lime juice
1 dash grenadine

Shake ingredients with ice and strain into a sugar-rimmed cocktail glass.

Berries 'n' Cream

½ oz. Captain Morgan
  Original Spiced Rum
¾ oz. wild-berry
  schnapps
3 oz. strawberry cocktail
  mix
2 oz. heavy cream
2 tbsp. raspberries or
  strawberries in syrup
8 oz. crushed ice

Mix ingredients in blender until smooth and creamy. Serve in specialty glass. Top with strawberries, blueberries, raspberries or combination.

Black Devil

1 oz. dark rum
¼ oz. dry vermouth

Shake ingredients with ice and strain into a chilled cocktail glass. Add splash of ice water. Garnish with a black olive.

Black Widow

¾ oz. dark rum
½ oz. Southern Comfort
1 oz. sweet & sour mix

Shake with ice cubes. Strain into stemmed cocktail glass. Garnish with lemon twist.

Blue Hawaiian

1 oz. dark rum
¼ oz. blue curaçao
1 oz. pineapple juice
½ oz. heavy cream
1 tsp. coconut cream

Shake ingredients with ice and strain into a chilled cocktail glass.

Blue Passion

¾ oz. Captain Morgan
    Original Spiced Rum
½ oz. blue curaçao
5 oz. sweet & sour mix
8 oz. crushed ice

Shake well with crushed ice and serve in a Collins glass. Garnish with a pineapple flag.

Bolero Cocktail

1 oz. dark rum
¼ oz. apple brandy
2 dashes sweet vermouth

Stir ingredients well with crushed or shaved ice. Strain into a chilled cocktail glass.

Bossa Nova

¾ oz. dark rum
¼ oz. apricot brandy
¼ oz. Galliano liqueur
5 oz. pineapple juice
½ oz. lemon juice

Combine ingredients in a cocktail shaker. Shake well. Pour into an ice cube–filled specialty glass. Garnish with pineapple fruit flag.

Breeze Punch

1¼ oz. dark rum
3 oz. passion-fruit juice
1 oz. sweet & sour mix

Shake ingredients with ice. Strain into a chilled cocktail glass.

Brown Derby

1¼ oz. dark rum
½ oz. lime juice
⅙ oz. maple syrup

Shake well with ice. Strain over ice cubes in an old-fashioned glass. Garnish with lime slice.

Calypso Cooler

½ oz. Captain Morgan
    Original Spiced Rum
½ oz. peach schnapps
¼ oz. dark rum
2 oz. orange juice
1 oz. grenadine
1 oz. lime juice
2 oz. lemon-lime soda

Shake all but soda well. Pour into ice cube–filled Collins or specialty glass. Top with lemon-lime soda. Garnish with an orange flag.

Captain Morgan's Daiquiri

1 oz. Captain Morgan
    Original Spiced Rum
¼ oz. cherry liqueur
1 oz. sweet & sour mix

Shake vigorously in crushed ice–filled cocktail shaker. Strain into a stemmed cocktail glass. Garnish with lime wheel.

Captain's Margarita

1 oz. Captain Morgan
    Original Spiced Rum
½ oz. triple sec
8 oz. frozen limeade
8 oz. ice

Blend all ingredients until smooth. Serve in margarita glass.

Captain's Peach Daiquiri

1 oz. Captain Morgan
    Original Spiced Rum
¼ oz. peach schnapps
¼ oz. lime juice
1 splash club soda

Pour rum, schnapps, and lime juice over crushed ice in margarita or daiquiri glass. Top with club soda and stir to blend. Garnish with thin lime slice.

Captain's Tropical Spiced Tea

1¼ oz. Captain Morgan
    Original Spiced Rum
5 oz. iced tea
½ tsp. lemon juice

Combine all ingredients over ice in a highball glass. Stir. Garnish with a lemon wedge.

Caribbean Cooler

¾ oz. dark rum
½ oz. apricot brandy
1 oz. cream of coconut
1 oz. heavy cream
8 oz. crushed ice

Whirl in a blender at low speed for 10 to 15 seconds. Pour into a wineglass. Garnish with grated coconut and a maraschino cherry.

Caribbean Smuggler

¾ oz. dark rum
½ oz. triple sec
1 oz. orange juice
1 oz. margarita mix
½ oz. simple syrup
3 oz. lemon-lime soda

Shake first five ingredients well. Pour into ice cube–filled specialty glass. Top with lemon-lime soda. Garnish with lime wheel and orange flag.

Caribe Cocktail

¼ oz. dark rum or
    Captain Morgan
    Original Spiced Rum
1 oz. pineapple juice
½ oz. lemon juice

Shake with ice cubes. Strain into stemmed cocktail glass. Garnish with lime wheel.

Caribbean Chat

1 oz. Captain Morgan
    Original Spiced Rum
¼ oz. white crème de
    cacao
3 oz. orange juice
1½ oz. club soda

Pour rum, crème de cacao, and orange juice over ice in a highball glass. Stir. Add soda and stir gently.

Chilly Chocolate Mint

¾ oz. dark rum
½ oz. peppermint
    schnapps
1 oz. cream of coconut
1 oz. chocolate syrup
1 oz. heavy cream
8 oz. crushed ice

Mix ingredients in blender until smooth and creamy. Serve in specialty glass. Garnish with whipped cream and maraschino cherry.

Ciao Baby

1¼ oz. dark rum
2 oz. frozen strawberries,
    in syrup
1 oz. Collins mix
½ oz. grenadine
8 oz. crushed ice

Blend all ingredients until slushy.

Cinnamon Toast

1¼ oz. Captain Morgan
    Original Spiced Rum
6 oz. hot apple cider

Rim glass with sugar and cinnamon. Add hot cider and rum.

Citrus Cooler

¾ oz. dark rum
½ oz. triple sec
2 oz. orange juice
2 oz. sweet & sour mix
1 oz. lime juice
2 oz. lemon-lime soda

Combine first five ingredients in a large ice cube–filled specialty glass. Top with lemon-lime soda. Garnish with a lime wheel.

Co-Co Cow

1¼ oz. Captain Morgan
    Original Spiced Rum
2 oz. Half-and-Half
1 oz. cream of coconut

Blend all ingredients in a blender with a scoop of crushed ice.

Coconut Climber

¾ oz. Captain Morgan
  Original Spiced Rum
½ oz. mango liqueur
2 oz. cream of coconut
2 oz. Half-and-Half
1 oz. orange juice
1 tbsp. grenadine
8 oz. crushed ice

Shake well with crushed ice. Pour into highball glass. Garnish with toasted coconut.

Coconut Daiquiri

1¼ oz. dark rum
2 oz. sweet & sour mix
1½ oz. cream of coconut
8 oz. crushed ice

Mix in blender until smooth. Serve in wineglass. Garnish with lime wheel.

Country & Western

1¼ oz. dark rum
1 oz. pineapple juice
1 oz. orange juice
1 oz. cream of coconut

Blend all ingredients in blender with a scoop of crushed ice.

Cuba Libre

1¼ oz. dark rum
juice of ½ lime
6 oz. cola

Fill Collins glass with ice cubes. Add rum and lime juice. Top with cola and stir. Garnish with lime slice.

Daiquiri

1¼ oz. dark rum
juice of ½ lime
1 tsp. bar sugar

Shake with ice. Strain into a prechilled cocktail glass.

Eve's Apple Daiquiri

1¼ oz. Captain Morgan
  Original Spiced Rum
2 oz. sweet & sour mix
2 oz. frozen apple juice,
  undiluted concentrate
8 oz. crushed ice

Mix well in blender until smooth. Serve in round wineglass. Garnish with apple wedge or lime wheel.

Falling Star

1¼ oz. Captain Morgan
    Original Spiced Rum
¼ oz. lime juice
2 oz. orange juice
2 oz. tonic water

Pour rum, lime juice, and orange juice over ice in a glass. Stir. Add tonic and stir gently.

Florida Daiquiri

1 oz. dark rum
¼ oz. cherry liqueur
½ oz. sweet & sour mix
½ oz. grapefruit juice
1 tsp. bar sugar
8 oz. shaved ice

Shake vigorously with shaved ice. Pour contents into large cocktail glass. Garnish with a citrus wheel and a maraschino cherry.

Florida Freeze

1¼ oz. dark rum
1¼ oz. cream of coconut
2 oz. pineapple juice
1 oz. orange juice
6 oz. crushed ice

Blend until slushy.

Florida Punch

1 oz. dark rum
¼ oz. Cognac
1 oz. grapefruit juice
1 oz. orange juice

Shake with ice. Strain into a highball glass filled with crushed ice. Garnish with an orange slice.

Floridita Daiquiri

1 oz. dark rum
¼ oz. cherry liqueur
½ oz. sweet & sour mix
½ oz. grapefruit juice
1 tsp. bar sugar
8 oz. shaved ice

Shake vigorously with shaved ice. Pour contents into large cocktail glass. Garnish with citrus wheel and maraschino cherry.

Fort Lauderdale

1 oz. dark rum
¼ oz. sweet vermouth
juice of ¼ lime
juice of ¼ orange

Shake ingredients with ice. Strain into chilled cocktail glass. Garnish with orange slice and maraschino cherry.

Fox Trot

1¼ oz. dark rum
1 dash curaçao
⅓ oz. lemon or lime juice
½ tsp. bar sugar

Shake with crushed or shaved ice. Strain into a chilled cocktail glass.

Frozen Daiquiri

1¼ oz. dark rum
juice of ½ lime
1 tsp. bar sugar
4 oz. crushed ice

Whirl all in a blender until smooth. Pour into wineglass. Garnish with lime slice.

Fuzzy Charlie

¾ oz. Captain Morgan
  Original Spiced Rum
½ oz. peach schnapps
2 oz. piña colada mix
4 oz. orange juice

Shake ingredients with crushed or shaved ice. Strain over ice cubes into a Collins glass. Garnish with an orange slice.

Fuzzy Charlie II

¾ oz. dark rum
¼ oz. crème de banana
¼ oz. cream of coconut
2 oz. pineapple juice
ginger ale

Shake rum, crème de banana, cream of coconut, and pineapple juice vigorously with ice. Strain over ice cubes in tall glass. Top with ginger ale. Or blend with crushed ice to serve as frozen drink. Garnish with pineapple spear.

Ginger Colada

¾ oz. dark rum
½ oz. ginger-flavored
  brandy
4 oz. pineapple juice
1 oz. cream of coconut
8 oz. crushed ice

Combine all ingredients in blender. Blend until slushy.

Ginger Snap

¾ oz. Captain Morgan
  Original Spiced Rum
½ oz. ginger-flavored
  brandy
4 oz. eggnog
1 ginger snap

Whirl ingredients in blender. Garnish with additional ginger snap for dunking.

Havana Beach Cocktail

1¼ oz. dark rum
1¼ oz. pineapple juice
4 dashes lemon juice

Shake ingredients with ice. Strain into a chilled cocktail glass.

Hurricane

¾ oz. dark rum
½ oz. rum
juice of ½ lime
1 tbsp. passion-fruit juice

Combine rums and juice. Shake well. Pour into a crushed ice–filled specialty glass. Garnish with lime wheel.

Hurricane II

¾ oz. dark rum
½ oz. rum
3 oz. passion-fruit or
   mango juice
2 oz. sweet & sour mix

Combine ingredients. Shake well. Pour into a crushed ice–filled Hurricane or specialty glass. Garnish with lime wheel and fruit flag.

Ice Breaker

½ oz. Myers's Original
   Dark Rum
¼ oz. crème de noya
¼ oz. Cognac
¼ oz. gin
2 oz. lemon juice
1 oz. orange juice

Shake ingredients vigorously in ice cube–filled mixing glass. Pour into specialty glass. Garnish with fruit flag.

Jamaican Blues

1 oz. dark rum
¼ oz. blue curaçao
2 oz. cream of coconut
2 oz. pineapple juice
8 oz. crushed ice

Mix well in blender until smooth. Serve in specialty glass. Garnish with pineapple fruit flag.

Key Lime Quencher

1¼ oz. dark rum
1½ oz. lime juice
3 oz. heavy cream
1 oz. cream of coconut
1 tsp. bar sugar
12 oz. crushed ice

Combine ingredients in blender until smooth. Serve in specialty glass. Garnish with lime wheel and sprinkle of graham cracker crumbs.

Key West Song

1¼ oz. Captain Morgan
   Original Spiced Rum
2 oz. orange juice
1 oz. cream of coconut

Blend all ingredients in a blender with a scoop of crushed ice.

Kingston

¾ oz. rum
½ oz. gin
½ oz. lime juice
3 dashes grenadine

Shake ingredients with crushed or shaved ice. Strain into a chilled cocktail glass.

Lei Lani

1¼ oz. dark rum
1 oz. orange juice
½ oz. lemon juice
½ oz. pineapple juice
½ oz. papaya juice
1 dash grenadine
2 oz. soda water

Pour all ingredients except soda water into ice cube–filled highball. Stir well. Top with soda water. Garnish with fruit flag or pineapple wedge.

Lichee Nut Cocktail

1 oz. dark rum or Captain
   Morgan Original
   Spiced Rum
¼ oz. cherry liqueur
1 oz. sweet & sour mix
1 tsp. sugar
3 whole lichee nuts
8 oz. shaved ice

Blend thoroughly in blender. Pour into specialty glass. Garnish with lime wheel and maraschino cherry.

Lounge Lizard

1¼ oz. dark rum
1 oz. pineapple juice
1 oz. orange juice
1 oz. sour mix
½ oz. grenadine

Pour ingredients over ice. Serve in old-fashioned glass.

Lounge Lizard II

1¼ oz. dark rum
3 oz. orange juice
1½ oz. cranberry juice

Pour ingredients over ice. Serve in old-fashioned glass.

Madras

¾ oz. Captain Morgan
　Original Spiced Rum
½ oz. triple sec
2 oz. pineapple juice
2 oz. cranberry juice
1 oz. cream of coconut
8 oz. crushed ice

Blend until slushy. Garnish with fresh mint.

Mai Tai

1 oz. dark rum
¼ oz. curaçao
1 tsp. grenadine
juice of ½ lime
1 tsp. bar sugar

Shake with ice. Strain over ice cubes into an old-fashioned glass. Garnish with lime slice.

Mai Tai II

1 oz. dark rum or Captain
　Morgan Original
　Spiced Rum
¼ oz. orange curaçao
1 oz. lime juice
1 tsp. sugar

Shake with ice. Strain over ice into an old-fashioned glass. Garnish with lime and pineapple stick.

Mai Tai Mai

1 oz. Captain Morgan
　Original Spiced Rum
¼ oz. apricot liqueur
3 oz. pineapple juice
1 tsp. grenadine
1½ oz. lemon-lime soda

Pour first four ingredients over ice in old-fashioned glass. Stir. Add the soda and stir gently.

Mango Daiquiri

1 oz. dark rum or Captain
　Morgan Original
　Spiced Rum
¼ oz. orange curaçao
3 oz. mango juice
1½ oz. sweet & sour mix
8 oz. shaved ice

Blend thoroughly in blender. Pour into specialty glass. Garnish with mango stick or fruit flag.

Mary Pickford

1¼ oz. dark rum
1¼ oz. pineapple juice
3 dashes grenadine

Shake ingredients with ice. Strain into a chilled cocktail glass.

Melon Spritz

1 oz. Captain Morgan
  Original Spiced Rum
¼ oz. melon liqueur
4 oz. pineapple juice
1 oz. club soda

Pour rum, liqueur, and juice over ice in a glass. Stir. Add the soda and stir gently.

Mojito

1¼ oz. dark rum
juice of ½ lime
1 tsp. sugar
5 mint leaves
2 oz. club soda

Shake rum, juice, sugar, and mint leaves with ice. Strain into a highball glass filled with crushed ice. Top with club soda.

Morgan Madras

1¼ oz. Captain Morgan
  Original Spiced Rum
4 oz. orange juice
1 splash cranberry juice

Pour rum over ice in highball glass. Add juices. Garnish with an orange slice and maraschino cherry.

Myers's Heatwave

¾ oz. Myers's Original
  Dark Rum
½ oz. peach schnapps
6 oz. pineapple juice
1 splash grenadine

Pour rum and schnapps over ice in a tall glass. Fill with juice and a splash of grenadine. Stir. Garnish with a pineapple wedge and a maraschino cherry.

The Myers's Sharkbite

1¼ oz. Myers's Original
  Dark Rum
3 oz. orange juice
1 dash grenadine

Pour over ice in an old-fashioned glass.

Myrtle Bank Punch

1⅛ oz. dark rum or
  Captain Morgan
  Original Spiced Rum
¼ oz. grenadine
1 oz. lime juice
1 tsp. sugar
⅛ oz. cherry liqueur or
  Kirschwasser

Mix rum, grenadine, lime juice and sugar into 10-oz. glass filled with crushed ice. Top with cherry liqueur. Garnish with fruit flag or lime wheel.

New Orleans Buck

1¼ oz. dark rum
½ oz. lime juice
½ oz. orange juice
4 oz. ginger ale

Shake rum and juices with ice. Strain into a highball glass over ice cubes. Top with ginger ale and stir. Garnish with slice of lime.

Northside Special

1¼ oz. dark rum or
  Captain Morgan
  Original Spiced Rum
2 oz. orange juice
½ oz. lemon juice
1 oz. soda water

Add ingredients to ice-filled 12-oz. glass. Stir lightly. Garnish with fruit flag.

Palm Beacher

1 oz. dark rum
¼ oz. amaretto
6 oz. orange juice

Pour all ingredients over ice in a glass. Stir.

Passion Colada

1¼ oz. dark rum
3 oz. passion-fruit nectar
1 oz. cream of coconut
8 oz. crushed ice

Mix well in blender until smooth. Serve in wineglass. Garnish with tropical edible flower or fruit flag.

Peach Daiquiri

1 oz. dark rum
¼ oz. triple sec
juice of ½ lime
1 tsp. bar sugar
1 peach, pitted
1 cup crushed ice

Whirl in a blender until smooth. Pour into wineglass.

Peach Melba

½ oz. Captain Morgan
  Original Spiced Rum
¾ oz. raspberry liqueur
2 oz. peach cocktail mix
1 oz. heavy cream
2 peach halves
8 oz. crushed ice

Combine ingredients until smooth and creamy in blender. Serve in specialty glass. Top with raspberry syrup, fresh raspberries, or in syrup.

Peach Punch

¾ oz. Captain Morgan
  Original Spiced Rum
½ oz. peach schnapps
4 oz. orange juice
2 oz. piña colada mix

Blend until frozen. Garnish with fresh peach.

Peachy Colada

1 oz. Captain Morgan
  Original Spiced Rum
¼ oz. peach schnapps
4 oz. pineapple juice
½ oz. cream of coconut
12 oz. crushed ice

Blend until slushy.

Piña Colada

1¼ oz. dark rum
2 oz. pineapple juice
1 oz. cream of coconut
4 oz. crushed ice

Whirl in a blender until smooth. Pour into wineglass. Garnish with pineapple stick and maraschino cherry.

Pink Lemonade

1¼ oz. rum
3 oz. cranberry juice
2 oz. club soda
juice of ¼ lemon

Pour rum over ice and add cranberry juice. Top with club soda and lemon juice. Garnish with lemon twist.

Pink Orchid

1¼ oz. Captain Morgan
  Original Spiced Rum
2 oz. cranberry juice
2 oz. pineapple juice

Blend with crushed ice. Garnish with fresh mint.

Pinky & the Captain

1¼ oz. Captain Morgan Original Spiced Rum
5 oz. grapefruit juice

Combine in an ice cube–filled highball glass. Garnish with pink grapefruit section or lime wheel.

Planter's Punch

1¼ oz. dark rum
2 oz. orange juice
2 oz. pineapple juice
¼ oz. lime juice
¼ oz. lemon juice
1 tsp. bar sugar
1 dash grenadine

Shake with ice. Strain over ice in a highball glass. Garnish with orange slice and maraschino cherry.

Princess Morgan

¾ oz. Captain Morgan Original Spiced Rum
¼ oz. crème de banana
2½ oz. orange juice
2 oz. club soda

Pour the rum, crème de banana, and orange juice over ice in a glass. Stir. Add the soda and stir gently.

Queen's Park Swizzle

1¼ oz. dark rum or Captain Morgan Original Spiced Rum
juice of ½ large lime
1 mint leaf
½ oz. sweet & sour mix
½ oz. simple syrup

Squeeze lime and drop shell into specialty glass. Add mint leaf. Add shaved ice and remaining ingredients. Stir until glass is frosty. Garnish with mint leaves.

R & B

1¼ oz. Captain Morgan Original Spiced Rum
2 oz. orange juice
2 oz. pineapple juice
1 splash grenadine

Pour ingredients over ice.

Roman Punch

1 oz. raspberry syrup
1 oz. lemon juice
½ oz. dark rum
½ oz. Cognac
⅛ oz. port

Place syrup and lemon juice in specialty glass. Fill with crushed ice and add rum and Cognac. Stir. Top with port. Garnish with strawberry or lemon wheel.

Rum and Cola

1¼ oz. dark rum
6 oz. Cola

Pour rum over ice cubes in a highball glass. Fill with Cola. Stir. Garnish with lime wedge.

Rum and Ginger

1¼ oz. dark rum
6 oz. ginger ale

Pour rum over ice cubes in a highball glass. Fill with ginger ale. Stir. Garnish with a lime wedge.

Rum Collins

1¼ oz. dark rum
1 tsp. bar sugar
juice of ½ lemon
6 oz. club soda

In tumbler combine rum, sugar, and lemon juice with ice. Strain over crushed ice into 14-oz. tall glass. Top with club soda. Garnish with lemon slice.

Rum Fizz

¾ oz. dark rum
½ oz. flavored brandy
    (apricot, cherry, peach,
    or ginger)
½ oz. sweet & sour mix
6 oz. soda water

Shake ingredients. Pour into ice-filled highball glass. Top with soda water. Garnish with lime.

Rum Julep

1¼ oz. dark rum
⅙ oz. simple syrup
2 mint leaves

In an old-fashioned glass, muddle simple syrup with mint leaves. Fill glass with shaved or crushed ice and pour in rum. Stir. Garnish with mint sprig.

Rum Rickey

1¼ oz. dark rum
juice of ½ lime
6 oz. club soda

Pour rum and lime juice over ice in a highball glass. Add soda. Stir. Garnish with lime wedge.

Rum Runner

¾ oz. Captain Morgan
    Original Spiced Rum
¼ oz. blackberry liqueur
¼ oz. crème de banana
4 oz. orange juice
½ oz. grenadine
8 oz. crushed ice

Blend all ingredients until slushy. Serve in specialty glass.

Rum Sour

1¼ oz. dark rum
juice of ½ lemon
½ tsp. bar sugar

Shake with ice. Strain into prechilled sour glass. Garnish with lemon slice and maraschino cherry.

Rummy Sour

1¼ oz. Captain Morgan
   Original Spiced Rum
1¾ oz. lemon-lime mix
8 oz. crushed ice

Blend in blender with crushed ice. Serve in a specialty glass.

Scorpion

¾ oz. dark rum
¼ oz. Cognac
¼ oz. almond syrup
1½ oz. orange juice
1½ oz. lemon juice
½ cup crushed ice

Blend ingredients with crushed ice in blender for 15 seconds. Pour into an old-fashioned glass over ice cubes. Garnish with orange slice and mint sprig.

Singing Orchard

1 oz. dark rum
¼ oz. raspberry liqueur
4 oz. pineapple juice
1 oz. cream of coconut
3 dashes grenadine

Thoroughly blend first four ingredients with a large scoop of crushed ice. Pour into large goblet and top with grenadine. Garnish with pineapple flag or flower.

Spiced Banana Daiquiri

1 oz. Captain Morgan
   Original Spiced Rum
¼ oz. crème de banana
2 oz. sweet & sour mix
½ banana
8 oz. shaved ice

Blend ingredients thoroughly in blender. Pour into specialty glass. Garnish with banana wheel and maraschino cherry.

Strawberry Banana Colada

1¼ oz. dark rum
2 oz. cream of coconut
2 oz. strawberries
1 banana
8 oz. crushed ice

Mix well in blender until smooth. Serve in specialty glass. Garnish with strawberry and banana round on pick.

Strawberry Daiquiri

1 oz. dark rum
¼ oz. triple sec
juice of ½ lime
½ cup strawberries
1 tsp. bar sugar
1 cup crushed ice

Whirl all in a blender until smooth. Pour into wineglass.

Strawberry Daiquiri II

1¼ oz. Captain Morgan
   Original Spiced Rum
1¾ oz. sweet & sour mix
3 oz. frozen strawberries

Blend all ingredients with a scoop of crushed ice.

Sunnier Sour

1¼ oz. dark rum
¼ oz. lemon juice
1½ oz. grapefruit juice
½ tsp. superfine sugar
4 oz. club soda

Shake rum, lemon juice, grapefruit juice, and sugar with ice until frosty. Strain over ice cubes in a highball glass. Fill with club soda. Stir. Garnish with a grapefruit wedge.

Sunniest Sour

1¼ oz. dark rum
½ oz. lemon juice
3 oz. orange juice
½ tsp. superfine sugar
3 oz. club soda

Shake rum, lemon juice, orange juice, and sugar with ice until frosty. Strain over ice cubes in a highball glass. Fill with club soda. Garnish with an orange wedge.

Sunny Sour

1¼ oz. dark rum
¼ oz. lemon juice
½ tsp. superfine sugar

Shake rum, lemon juice, and sugar with crushed or shaved ice until frosty. Strain into cocktail glass. Garnish with a lemon wedge and cherry.

Top Ten

1¼ oz. Captain Morgan
   Original Spiced Rum
2 oz. cola
1 oz. cream of coconut
1 oz. heavy cream
1 scoop crushed ice

Blend all ingredients in blender.

Tropic Freeze

1 ¼ oz. Captain Morgan
  Original Spiced Rum
2 oz. orange juice
2 oz. pineapple juice
1 ½ oz. cream of coconut
½ oz. grenadine
12 oz. crushed ice

Mix well in blender until smooth. Serve in specialty glass. Garnish with pineapple fruit flag.

Tropical Paradise

1 ¼ oz. Captain Morgan
  Original Spiced Rum
2 oz. orange juice
2 oz. cream of coconut
¼ oz. grenadine
½ banana
8 oz. crushed ice

Mix well in blender until smooth. Serve in specialty glass. Garnish with pineapple fruit flag, and palm tree stirrer.

Turtledove

1 oz. dark rum
¼ oz. amaretto
4 oz. orange juice
12 oz. crushed ice

Blend until slushy.

Union Jack

¾ oz. dark rum
½ oz. applejack
2 oz. sweetened lemon
  juice
3 dashes grenadine

Shake rum, applejack, and lemon juice with ice. Strain into a chilled wineglass. Top with grenadine.

Very Berry Colada

½ oz. dark rum
¾ oz. wild berries
  schnapps
2 oz. cream of coconut
2 oz. pineapple juice
8 oz. crushed ice

Mix in blender until smooth. Serve in specialty or wineglass. Garnish with 3 berries on a pick or a strawberry.

Voyager

1 oz. Captain Morgan
  Original Spiced Rum
8 oz. hot apple cider
¼ oz. crème de banana

Pour the cider into a mug. Stir in the rum and the banana liqueur.

Waikiki Tiki

1¼ oz. dark rum
3 oz. orange juice
2 oz. pineapple juice

Pour all ingredients over ice in a glass. Stir.

Wrath Of Grapes

1¼ oz. dark rum
4 oz. grape juice
1 oz. sweet & sour mix

Combine ingredients in ice cube–filled Collins glass. Shake well. Garnish with lime wheel or fresh grapes.

Yellow Bird

½ oz. dark rum or
    Captain Morgan
    Original Spiced Rum
¼ oz. Galliano
½ oz. crème de banana
2 oz. pineapple juice
8 oz. crushed ice

Shake well with crushed ice. Pour into highball glass or specialty glass. Garnish with pineapple flag. Add more ice if necessary.

Yellow Bird II

¾ oz. Captain Morgan
    Original Spiced Rum
¼ oz. crème de banana
¼ oz. Galliano
2 oz. orange juice
2 oz. pineapple juice
1 oz. lemon juice

Combine ingredients in a cocktail shaker. Shake well. Pour into an ice cube–filled specialty glass. Garnish with fruit flag.

SCOTCH

Though famous for its wailing bagpipes, majestic highlands and mythical Loch Ness Monster, Scotland is probably most well known for a spirit—Scotch. Perhaps the world's oldest spirit, Scotch whisky is so much a part of its country's lore, that over 3,500 brands are manufactured on the peaty soil of Scotland.

> *O whisky, soul o' play and pranks,*
> *Accept a bardie's gratefu' thanks.*
> —Bobbie Burns

Scotland makes two excellent types of Scotch: blended whisky and single malt. Single malts, often called the true whisky of Scotland, are distilled from pure water and varying degrees of malted barley. Made in over a hundred distilleries, single malt whiskies vary in taste according to numerous factors: the location, the source of the barley, the malting process, the amount of peat, the water source, and the size and shape of the still. The Glenlivet was designated the first legal distillery and is often referred to as the Father of all Scotch. Until 1863 all Scotch whiskies were single malt. It was then that William Sanderson is said to have begun the practice of blending whiskies from different distilleries, giving rise to the second type of Scotch—blended whisky. This made a smoother elixir that was far more palatable for non-Scots and led to worldwide popularity.

Blended Scotch is now more popular than single malt Scotch, and the most demanded blend is one combining single malt and grain whiskies. Although, both malt and grain Scotch whiskies must age for a legal minimum of three years, most age much longer. In fact premium brands such as Chivas Regal age for at least twelve.

Scotch whisky is distilled in four principal areas: the Highlands, the Lowlands, Islay, and Campbeltown. The Highlands provide the light full-bodied single malts that form the backbone of all fine blended Scotch. This whisky is especially fragrant. The Lowland malts are also light, but less smoky and are soft, with only a hint of peat. Islay whiskies are particularly thick and peaty, and their popularity is increasing of late. Campbeltown spirits are rich and full-bodied, but the number of distillers of this seasoned whisky has been steadily declining.

Scotch whisky has always been an integral part of Gaelic daily life. Not only would Scots drink it two or three times a day—much as the English now drink tea—but they took it along as a traveling companion, anesthetic, medical salve, disinfectant, and an all-around best friend.

As the twentieth century began, sales in the British Isles started to plummet due to the availability of many more types of spirits. In fact many attribute the ongoing popularity of Scotch whisky to American consumption. The worldwide depression in the 1930s led to the virtual evaporation of the Scotch distilleries, leaving only fifteen existing at one point. But shortly thereafter, Prohibition was repealed in the United States and Scotch began to flow overseas as well as across the Highlands. In 1937 Seagram began to build vast libraries of rare Scotch whiskies. Then-president of Seagram, Samuel Bronfman, summed up the making of Scotch whisky as follows: "Distilling is a science, blending is an art. Blending has, in fact, become the art of Scotland." And with a recent rise in the popularity of single malts, Scotch whisky is being savored by more imbibers across the world than ever before.

Affinity Cocktail

¾ oz. Scotch
¼ oz. dry vermouth
¼ oz. sweet vermouth
2 dashes bitters

Stir with ice and strain into a chilled cocktail glass. Garnish with a lemon peel and cherry.

Aggravation

¾ oz. Scotch
½ oz. coffee brandy
3 oz. Half-and-Half
4 oz. crushed ice

Shake with crushed ice. Pour into rocks glass.

Bairn

¾ oz. Scotch
½ oz. triple sec
1 dash orange bitters

Shake with ice. Strain over ice cubes in old-fashioned glass.

Balmoral Cocktail

¾ oz. Scotch
¼ oz. Lillet rouge
¼ oz. Lillet blanc
3 dashes Angostura bitters

Combine all ingredients in mixing glass with ice cubes. Stir well. Strain into chilled cocktail glass.

Beadlestone

¾ oz. Scotch
½ oz. dry vermouth

Stir ingredients with ice cubes in a mixing glass. Strain into chilled cocktail glass.

Bobby Burns Cocktail

¾ oz. Scotch
½ oz. sweet vermouth
2 dashes Benedictine

Stir ingredients with ice and strain into a chilled cocktail glass. Garnish with lemon peel.

Charmer

1 oz. Scotch
¼ oz. blue curaçao
1 dash dry vermouth
1 dash orange bitters

Mix all with cracked ice in a cocktail shaker. Strain into chilled cocktail glass.

Derby Fizz

¾ oz. Scotch
½ oz. triple sec
½ oz. lemon juice
½ tsp. bar sugar
1 whole egg
sparkling water

Combine all ingredients except water with cracked ice in a cocktail shaker. Shake vigorously. Pour over ice cubes into chilled Collins glass. Fill with sparkling water and stir gently.

Dry Rob Roy

1⅛ oz. Scotch
⅛ oz. dry vermouth

Serve in old-fashioned glass over ice. Garnish with olive.

Glasgow

1¼ oz. Scotch
1 tsp. dry vermouth
1 tbsp. lemon juice
1 tsp. almond extract

Combine all ingredients with cracked ice in a cocktail shaker. Shake well. Strain over ice into chilled old-fashioned glass.

Godfather

¾ oz. Scotch
½ oz. amaretto

Serve in an old-fashioned glass over ice.

Highland Cooler

1¼ oz. Scotch
1 tsp. sugar
1½ oz. club soda
2 oz. ginger ale

In a highball glass, dissolve the sugar in club soda. Add ice cubes and Scotch. Top with ginger ale and stir. Garnish with a twist of lemon peel.

Hole-in-One Cocktail

¾ oz. Scotch
½ oz. dry vermouth
2 dashes lemon juice
1 dash orange bitters

Shake ingredients with crushed or shaved ice. Strain into a chilled cocktail glass.

Hoot Mon

¾ oz. Scotch
¼ oz. Lillet blanc
¼ oz. sweet vermouth

Combine all ingredients with cracked ice in a cocktail shaker. Shake well. Strain into chilled cocktail glass.

Hop Scotch

1 oz. Scotch
¼ oz. Cointreau
2 dashes orange bitters

Fill highball glass with ice cubes. Add ingredients. Stir.

Loch Lomond

1¼ oz. Scotch
½ oz. simple syrup
3–5 dashes Angostura
    bitters

Combine all ingredients with cracked ice in a cocktail shaker. Shake well. Strain into chilled cocktail glass.

Loch Ness Mystery

¾ oz. Scotch
¼ oz. apricot brandy
⅛ oz. orange curaçao
2 oz. grapefruit juice
¼ oz. lime juice

Shake all ingredients with ice. Strain into a Collins glass filled with crushed ice. Garnish with lime wedge.

Mamie Taylor

1¼ oz. Scotch
juice of ½ lime
6 oz. ginger ale

Pour Scotch and lime juice into a Collins glass over ice cubes. Top with ginger ale and stir. Garnish with a slice of lemon.

Mint Sunrise

¾ oz. Scotch
¼ oz. brandy
¼ oz. curaçao

Pour all into a chilled highball glass over ice cubes. Stir gently. Garnish with lemon slice and mint sprig.

Modern Cocktail

1¼ oz. Scotch
1 tsp. dark rum
1 tsp. Pernod
1 tsp. lemon juice
3–5 dashes orange bitters

Combine all with cracked ice in a cocktail shaker. Shake well and pour into chilled od-fashioned glass. Garnish with maraschino cherry.

Perfect Rob Roy

1 oz. Scotch
⅛ oz. dry vermouth
⅛ oz. sweet vermouth

Serve in old-fashioned glass over ice. Garnish with lemon twist.

Remsen Cooler

1¼ oz. Scotch
1 tsp. simple syrup
sparkling water

Pour Scotch and syrup into a chilled Collins glass filled with ice cubes. Fill with sparkling water and stir gently. Garnish with lemon twist.

Rusty Aggravation

½ oz. Scotch
½ oz. coffee brandy
¼ oz. Drambuie
2 oz. Half-and-Half

Combine ingredients in an ice cube–filled highball glass.

Rusty Nail

1 oz. Scotch
¼ oz. Drambuie

Serve in old-fashioned glass over ice.

Scotch Buck

1¼ oz. Scotch
½ oz. lime juice
6 oz. ginger ale

Shake Scotch and lime juice with ice. Strain over ice cubes in a highball glass. Fill with ginger ale. Garnish with a lime slice.

Scotch Cobbler

1 oz. Scotch
¼ oz. white curaçao
½ oz. honey

Combine all ingredients with cracked ice in a cocktail shaker. Shake well and strain into chilled old-fashioned glass over ice cubes. Garnish with mint sprig.

Scotch Holiday Sour

¾ oz. Scotch
¼ oz. Cherry Heering
¼ oz. sweet vermouth
1 oz. lemon juice

Combine all ingredients with cracked ice in a cocktail shaker. Shake well and strain into chilled sour glass. Garnish with lemon slice.

Scotch Mist

1¼ oz. Scotch

Pour into old-fashioned glass filled with shaved ice. Garnish with lemon twist.

The Rob Roy was created in homage to the eighteenth-century romantic figure and Scottish freebooter, Robert McGregor—captured in legend as Rob Roy. McGregor's swashbuckling efforts to keep his highland clan fed and secure from the divisive forces of his country calls for frequent comparisons to the famed British outlaw Robin Hood. During the Jacobite rebellion of 1715, which pitted the Scots against the Brits, McGregor's clan removed itself from allegiances with either side, plundering each impartially and gaining further independence for his clan.

The drink, using Scotch whisky, is a variation on the manhattan and perhaps is the most commonly requested Scotch cocktail today.

Rob Roy

1 oz. Scotch
¼ oz. sweet vermouth

Shake with ice and strain into cocktail glass.

Scotch Old-Fashioned

1¼ oz. Scotch
1 sugar cube
1 tsp. water
1 dash bitters

In an old-fashioned glass, muddle sugar with water and bitters. Add ice cubes and Scotch. Garnish with lemon twist, orange slice, and maraschino cherry.

Scotch Orange Fix

1¼ oz. Scotch
1 oz. lemon juice
½ tsp. bar sugar
1 tbsp. triple sec

Combine all ingredients except triple sec with cracked ice in a cocktail shaker. Shake well and strain into chilled high-ball glass over ice cubes. Drop orange twist in drink and float triple sec on top.

Scotch Rickey

1¼ oz. Scotch
juice of ½ lime
6 oz. club soda

Pour Scotch and lime juice into a high-ball glass. Add soda and ice. Stir. Garnish with lime wedge.

Scotch Smash

1 ¼ oz. Scotch
8 fresh mint leaves
1 tbsp. honey
1 dash orange bitters

Muddle mint leaves with honey in the bottom of a chilled highball glass. Fill the glass with crushed ice and add the Scotch. Stir well and top off with the bitters. Garnish with mint sprig.

Scotch Solace

1 oz. Scotch
¼ oz. triple sec
½ oz. honey
4 oz. milk
1 oz. heavy cream
⅛ tsp. grated orange rind

Put Scotch, triple sec, and honey in a highball glass. Stir until blended. Add ice cubes. Add milk, cream, and orange rind. Stir well.

Scotch Sour

1 ¼ oz. Scotch
juice of ½ lemon
½ tsp. bar sugar

Shake with ice. Strain into chilled sour glass. Garnish with lemon slice and maraschino cherry.

Scotch Swizzle

1 ¼ oz. Scotch
¼ oz. lime juice
½ tsp. sugar
1 dash bitters
6 oz. club soda

Mix lime juice, sugar, and bitters in a Collins glass. Fill ⅔ full of crushed or shaved ice and stir. Add Scotch and top with soda. Stir again and serve with a swizzle stick.

Secret

1 oz. Scotch
¼ oz. white crème de menthe
sparkling water

Combine Scotch and liqueur with cracked ice in cocktail shaker and shake well. Strain into chilled highball glass over ice cubes and fill with sparkling water. Stir gently.

Stone Fence

1¼ oz. Scotch
1 dash Angostura bitters
sparkling apple cider

Pour Scotch and bitters into a chilled highball glass over ice cubes. Fill with cider and stir.

TEQUILA

The desert has always been a place of mystery, a seemingly desolate terrain devoid of any riches and inhospitable to the living. But things aren't always what they seem. Take the blue *agave*, for instance. The unappetizing cactuslike plant, native to infertile, rocky soil, is the source of Mexico's national spirit, tequila. Growing as high as ten feet, the blue agave (known as the "century plant" north of the border) sports a cluster of swordlike leaves that are as beautiful as they are intimidating. Once every eight to twelve years, when the sap rushes to the base of the plant, the plant blooms and the leaves then wither away, leaving a 20- to 30-foot flowering stalk—with a pineapplelike center weighing 75 to 150 pounds—ready for harvesting.

There are three basic types of tequila: silver, gold, and *añejo*. Silver tequila is created for immediate consumption by using distilled water to reduce the spirit to approximately 80 proof. The famed gold tequila is aged in oak vats for as long as four years to give it its amber glow and rich flavor. The finest tequila, the *añejo*—such as Patrón—is 100 percent blue agave and is aged for two to three years until it reaches perfect taste and character. Patrón *añejo* tequila is harvested exclusively from the mountainous Jalisco region, an area renowned for its warm climate and claylike soil. Prices for *añejo* can approach the same as those for premium Cognac.

The name *tequila* comes from the town of the same name, which in turn took its moniker from Tuiquila, the name of the Aztec tribe which inhabited the region of Jalisco near Guadalajara. And in fact, tequila's origins can be traced back to the golden days of the Aztecs, who regularly produced and drank *pulque*, a milky alcohol beverage made from the agave. When Spain conquered Mexico, the Spanish began to distill this beverage into *mezcal*, a brandylike drink—the precursor of tequila. By the 1950s, however, *pulque* was outlawed due to health concerns associated with its hazardous production process. But tequila was to flourish.

The earliest written accounts of tequila occur in the seventeenth century. Early tequila makers used to place the bulbous, sap-filled hearts of the blue agave in fire-filled pits, where they would cook, and exude the liquid called *aguamiel* ("honey water").

Today the hearts are split open and steamed for up to twenty-four hours. The sap then becomes concentrated and the starch turns to sugar—which is mechanically extracted from the hearts. The juices are then combined in large vats, where fermentation begins and continues for about two and a half days. Next, the spirit is distilled in copper pot stills at 28 proof. The condensed vapors from these stills, called tuba, will sit for fifteen days, then be redistilled to 104 proof.

Although some spirits are referred to as tequila, tequila is not considered authentic unless it adheres to Mexican law mandating that it contain at least 51 percent blue agave and be made only in the Mexican towns of Tequila, Arenal, Amatitian, or the region of Los Altos de Jalisco. These four areas alone produce the world's entire supply of tequila—turning out over 150 million liters of the spirit annually.

Rumor has it that the classic margarita was first concocted from a secret recipe by the Nicholas family, owners of the La Paz restaurants in the cities of Laguna Beach, Orange, and Fullerton, California. Now, thanks in part to the popularity of Mexican and Southwestern cuisines, the tangy drink is the third most popular drink consumed by Americans.

Acapulco Apple Margarita

¾ oz. tequila
4 oz. sweet & sour or margarita mix
3 oz. apple puree
½ oz. triple sec or simple syrup
12 oz. ice

Blend all ingredients until slushy. Serve in a margarita glass.

Acapulco Blue

¾ oz. tequila
½ oz. blue curaçao
½ oz. bar syrup
1 splash club soda

Rim whiskey sour glass with lime juice and salt. Place ½ orange slice in each glass. Add crushed ice, tequila, blue curaçao, bar syrup and club soda to fill. Stir lightly.

Acapulco Clam Digger

1¼ oz. tequila
3 oz. tomato juice
3 oz. clam juice
¾ tsp. horseradish
Tabasco sauce to taste
Worcestershire sauce to taste
1 splash lemon or lime juice

Mix all ingredients in a Collins glass with cracked ice. Garnish with slice of lemon or lime.

Añejo Banger

1 oz. gold tequila
6 oz. orange juice
¼ oz. Galliano

Blend tequila and orange juice with small scoop of crushed ice. Pour over rocks. Float Galliano. Garnish with orange wheel and cherry.

Añejo Pacifico

1¼ oz. tequila
½ oz. lime juice
½ oz. passion-fruit syrup

Chill over rocks. Strain. Serve in cocktail glass. Garnish with lime wheel.

Baja Banana-Boat Margarita

¾ oz. tequila
½ oz. crème de banana
6 oz. sweet & sour or margarita mix
1 banana
8 oz. crushed ice

Blend all ingredients until slushy. Serve in margarita glass.

Berta's Special

1¼ oz. tequila
1 tsp. honey
1 egg white
5–7 dashes orange bitters
juice of 1 lime
sparkling water

Combine all except sparkling water in a cocktail shaker. Shake vigorously. Pour over into a chilled Collins glass filled with ice cubes and top off with sparkling water. Garnish with lime slice.

Pace yourself and you will live a longer life.

—Mexican proverb

Bloody Maria

1¼ oz. tequila
juice of ½ lime
1 dash Tabasco
1 dash celery salt
6 oz. tomato juice

Pour tequila, lime juice, Tabasco, and celery salt over ice cubes in a highball glass. Fill with tomato juice. Stir. Garnish with a lime slice.

Border Passion Margarita

¾ oz. tequila
4 oz. sweet & sour or
  margarita mix
½ oz. triple sec
½ oz. Tropicana citrus-
  passion concentrate
8 oz. ice

Blend all ingredients until slushy. Serve in margarita glasses.

Blue Meanie

¾ oz. tequila
½ oz. blue curaçao
2 oz. sweet & sour mix

Salt rim of cocktail glass. Shake ingredients well with crushed ice and strain into glass. Garnish with a lime wheel.

Brave Bull

¾ oz. tequila
½ oz. coffee liqueur

Stir ingredients with ice. Strain into old-fashioned glass over ice cubes. Garnish with twist of lemon peel.

Bunny Bonanza

¾ oz. tequila
½ oz. apple brandy
3 dashes triple sec
½ oz. lemon juice
¾ tsp. maple syrup

Combine all ingredients in a cocktail shaker with cracked ice. Shake well. Strain into chilled old-fashioned glass and garnish with lemon slice.

Cactus Colada

1 oz. tequila
¼ oz. melon liqueur
4 oz. pineapple juice
½ oz. cream of coconut

Stir vigorously with ice. Strain into champagne glasses over crushed ice. Garnish with melon balls in season.

Cactus Margarita

1¼ oz. tequila
½ oz. pineapple concentrate
5 oz. sweet & sour or margarita mix
1 oz. cream of coconut
12 oz. ice

Blend all ingredients until slushy.

Cha-Cha-Cha Cherry Margarita

¾ oz. tequila
½ oz. triple sec
1 oz. red sour cherry concentrate
3 oz. sweet & sour or margarita mix
8 oz. ice

Blend all ingredients until slushy. Serve in margarita glass.

Changuirongo

1¼ oz. tequila
ginger ale

Pour into a chilled Collins glass filled with ice cubes. Stir and garnish with lime wedge.

Chapala

1 oz. tequila
¼ oz. triple sec
2 oz. orange juice
1 oz. lime juice
½ oz. grenadine

Combine all ingredients in a cocktail shaker. Shake well. Pour into chilled highball glass half filled with cracked ice and stir.

El Diablo

1 oz. tequila
¼ oz. crème de cassis
¼ oz. lime juice
5 oz. ginger ale

Pour tequila, cassis, and lime juice over ice in a tall glass. Fill with ginger ale. Stir. Garnish with a lime wedge.

Frostbite

¾ oz. tequila
¼ oz. crème de cacao
¼ oz. blue curaçao
2 oz. Half-and-Half

Combine all ingredients in a cocktail shaker with cracked ice. Shake well. Strain into chilled sour glass.

Frozen Cactus Colada

1 oz. tequila
¼ oz. melon liqueur
2 oz. pineapple juice
1 oz. cream of coconut
8 oz. crushed ice

Whirl all ingredients together in blender. Pour into colada glass.

Frozen Matador

1¼ oz. tequila
2 oz. pineapple juice
½ oz. lime juice

Combine all ingredients in a blender with ½ cup of cracked ice. Blend well. Garnish with lime slice.

Grand Matador

¾ oz. gold tequila
¼ oz. Cuarenta y Tres (Licor 43)
¼ oz. Grand Marnier

Shake well with ice. Strain over ice into an old-fashioned glass. Garnish with orange wedge.

Hibiscus Holiday Margarita

1¼ oz. tequila
½ oz. hibiscus cooler concentrate
4 oz. sweet & sour or margarita mix
½ oz. simple syrup
8 oz. ice

Blend all ingredients until slushy.

Margarita 43

1 oz. tequila
¼ oz. Cuarenta y Tres (Licor 43)
juice of ½ lime
juice of ½ lemon
1 dash bar sugar

Shake well with ice. Strain into large shot glass. Garnish with lime wedge.

Margarita

1 oz. tequila
¼ oz. triple sec
juice of ½ lime

Shake tequila, triple sec, and lime juice with ice. Dip rim of prechilled old-fashioned glass in lime juice, then in coarse salt to coat.

Mariachi Melon Margarita

1 oz. tequila
¼ oz. melon liqueur
4 oz. sweet & sour or
   margarita mix
12 oz. ice.

Blend all ingredients until slushy. Serve in a margarita glass.

Matador

1¼ oz. tequila
2 oz. pineapple juice
½ oz. lime juice

Shake with ice. Strain over ice cubes in an old-fashioned glass. Garnish with a lime slice.

Mexican Berry

1 oz. tequila
¼ oz. Cointreau
4 oz. cranberry juice
1 dash lime juice

Shake well with ice. Strain over ice into large goblet glass. Garnish with lime wheel.

Mexicana

1¼ oz. tequila
2 oz. pineapple juice
1 oz. lime juice
¼ tsp. grenadine

Combine all ingredients in a cocktail shaker with cracked ice. Shake well. Strain into chilled highball glass.

Nuclear Meltdown

¾ oz. tequila
½ oz. alize (or ½ oz.
   Cognac and ½ oz.
   passion-fruit syrup)

Shake well with ice. Strain. Serve in shot or up glasses.

Olé

¾ oz. tequila
½ oz. coffee liqueur
1 tsp. simple syrup
1 tbsp. Half-and-Half

Stir all in a mixing glass, except Half-and-Half. Pour into a chilled cocktail glass over crushed ice. Float Half-and-Half on top.

Patrón Blue Boss

1 oz. Patrón Silver
¼ oz. blue curaçao
¼ oz. grenadine

Pour Patron Silver and blue curaçao into cocktail shaker over ice. Shake. Strain into shot glass. Sink grenadine to bottom of glass.

Patrón Cruiser

1¼ oz. Patrón Silver
3 oz. cranberry juice
3 oz. lemon-lime soda
¼ oz. fresh lime juice

Pour all ingredients into a tall glass filled with ice. Garnish with a mint sprig.

Patrón Inferno

1¼ oz. Patrón Silver,
    chilled
juice of ¼ medium fresh
    lime
3 splashes Tabasco sauce
freshly ground pepper

Pour all ingredients into shot glass. Top with freshly ground pepper. The flavor is pure heat!

Patrón Matador

1¼ oz. Patrón Silver
4 oz. pineapple juice
1 oz. lime juice
1 splash grenadine

Combine all ingredients and serve over crushed ice.

Patrón Silver Sunrise

1¼ oz. Patrón Silver,
    chilled
2 oz. fresh orange juice
2 oz. fresh grapefruit juice
juice of ¼ lime
1 splash bitters

Pour all ingredients into a large ice–filled glass. Stir.

Peach Margarita

1 oz. tequila
½ oz. peach liqueur
2 oz. lime juice
1 tbsp. triple sec

Rim a chilled cocktail glass with salt. Combine ingredients in a cocktail shaker with cracked ice. Shake well. Garnish with peach slice.

Piñata

¾ oz. tequila
½ oz. crème de banana
1½ oz. lime juice

Combine all ingredients in a cocktail shaker with cracked ice. Shake well. Strain into chilled cocktail glass.

Pineapple Cancun Margarita

1¼ oz. tequila
4 oz. sweet & sour or
   margarita mix
1 oz. pineapple or papaya
   concentrate
½ oz. simple syrup
12 oz. ice

Blend all ingredients until slushy.

Rosita

½ oz. tequila
½ oz. Campari
⅛ oz. dry vermouth
⅛ oz. sweet vermouth

Combine all ingredients in a mixing glass with cracked ice. Stir well. Pour into chilled old-fashioned glass. Garnish with lemon twist.

T.L.C. (Tequila, Lime, Campari)

¾ oz. tequila
½ oz. Campari
juice of ¼ lime

Fill tall glass with ice, then add tequila, Campari, and lime juice. Top with club soda. Garnish with lime wheel.

T.L.C. (Tequila, Lime, Cognac)

¾ oz. tequila
juice of ¼ lime
½ oz. Cognac

Shake well with ice. Strain into wineglass. Fill with ice. Garnish with wedge of lime.

T.L.C. (Tequila, Lime, Cola)

1¼ oz. tequila
juice of ½ lime
5 oz. cola

Fill tall glass with ice and add tequila and lime. Top with cola. Garnish with lime wheel.

T.T.T. (Tequila, Triple Sec, Tonic)

1 oz. tequila
¼ oz. triple sec
2 oz. tonic

In wineglass stir tequila and triple sec with ice. Top with tonic and add lime spiral.

Tequila Colada

1¼ oz. tequila
2 oz. sweet & sour mix
2 oz. cream of coconut
8 oz. crushed ice

Mix well in blender until smooth. Serve in specialty glass rimmed with crushed toasted coconut. Garnish with lime fruit flag.

Tequila Collins

1¼ oz. tequila
1 tsp. bar sugar
juice of ½ lemon
6 oz. club soda

Shake tequila, sugar, and lemon juice with ice. Strain over crushed ice in a Collins glass. Fill with soda. Stir. Garnish with lemon slice.

Tequila Fizz

1¼ oz. tequila
juice of ½ lemon
¾ oz. grenadine
1 egg white
4 oz. ginger ale

Shake tequila, lemon juice, grenadine, and egg white well with ice and strain into Collins glass over ice cubes. Fill with ginger ale.

Tequila Martini

¾ oz. tequila
½ oz. dry vermouth

Stir with ice. Strain into chilled cocktail glass. Garnish with an olive.

Tequila Rickey

1¼ oz. tequila
juice of ½ lime
6 oz. club soda

Pour tequila and lime juice over ice in a highball glass. Add soda. Stir. Garnish with lime wedge.

Tequila Sour

1¼ oz. tequila
juice of ½ lemon
½ tsp. bar sugar

Shake with ice. Strain into chilled sour glass. Garnish with lemon slice and maraschino cherry.

Tequila Sunburst

¾ oz. tequila
½ oz. alize (or ½ oz.
    Cognac and ½ oz.
    passion-fruit syrup)
4 oz. orange juice
1 dash grenadine

Shake well with ice. Strain into Hurricane glass. Fill with ice. Garnish with orange slice.

Tequila Sunrise

1¼ oz. tequila
1 tsp. grenadine
6 oz. orange juice

Pour tequila and grenadine over ice cubes in a highball glass. Fill with orange juice. Stir. Garnish with an orange slice.

Tequila Tango

¾ oz. tequila
½ oz. amaretto
2 oz. orange juice
1 splash of lemon-lime
   soda

Stir first three ingredients with ice cubes in wine goblet. Top with splash of soda. Garnish with two thin orange halves, sliced and fanned.

Tequini

1 oz. tequila
¼ oz. dry vermouth

Stir with ice. Strain into prechilled martini glass. Garnish with pickled jalapeño pepper.

Tijuana Bulldog

¾ oz. tequila
½ oz. coffee brandy
3 oz. milk
1 oz. cola

Combine in an ice cube–filled Collins glass.

Tijuana Blues Margarita

1 oz. tequila
¼ oz. blue curaçao
4 oz. sweet & sour or
   margarita mix
8 oz. ice

Blend all ingredients until slushy. Serve in a margarita glass.

Tequila Sunset Margarita

1 oz. tequila
¼ oz. triple sec or simple
   syrup
4 oz. sweet & sour or
   margarita mix
1 oz. strawberry or guava
   concentrate
½ oz. mango concentrate
8 oz. ice

Blend all ingredients until slushy. Serve in a margarita glass.

Tucson Tumbler

1¼ oz. tequila
2 oz. pineapple juice
1 oz. cream of coconut
1 oz. cranberry juice
1 oz. grenadine

Shake ingredients well. Pour into ice cube–filled highball glass. Garnish with orange flag.

Bar Game

◆ *The Game:* A wine glass is resting on two nickels and a dime is slid between them. How can you remove the dime without touching the glass or poking at it?

◆ *The Solution:* Gently pull the table-cloth in the direction of its weave and the dime will magically slide out from under the glass.

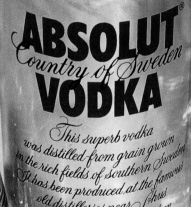

VODKA

Considered among the most versatile of spirits, vodka is a key ingredient in many popular drinks. However, when vodka first came to the United States, it was an acquired taste. The wonders of vodka were the secrets of Eastern European immigrants who consumed it chilled or straight. This did not appeal to Americans who were accustomed to spirits with complex personalities, like whiskies and rums.

I must get out of these wet clothes and into a dry vodka martini.

—Alexander Woollcott

Vodka's versatility in mixed drinks was discovered shortly after World War II. A West Coast restaurateur, trying to unload excess ginger ale, blended various combinations and created a drink that he dubbed the Moscow Mule—vodka, ginger ale, and lime. The drink caught on at his restaurant, and the vodka rage caught on in Hollywood. In 1955, vodka sales accounted for three percent of the U.S. spirits market; by 1982, it accounted for 22 percent. Today, vodka sales account for 25 percent of the U.S. spirits market.

Vodka was first produced in the fourteenth century in Europe through a traditional distallation process that renders a high-proof spirit. The proof of a spirit reflects its alcohol content, and the higher alcohol content makes the flavor of the source fruit, grain, or starch more subtle. Vodka can be produced from starches or grains such as corn and wheat. Grain vodka is considered to be of higher quality. Vodka is distilled from a fermented mash that parallels the production of whisky. Both vodka and whisky rely on pure water and natural grains, however, whisky is distilled at low proof to retain flavor, whereas vodka is distilled at high proof to produce a neutral spirit.

Flavored vodkas such as Sweden's Absolut Citron and Kurant, have increased in popularity, adding a new dimension to traditional mixed drinks while inspiring new ones.

Absolut Citron Blue Lemonade

¾ oz. Absolut Citron
½ oz. blue curacao
4 oz. lemonade

Shake with gusto. Pour into an ice cube-filled Collins glass. Garnish with a lemon wedge.

Absolut Kurant Collins

1 oz. Absolut Kurant
¼ oz. crème de cassis
3 oz. Collins mix
2 oz. club soda

Combine Absolut Kurant, crème de cassis, and Collins mix in an ice cube–filled Collins glass. Top with soda.

Absolut Kurant Kir

¾ oz. Absolut Kurant,
    chilled
½ oz. crème de cassis
brut Champagne or white
    wine

Pour Absolut Kurant and cassis into a Champagne flute. Fill with wine or Champagne.

Absolut Kurant Margarita

¾ oz. Absolut Kurant
½ oz. orange curaçao
½ oz. lemon juice

Shake all ingredients with ice. Serve straight up or on the rocks in a margarita glass rimmed with salt. Garnish with a lemon twist.

Absolut Kurant Sunrise

1¼ oz. Absolut Kurant
6 oz. orange juice
1 splash grenadine

Pour vodka over ice in an old-fashioned glass. Fill with orange juice and grenadine. Stir.

Absolut Peppar Bloody Mary

1¼ oz. Absolut Peppar
6 oz. tomato juice

Mix with ice in a Collins glass. Garnish with a lime wedge and a celery stalk.

Absolut Peppar Ragin' Cajun

1¼ oz. Absolut Peppar
5 oz. tomato juice
2 dashes salt
cayenne pepper to taste

Serve over ice in a Collins glass. Garnish with a lime wedge and a celery stalk.

Absolut Peppar Salty Dog

1¼ oz. Absolut Peppar
5 oz. grapefruit juice

Serve over ice in a old-fashioned glass rimmed with coarse salt.

Algonquin Bloody Mary

1¼ oz. vodka
3 oz. tomato juice
juice of ½ lime
6–8 dashes Worcestershire sauce
Tabasco sauce to taste
salt to taste
pepper to taste

Combine all ingredients in a cocktail shaker with cracked ice. Shake quickly. Strain into highball glass over ice. Drop in a lime wedge.

Anna's Banana

1¼ oz. vodka
1 oz. lime juice
½ small banana, peeled and sliced thin
1 tsp. honey or almond syrup

Combine all ingredients in a blender with ½ cup of cracked ice. Blend at medium speed. Pour into chilled white-wine glass and garnish with lime.

Aqueduct

¾ oz. vodka
¼ oz. curaçao
¼ oz. apricot brandy
½ oz. lime juice

Shake ingredients with ice and strain into a prechilled cocktail glass. Garnish with orange peel.

Ballet Russe

¾ oz. vodka
½ oz. crème de cassis
3 oz. sweet & sour mix
4 oz. crushed ice

Shake with crushed ice. Pour into old-fasioned glass.

Banana Chi Chi

¾ oz. vodka
½ oz. crème de banana
2 oz. pineapple juice
2 oz. cream of coconut
½ banana
8 oz. crushed ice

Blend ingredients thoroughly. Pour into specialty glass. Garnish with a banana spear.

Bay Breeze

1¼ oz. vodka
3 oz. pineapple juice
2 oz. cranberry juice

Combine ingredients in ice cube–filled highball glass. Garnish with a lime wedge.

Belmont Stakes

¾ oz. vodka
¼ oz. rum
¼ oz. strawberry liqueur
½ oz. lime juice
1 tsp. grenadine

Combine all ingredients in a cocktail shaker with cracked ice. Shake well. Strain into chilled cocktail glass. Garnish with lime wedge and orange slice.

Black Russian

¾ oz. vodka
½ oz. coffee liqueur

Shake with ice. Strain over ice cubes in an old-fashioned glass.

Blackberry Sip

¾ oz. vodka
½ oz. blackberry brandy
2 oz. sweet & sour mix

Shake well with crushed ice. Strain into chilled cocktail glass. Garnish with lemon wedge.

Bloody Bull

1¼ oz. vodka
3 oz. Bloody Mary mix
3 oz. beef broth

Combine in a large ice cube–filled highball or specialty glass. Garnish with a celery stalk and lime wedge.

Bloody Caesar

1¼ oz. vodka
6 oz. Clamato (clam-
    tomato cocktail)
1 dash Tabasco

Pour vodka over ice in a goblet. Add Tabasco. Fill with Clamato juice. Stir. Garnish with a lime wedge.

Bloody Mary

1¼ oz. vodka
6 oz. tomato juice
½ tsp. Worcestershire
    sauce
1 dash lemon juice
2–3 drops Tabasco
salt and pepper

Shake with ice and strain into highball glass over ice. Garnish with lime wedge and celery stalk.

Blue Bayou

¾ oz. vodka
½ oz. blue curaçao
3 oz. pineapple juice
3 oz. grapefruit juice

Shake well and pour into a crushed ice–filled glass. Garnish with a fruit flag.

Blue Lemonade

¾ oz. vodka
½ oz. blue curaçao
4 oz. lemonade

Shake well. Pour into ice cube–filled Collins glass. Garnish with lemon wedge.

Blue Shark

¾ oz. vodka
½ oz. tequila
several dashes blue
curaçao

Combine all ingredients in a cocktail shaker with cracked ice. Shake well. Strain into chilled old-fashioned glass.

Bullshot
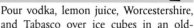

1¼ oz. vodka
1 tsp. lemon juice
3–4 drops Worcestershire
sauce
1 dash Tabasco sauce
4 oz. beef bouillon,
chilled

Pour vodka, lemon juice, Worcestershire, and Tabasco over ice cubes in an old-fashioned glass. Fill with bouillon—either premixed from a cube or canned. Stir.

Bullfrog

1¼ oz. vodka
1 tsp. triple sec
limeade

Pour vodka and triple sec over ice cubes into a chilled highball glass. Stir. Top off with limeade. Stir again and garnish with slice of lime.

Cajun Martini

1¼ oz. vodka
1 dash dry vermouth
pickled jalapeño pepper

Combine vodka and vermouth in a mixing glass with cracked ice and stir well. Strain into cocktail glass. Drop in the jalapeño.

Californian

1¼ oz. vodka
3 oz. orange juice
3 oz. grapefruit juice

Combine in an ice cube–filled highball glass.

Cape Codder

1¼ oz. vodka
6 oz. cranberry juice

Pour vodka over ice cubes in a highball glass. Fill with cranberry juice. Stir.

Cape Colada

¾ oz. vodka
½ oz. peach schnapps
2 oz. cranberry juice
2 oz. cream of coconut
1 oz. sweet & sour mix
8 oz. crushed ice

Blend thoroughly. Pour into specialty glass. Garnish with pineapple flag or cranberry pick.

Chi-Chi

1¼ oz. vodka
2 oz. pineapple juice
1 oz. cream of coconut
8 oz. crushed ice

Mix well in blender until smooth. Pour into wine goblet or specialty glass. Garnish with pineapple fruit flag.

Coconut Bon-Bon

1 oz. vodka
¼ oz. Vandermint liqueur
1½ oz. cream of coconut
1 oz. heavy cream
8 oz. crushed ice

Mix in blender until smooth. Serve in specialty or wine glass. Garnish with chocolate shavings, and maraschino cherry.

Copperhead

1¼ oz. vodka
6 oz. ginger ale

Combine in an ice cube–filled Collins glass. Garnish with lime wedge.

Cosmopolitan

¾ oz. vodka
½ oz. triple sec
1 oz. cranberry juice
½ oz. lime juice

Combine all ingredients in a cocktail shaker with cracked ice. Shake well. Strain into chilled cocktail glass.

Cossack

¾ oz. vodka
½ oz. Cognac
1 oz. lime juice
½ tsp. bar sugar

Combine all ingredients in a cocktail shaker with cracked ice. Shake well. Strain into chilled cocktail glass.

Count Stroganoff

¾ oz. vodka
¼ oz. crème de cacao
¼ oz. Cointreau

Combine all ingredients in a cocktail shaker with cracked ice. Shake well. Strain into chilled old-fashioned glass.

Creamy Screwdriver

1¼ oz. vodka
6 oz. orange juice
½ tsp. bar sugar
1 egg yolk

Combine all ingredients in a blender with cracked ice. Blend until smooth. Pour into chilled Collins glass over ice cubes.

Fashion Passion

1¼ oz. vodka
2 oz. grapefruit juice
2 oz. grape juice

Shake well. Serve in ice cube–filled Collins glass. Garnish with two red grapes on pick or lime wheel.

Florida Banana

¾ oz. vodka
½ oz. crème de banana
3 oz. orange juice
1 oz. cream of coconut
1 medium banana
8 oz. crushed ice

Mix well in blender until smooth. Serve in specialty glass. Garnish with orange, maraschino cherry, banana round, and fruit flag.

Flying Grasshopper

1 oz. vodka
⅛ oz. green crème de
  menthe
⅛ oz. white crème de
  menthe

Combine all ingredients in a blender with cracked ice. Blend at low speed until slushy. Pour into chilled old-fashioned glass.

Georgia Peach

¾ oz. vodka
½ oz. peach brandy
1 tsp. lemon juice
2 oz. fresh peach
1 tsp. peach preserves

Combine all ingredients in a blender with cracked ice. Blend until smooth. Pour into chilled highball glass.

Ginza Mary

¾ oz. vodka
½ oz. sake
2 oz. tomato juice
½ oz. lemon juice
3–5 dashes Tabasco sauce
2 dashes soy sauce
ground pepper to taste

Combine all ingredients in a mixing glass with cracked ice. Stir well. Pour into chilled old-fashioned glass.

Gorky Park

1¼ oz. vodka
1 oz. sweet & sour mix
1 tsp. grenadine
1 dash bitters

Shake well with crushed ice. Strain into chilled cocktail glass. Garnish with strawberry or paper Russian flag.

Greyhound

1¼ oz. vodka
5 oz. grapefruit juice

Combine in an ice cube–filled highball glass.

Harvey Wallbanger

¾ oz. vodka
6 oz. orange juice
½ oz. Galliano

Fill Collins glass with ice. Add vodka and orange juice. Top with Galliano.

Hawaiian Lemonade

1¼ oz. vodka
4 oz. lemonade
2 oz. pineapple juice

Shake well. Serve in a crushed ice–filled Collins or specialty glass. Garnish with lemon wheel or pineapple flag.

Ice Pick

1¼ oz. vodka
6 oz. iced tea
½ oz. lemon juice

Combine in an ice cube–filled iced tea glass or Collins glass. Garnish with lemon wedge or mint sprig.

Kamikaze

¾ oz. vodka
½ oz. triple sec
1 oz. lime juice

Shake and serve over ice in old-fashioned glass or serve straight up.

Kremlin Kernel

1¼ oz. vodka
1 oz. simple syrup
½ oz. water

Shake well with crushed ice. Strain into chilled cocktail glass. Garnish with 3–4 mint leaves torn in half.

Kretchma Cocktail

¾ oz. vodka
½ oz. crème de cacao
1 oz. lemon juice
2 dashes grenadine

Combine all ingredients in a cocktail shaker with cracked ice. Shake well. Strain into chilled cocktail glass.

Licorice Slush

½ oz. vodka
¾ oz. anisette
1 scoop lemon sherbet

Combine in blender until slushy. Pour into a tall, narrow highball glass. Garnish with a licorice stick or mint sprig.

Mad Hatter

1¼ oz. vodka
2 oz. cranberry juice
2 oz. orange juice
1 oz. sweet & sour mix

Combine in an ice cube–filled Collins glass. Garnish with lime wedge.

Melon Vodka Margarita

1 oz. vodka
¼ oz. melon liqueur
4 oz. sweet & sour mix
12 oz. crushed ice

Blend all ingredients until slushy. Served in a prechilled margarita glass rimmed with salt.

Melonball

¾ oz. vodka
½ oz. melon liqueur
2 oz. orange juice

Shake well with crushed ice. Strain into cocktail glass.

Moscow Mule

1¼ oz. vodka
juice of ½ lime
6 oz. ginger beer

Pour vodka over ice in a highball glass. Squeeze lime over drink and drop into glass. Fill with ginger beer. Stir.

Mudslide

½ oz. vodka
½ oz. coffee liqueur
¼ oz. Irish cream liqueur

Combine all ingredients with cracked ice in a cocktail shaker. Shake well and strain into chilled cocktail glass.

"Multiple Orgasm"

¼ oz. vodka
½ oz. amaretto
½ oz. Tia Maria
2 oz. Half-and-Half

Shake well with crushed ice. Strain into cocktail glass.

New Orleans Night

¾ oz. vodka
½ oz. praline liqueur
2 oz. cream of coconut
1 oz. heavy cream
8 oz. crushed ice

Mix well in blender until smooth. Serve in wineglass. Garnish with whipped cream.

North Star

¼ oz. vodka
½ oz. blue curaçao
¼ oz. Captain Morgan
  Original Spiced Rum
¼ oz. apricot brandy
2 oz. sweet & sour mix
1 oz. orange juice
1 oz. pineapple juice

Shake well. Pour into a crushed ice–filled specialty glass. Garnish with a sprig of mint.

Orange Crusher

¾ oz. vodka
½ oz. triple sec
2 oz. orange juice

Shake well with crushed ice. Strain into cocktail glass.

Pineapple Lemonade

1¼ oz. vodka
3 oz. pineapple juice
fresh lemonade

Pour vodka and pineapple juice into a chilled Collins glass over ice cubes. Fill with lemonade and stir.

Pink Baby

1 oz. vodka
¼ oz. cherry liqueur
2 oz. sweet & sour mix

Shake well with crushed ice. Strain into chilled cocktail glass. Garnish with maraschino cherry.

Pink Panther

¾ oz. vodka
¼ oz. dry vermouth
⅛ oz. crème de cassis
1 oz. orange juice
½ egg white

Combine all ingredients in a cocktail shaker with cracked ice. Shake well. Strain into chilled cocktail glass.

Polar Ice Cap

¾ oz. vodka
½ oz. coffee brandy
2 oz. heavy cream
1 oz. cream of coconut
8 oz. crushed ice

Mix well in blender until smooth. Pour into chilled cocktail glass. Garnish with whipped cream.

Polynesian Cocktail

¾ oz. vodka
½ oz. cherry brandy
½ oz. lime juice
½ oz. lemon juice

Rim a chilled cocktail glass with sugar. Combine ingredients with cracked ice in a cocktail shaker and shake well. Strain into the cocktail glass.

Polynesian Pepper Pot

¾ oz. vodka
½ oz. rum
½ cup pineapple juice
½ oz. almond syrup
1 tsp. lemon juice
3–5 dashes Tabasco sauce
¼ tsp. cayenne pepper, or
    to taste
curry powder

Combine all ingredients except curry in a cocktail shaker with cracked ice. Shake well. Strain into chilled highball glass. Sprinkle curry powder on top.

Prairie Oyster

1¼ oz. vodka
1 egg yolk
3 oz. tomato juice
1 dash Worcestershire
    sauce
1 dash Tabasco sauce

Drop unbroken yolk in bottom of chilled wineglass. In a separate glass combine remaining ingredients. Stir with four cubes of ice. Strain. Pour over egg yolk. Serve salt and pepper on the side.

Purple Passion

1¼ oz. vodka
6 oz. grape juice

Pour vodka over ice cubes in a highball glass. Fill with grape juice. Stir.

Rainbow

1 oz. vodka
½ oz. grenadine
5 oz. Collins mix
¼ oz. blue curaçao

Pour grenadine into an empty Hurricane glass. Fill with crushed ice. Combine vodka and Collins mix in shaker, pour into glass. Top with blue curaçao. Garnish with fruit flag.

Red Snapper

1¼ oz. vodka
3 oz. tomato juice
3–5 dashes Worcester-
    shire sauce
dash of lemon juice
salt to taste
freshly ground pepper to
    taste
cayenne pepper to taste

Combine all ingredients except vodka and tomato juice in a cocktail shaker. Shake well. Add ice cubes, vodka, and tomato juice and shake again. Pour into chilled highball glass. Garnish with celery rib.

Rock and Rye Cooler

¾ oz. vodka
½ oz. rock and rye
½ oz. lime juice
6 oz. bitter lemon soda

Shake vodka, rock and rye, and lime juice with ice. Strain into Collins glass over ice cubes. Add soda and stir. Garnish with slice of lime.

Russian Rose

1 oz. vodka
¼ oz. grenadine
1 dash orange bitters

Combine all ingredients in a cocktail shaker with cracked ice. Shake well. Strain into chilled cocktail glass.

Salt Lick

1¼ oz. vodka
2 oz. bitter lemon soda
2 oz. grapefruit juice

Combine in an ice cube–filled wineglass rimmed with salt. Garnish with lemon wheel.

Salty Dog

1¼ oz. vodka
6 oz. grapefruit juice
¼ tsp. salt

Pour vodka over ice in a highball glass. Mix in salt and grapefruit juice.

Scandinavian Martini

¾ oz. vodka
½ oz. akvavit liqueur
1 oz. sweet & sour mix

Shake well with crushed ice. Strain into chilled cocktail glass. Garnish with cocktail onions.

Screwdriver

1¼ oz. vodka
6 oz. orange juice

Pour vodka over ice in a highball glass. Fill with orange juice.

Seabreeze

¾ oz. vodka
¼ oz. melon liqueur
¼ oz. raspberry liqueur
5 oz. pineapple juice
8 oz. crushed ice

Shake well with crushed ice. Pour into Collins glass. Add more ice if necessary.

Summer Lemonade

1 oz. vodka
¼ oz. orange curaçao
1½ oz. sweet & sour mix
1½ oz. lemon-lime soda

Combine in an ice cube–filled Collins glass. Garnish with lemon wheel.

Summer Sailor

¾ oz. vodka
½ oz. triple sec
4 oz. grapefruit juice

Pour into ice cube–filled highball glass.

Vodka Collins

1¼ oz. vodka
juice of ½ lemon
1 tsp. bar sugar
6 oz. club soda

Shake all but soda with ice. Strain over crushed ice in a Collins glass. Fill with soda. Stir. Garnish with lemon slice.

Vodka Cooler

1¼ oz. vodka
½ tsp. sugar
peel of 1 lemon, cut in
  continuous spiral
6 oz. club soda

In highball glass, dissolve sugar in vodka. Add crushed ice and lemon peel. Top with club soda and stir.

Vodka Fizz

1¼ oz. vodka
juice of ½ lemon
juice of ½ lime
2 tsp. bar sugar
6 oz. club soda

Shake all but soda with ice. Strain over ice cubes in a tall glass. Fill with club soda. Stir. Garnish with lemon slice.

Vodka Gimlet

1¼ oz. vodka
½ oz. lime juice

Shake with ice. Strain into prechilled cocktail glass.

Vodka Grasshopper

½ oz. vodka
½ oz. green crème de
  menthe
¼ oz. white crème de
  cacao

Combine all ingredients in a cocktail shaker with cracked ice. Shake well. Strain into chilled cocktail glass.

Vodka Martini

1 oz. vodka
¼ oz. dry vermouth

Stir with ice. Strain into prechilled cocktail glass. Garnish with an olive.

Vodka Rickey

1¼ oz. vodka
juice of ½ lemon
6 oz. club soda

Pour vodka and lime juice in ice cube–filled highball glass. Add soda, stir. Garnish with lime wedge.

Vodka Sling

1 ¼ oz. vodka
1 tsp. bar sugar
1 tsp. water
juice of ½ lemon

In an old-fashioned glass dissolve sugar in water and lemon juice. Add ice cubes and vodka. Garnish with lemon twist.

Vodka Sour

1 ¼ oz. vodka
juice of ½ lemon
½ tsp. bar sugar

Shake with ice. Strain into prechilled sour glass. Garnish with lemon slice and maraschino cherry.

Vodka Stinger

¾ oz. vodka
½ oz. white crème de menthe

Shake well with crushed ice. Pour into ice cube–filled old-fashioned glass.

Vodka Tonic

1 ¼ oz. vodka
6 oz. tonic water

Pour vodka over ice in a highball glass. Fill with tonic water. Squeeze a lime wedge over drink and drop into glass.

White Elephant

¾ oz. vodka
½ oz. white crème de cacao
4 oz. Half-and-Half

Combine in ice cube–filled highball glass.

White Russian

¾ oz. vodka
½ oz. coffee liqueur
2 oz. heavy cream

Pour coffee liqueur and vodka in an old-fashioned glass over ice cubes and fill with cream.

White Spider

1 oz. vodka
¼ oz. white crème de menthe

Stir ingredients with crushed or shaved ice. Strain into a chilled cocktail glass.

WHISKEY

For centuries the Irish and Scots have waged a battle about the origins of whiskey, as it's spelled in Ireland, or whisky, as it is across the North channel in Scotland. In Ireland the word first appeared as *uisgebeatha;* in Scotland, *uisebaugh.* Today the controversy continues and spans the Atlantic Ocean. In Ireland and the United States, it is spelled "whiskey"; in Scotland and Canada, it is spelled "whisky."

Irish or Scotch, American or Canadian, with or without the *e*, one thing holds true for whiskey: It is distilled from a fermented mash of grain at a maximum of 190 proof and removed from the still at between 80 and 110 proof, then bottled at a minimum of 80 proof.

Differences in the characteristics of the country's ingredients and distillation laws lend whiskey its distinct national and brand-name qualities. For instance, the primary distinction between Irish and Scottish versions is the drying process. The Scots use peat moss to dry their malt, which infuses the spirit with a smoky flavor, whereas the Irish use smokeless anthracite. Consequently, Irish whiskey is lighter than Scotch.

Whiskey's fermented grain mash is usually comprised of corn, rye, barley, or wheat. Distilled to a clear elixir, it is then aged in oak barrels, where it slowly develops its unique color, flavor, and aroma.

Of the many myths surrounding this spirit, the most popular is that age is synonymous with quality. It simply isn't true: It's tantamount to saying that all fifty-year-old people are smarter than all thirty-year-olds.

Whiskey is the life of man,
Whiskey, Johnny!
Oh, I'll drink whiskey
while I can,
Whiskey for my Johnny!
—Anonymous shanty

First-rate whiskey, such as Seagram's 7 Crown, begins with the grain. Just as the quality of grain differs, so too does the quality of the whiskey. Also determining the quality of whiskey is the quality of the water source. The finest distilleries are located near springs bubbling with crystal-clear water. But the grain and water must be mashed, fermented, distilled, and aged. Each of these sensitive processes can alter the taste and quality of the whiskey.

Like Scotch, there are two primary types of whiskey: straight or blended. Straight whiskeys are distilled from a base of 51 percent single grain and are aged in pot stills. Blended whiskeys are a seamless weave of a minimum of 20 percent straight whiskey and neutral grain spirits.

Canadian whisky (spelled without the *e*), such as Crown Royal or Seagram's V.O., are blended whiskies that are aged for at least three years before they are sold in the United States. Although Scottish immigrants began the Canadian whisky business, the whisky produced in Canada bears little resemblance to the spirit made in the motherland. Canadian whiskies are made from cereal grains blended, in continuous stills.

American whiskey is mostly blended, with Federal law stipulating at least 20 percent straight whiskey content. Two types of American whiskey differ from the standard variety. Bourbon whiskey is made from a special sour-mash process and aged in charred-oak barrels for at least two years. This corn-based liquor originated in the hills of Kentucky. Tennessee whisky is similar to Bourbon, but is filtered through sugar-maple charcoal and aged for a minimum of four years.

Although Scotch whisky is considered by many to be the world's finest, the Irish refuse to understate their fervor for this wonderful elixir. "An Irishman is lined with copper, and the beer corrodes it," Mark Twain once wrote, "but whiskey polishes the copper and is the saving of him." Whether in a Smash, Sour, or Squirt, this spirit is the passion of many of the world's drinkers—no matter how you spell it. The battle wages on, but all sides continue drinking this fine spirit.

Algonquin

¾ oz. whiskey
½ oz. dry vermouth
1 oz. pineapple juice

Shake with ice and strain into cocktail glass.

Allegheny Cocktail

½ oz. whiskey
½ oz. dry vermouth
¼ oz. blackberry brandy
¼ oz. lemon juice
1 dash bitters

Shake ingredients with ice and strain into chilled cocktail glass. Garnish with lemon twist.

Apricot Sour

1 oz. whiskey
¼ oz. apricot brandy
1 oz. sweet & sour mix

Shake well with crushed ice. Strain into a chilled sour glass. Garnish with fruit flag.

Banana Crown

1 oz. Seagram's 7 Crown
¼ oz. crème de banana
½ oz. cream of coconut
1 oz. pineapple juice

Blend all ingredients in a blender with a scoop of crushed ice.

Banana Scream

¾ oz. Seagram's 7 Crown
½ oz. crème de banana
3 oz. banana cocktail mix
2 oz. heavy cream
16 oz. crushed ice

Mix ingredients in electric blender till smooth and creamy. Serve in specialty glasses. Garnish with dollop of whipped cream with nutmeg sprinkle.

Blackthorn

1 oz. Irish whiskey
¼ oz. dry vermouth
1 dash anisette

Stir well with cubed ice. Strain into cocktail glass or serve on the rocks. Garnish with lemon twist.

Blackthorn Cocktail

¾ oz. Seagram's 7 Crown
¼ oz. dry vermouth
¼ oz. anisette

Stir well with crushed ice. Strain into chilled cocktail glass. Garnish with lemon twist.

Bloody 7

1¼ oz. Seagram's 7
    Crown
4 oz. tomato juice
2 dashes Worcestershire
    sauce
2 dashes Tabasco
celery salt and pepper to
    taste

Pour ingredients into ice cube–filled high-ball glass. Garnish with cucumber spear and lime wedge.

Boilermaker

1¼ oz. whiskey
10 oz. beer

Serve whiskey in a shot glass with a glass of beer on the side as a chaser. Makes two drinks

Bucking Irish

1¼ oz. Irish whiskey
5 oz. ginger ale

Combine in ice cube–filled highball glass. Garnish with lemon twist.

Canadian and Bitters

1¼ oz. Canadian whisky
1–2 dashes bitters
1 tsp. simple syrup

Shake with shaved or crushed ice. Strain into a chilled cocktail glass or over ice cubes in an old-fashioned glass.

Canadian Blackberry Fizz

1 oz. Canadian whisky
¼ oz. blackberry brandy
½ tsp. bar sugar
juice of ½ lemon
2 oz. club soda

Shake whisky, brandy, sugar, and lemon juice with ice. Strain into a tall glass filled with crushed ice. Top with club soda. Garnish with lemon slice.

Canadian Cocktail

1 oz. Canadian whisky
¼ oz. triple sec
1 dash bitters
1 tsp. sugar

Shake ingredients with ice. Strain into a chilled cocktail glass.

Canadian Old-Fashioned

1¼ oz. Canadian whisky
1 sugar cube
1 dash bitters
1 tsp. water

In an old-fashioned glass, muddle sugar with bitters and water. Add ice cubes and whisky. Garnish with lemon twist, orange slice, and maraschino cherry.

Cherry Sour

½ oz. whiskey
½ oz. cherry brandy
1 oz. orange juice
½ oz. lemon juice
½ tsp. bar sugar

Shake with ice. Strain into a chilled sour glass. Garnish with a lemon slice and a maraschino cherry.

Crown and Cola

1¼ oz. Crown Royal
4 oz. cola

Pour whisky over ice in Collins glass. Top with cola and garnish with lemon wedge.

Crownberry Royal

1¼ oz. Crown Royal
1½ oz. cranberry juice
1½ oz. lemon-lime soda

Shake well with crushed ice. Strain into a chilled cocktail glass. Garnish with a lime wheel or three cranberries on a pick.

Crown Jewels

1 oz. Crown Royal
¼ oz. white crème de menthe
3 oz. Half-and-Half
1 splash simple syrup

Combine in an ice cube–filled highball glass. Garnish with a maraschino cherry.

Crowning Glory

1 oz. Seagram's 7 Crown
¼ oz. amaretto
½ oz. cream of coconut
4 oz. pineapple juice
8 oz. crushed ice

Blend all ingredients until slushy. Serve in a specialty glass.

Dixie Whiskey

1¼ oz. whiskey
⅙ oz. lemon juice
½ tsp. powdered sugar
1 dash white crème de
   menthe
1 dash curaçao

Shake with ice. Strain over ice in an old-fashioned glass. Garnish with a mint sprig.

Dry Manhattan

1 oz. Canadian whisky
¼ oz. dry vermouth
1 dash bitters (optional)

Stir with ice. Strain into prechilled cocktail glass. Garnish with a maraschino cherry.

Everybody's Irish Cocktail

1 oz. Irish whiskey
¼ oz. chartreuse, green
4 dashes green crème de
   menthe

Stir ingredients with shaved or crushed ice. Strain into a chilled cocktail glass. Garnish with a green olive.

Hurricane Cocktail

½ oz. whiskey
½ oz. white crème de
   menthe
¼ oz. gin
1 oz. sweet & sour mix

Shake well with crushed ice. Strain into a chilled cocktail glass. Garnish with lemon wheel.

Hurricane III

¾ oz. whiskey
½ oz. apricot brandy
1 oz. orange juice
1 dash bitters

Shake all ingredients. Pour into an ice cube–filled old-fashioned glass. Garnish with orange wheel.

Irish Angel

¾ oz. Irish whiskey
¼ oz. light crème de
   cacao
¼ oz. white crème de
   menthe
1½ oz. heavy cream

Shake well with crushed ice. Strain into chilled cocktail glass or serve on the rocks.

Irish Cooler

1¼ oz. Irish whiskey
6 oz. club soda

Pour whiskey into a highball glass over ice cubes. Top with soda and stir. Garnish with a lemon peel spiral.

Irish Delight

1¼ oz. Irish whiskey
1½ oz. heavy cream

Combine in an ice cube–filled old-fashioned glass. Stir.

Irish Eyes

1 oz. Irish whiskey
¼ oz. green crème de menthe
2 oz. heavy cream

Shake well with crushed ice. Strain into chilled cocktail glass. Garnish with maraschino cherry.

Irish Horseman

¾ oz. Irish whiskey
¼ oz. triple sec
3 oz. sweet & sour mix
8 oz. crushed ice
¼ oz. raspberry liqueur

Combine whiskey, triple sec, and sweet & sour mix with crushed ice. Shake well. Pour into highball glass. Top with raspberry liqueur.

Irish Kiss

¾ oz. Irish whiskey
½ oz. peach schnapps
4 oz. ginger ale
2 oz. orange juice

Combine in an ice cube–filled Collins or specialty glass. Garnish with lime wheel.

Irish Knight

1 oz. Irish whiskey
1 tsp. dry vermouth
¼ tsp. Benedictine
1 oz. orange juice

Shake well with crushed ice. Strain into ice cube–filled old-fashioned glass. Garnish with orange twist.

Irish Magic

1 oz. Irish whiskey
¼ oz. white crème de cacao
5 oz. orange juice

Pour all ingredients over ice in a glass. Stir.

Irish Prince

1¼ oz. Irish whiskey
3 oz. tonic water

Combine in an ice cube–filled old fashioned glass. Stir. Garnish with lemon twist.

Irish Summer Coffee

1 oz. Irish whiskey
¼ oz. Irish cream liqueur
4 oz. cold coffee

Stir with cubed ice. Strain into wineglass or specialty coffee glass. Garnish with whipped cream if desired.

Ladies' Cocktail

1 oz. whiskey
4 dashes Pernod
4 dashes anisette
2 dashes bitters

Stir ingredients with crushed or shaved ice. Strain into a chilled cocktail glass. Garnish with a slice of fresh pineapple.

Manhasset

1 oz. whiskey
⅛ oz. dry vermouth
⅛ oz. sweet vermouth
½ oz. lemon juice

Shake ingredients with ice. Strain into a chilled cocktail glass. Garnish with a twist of lemon peel.

Manhattan

1 oz. Canadian whisky
¼ oz. sweet vermouth
1 dash bitters (optional)

Stir with ice in tumbler. Strain into a prechilled old-fashioned glass. Garnish with a maraschino cherry or serve on the rocks.

New Old-Fashioned

1¼ oz. whiskey
3 oz. lemon-lime soda
1 splash bitters

Combine in an ice cube–filled old-fashioned glass. Garnish with lemon twist, orange slice, maraschino cherry.

New Yorker Cocktail

1¼ oz. whiskey
juice of ½ lime
2 dashes grenadine
1 tsp. sugar

Shake ingredients with ice. Strain into a chilled cocktail glass. Garnish with twists of lemon and orange peel.

Old Fashioned

1¼ oz. Canadian whisky
1 sugar cube
1 dash bitters
1 tsp. water

In old-fashioned glass, muddle sugar with bitters and water. Add ice cubes and whisky. Garnish with lemon twist, orange slice, and maraschino cherry.

Patty's Pride

1 oz. Irish whiskey
¼ oz. peppermint schnapps
1 oz. club soda

Combine in an ice cube–filled old-fashioned glass.

Perfect Manhattan

1 oz. Crown Royal
⅛ oz. dry vermouth
⅛ oz. sweet vermouth
1 dash bitters (optional)

Stir with ice. Strain into prechilled cocktail glass. Garnish with a maraschino cherry.

Royal Chill

¾ oz. Crown Royal
¼ oz. amaretto
2 oz. heavy cream

Shake well with crushed ice. Serve in chilled cocktail glass.

Royal Family

1 oz. Crown Royal
¼ oz. cherry brandy
2 oz. sweet & sour mix

Shake well with crushed ice. Strain into ice cube–filled wineglass. Garnish with maraschino cherry.

Royal L.A.

1 oz. Crown Royal
¼ tsp. bar sugar
1 oz. club soda
1 dash bitters
¼ oz. triple sec

Mix whisky, sugar, soda, and bitters. Pour over ice. Float triple sec. Garnish with an orange slice and a maraschino cherry.

Royal Majic

1 oz. Crown Royal
¼ oz. amaretto
1½ oz. orange juice

Combine in an ice cube–filled glass.

Royal Milk Punch

1¼ oz. Crown Royal
5 oz. milk
1 splash simple syrup

Shake well to combine. Pour into ice cube–filled Collins glass. Garnish with maraschino cherry.

Royal Peach

¾ oz. Crown Royal
½ oz. peach schnapps
1 oz. orange juice
1 oz. club soda

Combine whisky, schnapps, and juice in ice cube–filled old-fashioned glass. Top with soda.

Royal Regalia

¾ oz. Crown Royal
½ oz. cherry brandy
2 oz. cranberry juice

Shake well with crushed ice. Strain into ice cube–filled old-fashioned glass.

Royal Schnapreme

½ oz. Crown Royal
¾ oz. peppermint schnapps
1 oz. soda water

Shake well with crushed ice. Strain into chilled cocktail glass.

Royal Splash

1¼ oz. Crown Royal
1 oz. sweet & sour mix
1 tsp. grenadine
3 oz. club soda

Combine Crown Royal, sweet & sour mix, and grenadine in ice cube–filled Collins glass. Top with soda. Garnish with lime wheel.

Royal Stinger

1 oz. Crown Royal
¼ oz. white crème de menthe

Shake well with crushed ice. Strain into chilled cocktail glass.

Royal Ward 8

1¼ oz. Crown Royal
2 oz. sweet & sour mix
½ oz. grenadine

Shake well with crushed ice. Strain into chilled cocktail glass. Garnish with maraschino cherry.

Salty John

1¼ oz. whiskey
6 oz. grapefruit juice

Pour into salt-rimmed, ice cube–filled highball glass.

Scepter

1¼ oz. Canadian whisky
3 oz. grapefruit juice
1 splash grenadine

Shake well to combine. Pour into ice cube–filled old-fashioned glass. Garnish with lime wedge.

Screwy 7 Fizz

1¼ oz. Seagram's 7 Crown
4 oz. orange juice
2 oz. club soda

Pour Seagram's 7 Crown and orange juice over ice in a glass. Stir. Add club soda and stir gently.

Seagram's 7 Sidecar

1 oz. Seagram's 7 Crown
¼ oz. triple sec
2 oz. sweet & sour mix

Shake well with crushed ice. Strain into chilled cocktail glass with sugared rim. Garnish with lime wheel.

7 Crown Collins

1¼ oz. Seagram's 7
    Crown
1 tsp. bar sugar
juice of ½ lemon
6 oz. club soda

In tumbler, combine whiskey, sugar, and lemon juice with ice. Strain over crushed ice into cocktail glass. Top with club soda. Garnish with lemon slice.

7 Crown Julep

1¼ oz. Seagram's 7
    Crown
1 tsp. simple syrup
4 mint leaves

In a tall glass, muddle simple syrup with mint leaves. Fill glass with shaved ice and pour in whiskey. Add more shaved ice. Garnish with mint sprig.

7 Crown Rickey

1¼ oz. Seagram's 7
    Crown
½ lime
6 oz. club soda

Pour Seagram's 7 Crown and lime juice over ice in a highball glass. Add soda. Stir. Garnish with a lime wedge.

7 Highball

1¼ oz. Seagram's 7
    Crown
5 oz. ginger ale

Combine in an ice cube–filled highball glass. Stir. Add lemon twist, if desired.

7 'n' Bitters

1¼ oz. Seagram's 7
    Crown
2 dashes bitters

Pour into ice cube–filled old-fashioned glass. Stir. Garnish with lemon twist.

7 Seas

¾ oz. Seagram's 7 Crown
½ oz. melon liqueur

Combine in an ice cube–filled highball glass. Garnish with pineapple segment.

7 & 7

1¼ oz. Seagram's 7
    Crown
6 oz. 7-Up

Pour Seagram's 7 Crown over ice cubes in highball glass. Fill with 7-Up. Stir.

7th Heaven

¾ oz. Seagram's 7 Crown
½ oz. amaretto
4 oz. orange juice

Combine in an ice cube–filled highball glass. Garnish with orange slice.

7th Sunset

1¼ oz. Seagram's 7 Crown
2 oz. cranberry juice
2 oz. sweet & sour mix

Combine Seagram's 7 Crown and cranberry juice in ice cube–filled Collins glass. Top with sweet & sour mix. Garnish with fruit flag.

Snake Bite

¾ oz. Canadian whisky
½ oz. peppermint schnapps

Shake well with crushed ice. Strain into pony glass.

South of the Border

1 oz. whiskey
¼ oz. triple sec
2 oz. sweet & sour mix

Shake well with crushed ice. Strain into chilled cocktail glass rimmed with salt. Garnish with lime wheel.

Strawberry 7

1¼ oz. Seagram's 7 Crown
4 strawberries
8 oz. crushed ice
3 oz. 7-Up

Blend first three ingredients for 10 seconds in blender. Pour into wineglass, top with 7-Up. Garnish with fresh strawberry.

Tipperary

¾ oz. Irish whiskey
¼ oz. sweet vermouth
⅛ oz. chartreuse, green
1 oz. club soda

Stir well with 5 to 6 ice cubes. Strain into chilled cocktail glass or serve on the rocks.

V.O. Canadian Cooler

1¼ oz. Seagram's V.O.
1 oz. sweet & sour mix
1 oz. orange juice
1 oz. lemon-lime soda

Serve on the rocks in a highball glass. Garnish with a cherry and an orange slice.

V.O. Manhattan

1 oz. Seagram's V.O.
¼ oz. sweet vermouth
1 dash bitters

Shake or stir with ice. Strain into prechilled old-fashioned glass or serve on the rocks. Garnish with a maraschino cherry.

Whiskey Cocktail

1¼ oz. whiskey
1 dash bitters
⅙ oz. simple syrup

Stir ingredients with crushed or shaved ice. Strain into a chilled cocktail glass. Garnish with a maraschino cherry.

Whisky Sour

1¼ oz. Canadian whisky
juice of ½ lemon
½ tsp. bar sugar

Shake with ice. Strain into prechilled sour glass. Garnish with lemon slice and maraschino cherry.

Whisky Fizz

1¼ oz. Canadian whisky
juice of ½ lemon
1 tsp. bar sugar
6 oz. club soda

In tumbler, shake whisky, lemon juice, and sugar with ice and strain into Collins glass over ice cubes. Fill with club soda and stir.

Whisky Rickey

1¼ oz. Canadian whisky
juice of ½ lime
6 oz. club soda

Pour whisky and lime juice into a highball glass. Add soda. Stir. Garnish with lime wedge.

Whisky Sling

1¼ oz. Canadian whisky
1 tsp. bar sugar
1 tsp. water
juice of ½ lemon

In old-fashioned glass, dissolve sugar in water and lemon juice. Add ice cubes and whisky. Stir. Garnish with lemon twist.

Zero Mint Julep

1 oz. whiskey
¼ oz. green crème de
menthe

Pour crème de menthe over crushed ice in an old-fashioned glass. Place in freezer until glass frosts over. Add whiskey. Stir gently. Garnish with mint sprig.

Bar Game

◆ *The Game:* Stand sideways against a wall, pressing your left shoulder, elbow, hip, and knee to the wall. Then try to lift your right leg.

◆ *The Solution:* It can't be done!

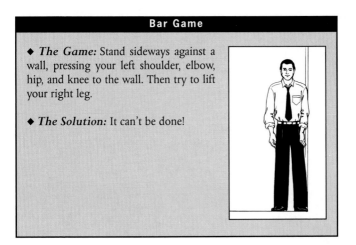

BEERS & ALES

Why did the Pilgrims land in Massachusetts instead of Virginia? As the *Mayflower* journal put it, "We could not now take time for further search or considerations, our victuals being spent, especially our beer." As much as they loved the "liquid bread," the Pilgrims were not the first to bring beer to America. Before their arrival Columbus documented that he was served a special corn brew by the Native Americans. While many undocumented types of beers surely existed in the colonial days, today the world has hundreds of large-label commercial brands available.

HOW BEER IS MADE

Beer is a brewed and fermented drink consisting of malted barley, hops, water, and yeast. Like wine making, beer brewing is simple in its natural process. But creating a quality beer is not simple and requires a brew master with a watchful eye.

First the barley is steeped—that is, the dry, hard grains are soaked in water for two days to soften them. Once softened, the barley is ready for germinating. The grains are placed in temperature- and humidity-controlled compartments for about a week, during which the barley will sprout into what is termed "green malt" and produce the enzyme amylase, an enzyme that enables the conversion of starch to sugar for fermentation.

The green malt is dried in a kiln to stop the sprouts from further development. Here, time and temperature controls are critical, as the amount of time the green malt spends in the kiln and the roasting temperature decide the degree of sweetness and the color of the end product. Once dried the barley malt is sifted through to extract the sprouts, after which the remaining malt is ground in a milling process.

After milling, hot water and milled barley are mixed in a mashing tun, creating a cereal mash, which causes the starch to change to sugar, forming a liquid called "wort." The wort is brewed in a large kettle for several hours and hops are added to enhance the aroma and flavor. Then the hops are filtered out, and the wort is chilled immediately, helping to produce a clear beer.

Pitched together with yeast in a large tank, the wort begins to ferment, producing carbon dioxide. After a week or so, depending upon the brew, the beer is ready for maturation, during which the beer will develop new characteristics in its flavor and aroma.

Lastly, the beer is either racked, canned, or bottled for the consumer. Racked beer is not filtered but kegged directly from the maturation tank. Kegs generally are not pasteurized because they are usually consumed quickly, while cans and bottles with potentially longer lives are pasteurized to avoid spoiling.

STYLES OF BEER

Beer categories vary depending on beer characteristics and geographic location because there is no industry standard as there is for whiskey. In fact, there are some 70 styles of beer. However, most beer is either ale or lager.

What the Pilgrims named beer was actually ale. Ale, unlike lager beer, is a top-fermenting brew. During fermentation the yeast floats to the top after feasting on the sugar, which gives it a distinct flavor. Ale is typically dark-hued, bitter, full-bodied, aromatic, and has a higher alcohol content than lager.

Under the ale heading fall many different types of beer:

Alt, a German beer, is generally high in hops, medium-bodied, and reddish-brown in color. Two name brands are Gaffel and Gilden.

Stout is a dark and full-bodied ale that is brewed with roasted barley for a stronger flavor and aroma. There are several kinds of stout. Among them is a dry stout, which is light on hops. International stouts tend to be stronger than U.S. blends.

Porter, a baby brother to stout, actually preceded its stronger counterpart and originated in London during the 1700s. It also has a dark color and is full-bodied with a bittersweet taste but has a lower alcohol content than a stout. Chocolate malt is added to create a robust porter and may be found in Sierra Nevada Porter. For a lighter and medium-bodied flavor, try a brown porter such as Samuel Smith's Taddy Porter.

Strong Ales all tend to have a powerful taste and a high alcohol content. There are three common variations: Scottish Ale, which is full-bodied and has less hops than English ale; Barley Wine (called wine because of the similarity in alcohol content), which is characterized by its hoppy nature; and English Old Ale, which typically is a draft ale that is identified by its sweet, nutty flavor.

Compared to ales, lagers tend to be crisper, drier, clearer, and more carbonated. Most American beers fall into the lager category. Lager encompasses a wide range of beer, from light to dry to dark. Light beer such as Coors Light and Miller Lite are light-bodied, pale in color, and lower in calories. Dry beer is also pale, but has a low alcohol content, which results in a diminished aftertaste. In contrast, the popular dark lagers are not only deeper in color but are aromatic and full-bodied. The exceptions are American dark lagers which change only in color.

Pilsner is a moderately hoppy, pale lager with a crisp, light- to medium-bodied flavor. A town in Czechoslovakia called Pilzen was famous for its beer, and breweries wishing to capitalize on the fame and emulate the taste of the lager named their beer after it.

Bockbier or Bock, which originated in Einbeck, Germany, can be either pale or dark, and is a full-bodied lager. Because of an old myth, bock used to be brewed only in the spring, but it is now brewed year round. A good bock is characterized by a sweet, malty taste. Another kind of bock is the Dopplebock, which is more intense and a dark-brown color.

Sake, usually thought of as a rice wine, is actually beer made from rice. The confusion is not surprising considering sake's resemblance to wine with its clear color and high alcohol content—usually 12–20 percent. Produced in Japan, Sake is traditionally served hot—about 100 degrees—in ceramic bottles. It may also be served on the rocks or at room temperature.

Other specialty beers include Lambic, or fruit beers, which are made by brewing into the beer different fruits, such as cherries and raspberries. Herb beers mix spices like garlic and pepper into the brew. And for those who love the taste of beer, but want to avoid the alcohol, many nonalcohol beers are available. By law they are required to have less than .5 percent alcohol by weight. To produce this beer the alcohol is either extracted or the beer is only partially fermented.

BUYING, STORING, AND SERVING

Beer is a perishable item, but following general rules will ensure quality and freshness. Beer should always be bought from a store that refrigerates its brew. Avoid stores that are lit with fluorescent lights or where the beer is placed in direct sunlight, as it may skunk—or compromise—the flavor of the beer. To help block out unwanted light, buy tinted brown or green bottles. Cans, while economical, may flavor the beer with a metallic taste.

Handle with care. Jostling beer can cause a chemical reaction that will change the flavor and scent of the beer. For storing purposes, beer should be kept in a cool place—preferably around 45°F—and temperature should not fluctuate or damage may occur. Unlike wine, beer should be stored upright and for short periods of time.

When serving beer always use a glass. This will release the carbon dioxide into the air instead of into the stomach. Before pouring, it is important to peel away any foil completely, as contact with the beer will taint the taste. Contrary to popular opinion, a beer should be poured in the center of the upright glass, not at a slant—all the better to release carbon dioxide. Temperature for serving varies with the type of beer served: ordinary beer at 45°F; choice lagers at 50°F; prime ales at 55°F; and porters at 60°F.

HOME-BREWING

Many of our forefathers brewed their own beer; George Washington brewed his own beer, as did Samuel Adams and Thomas Jefferson. Today, home-brewing serves as a hobby instead of a need, but it does have a strong following, with magazines and books dedicated to the subject. For the unsure beginner, complete home-brewing kits that are easy to use are now available at grocery stores for around twenty dollars.

MICROBREWERIES

With the advent of beer tasting and appreciation, the old philosophy that any beer will do has disappeared. Three hundred microbreweries that specialize in finer-quality beer have sprouted up across the United States to cater to the beer connoisseur. Technically capable of producing no more than 10,000 barrels a year, microbreweries contend that they take more time and care making their beer than do the major commercial breweries. As the brewmaster of Samuel Adams is famous for saying, "The major breweries spill more in a day than [microbreweries] bottle all year." These brews from the smaller micros tend to be fresher because they are not shipped great distances. Many local restaurants and bars now have regularly scheduled microbrewery sampling nights.

TASTING BEER

Appearance, aroma, flavor . . . the principles of beer tasting and wine tasting are similar.

Before opening the beer bottle, check the amount of space between the head of the beer and the bottle top. The space should equal no more than 1½ inches and no less than ½ inch for adequate breathing. Next look for sediment. There should only be a thin layer, and in commercial beers, there shouldn't be any.

Once the beer is poured, hold the glass against a white background to look at the clarity and color. A quality beer will be clear or brilliant with the color corresponding to that of its type. As for carbonation, small bubbles indicate the beer was carbonated naturally, while large bubbles mean the carbonation is artificially added.

Whereas evaluating the aroma of a wine requires olfactory subtleness, beer testing requires a sharp, deep sniff. Many beers will have fruity undertones in the aroma and a practiced nose will be able to discern the fruit scents. Wine connoisseurs will notice that the vocabulary of wine tasting is often interchangeable with that of beer tasting. For example, a herbaceous wine has the same meaning as a herbaceous beer.

The best time to taste beer is in the morning when the senses are the sharpest. Nibbling on white bread will cleanse the palate before trying a beer, and smoking should be avoided several hours before serious tasting. Mild-flavored beers should be served before strong-flavored beers, as well as light-bodied before full-bodied. When rating the flavor of beer, the beer should be swirled around the tongue. Repeat this twice so the flavor is clear in the mind. A good beer will be true to its character mainly in hoppiness, body, and maltiness. As always, personal preference is the most important factor.

WINE

It's believed that wine originated in the Middle East some 6,000 years ago. Ancient Greek, Etruscan, Minoan, and Egyptian civilizations were the first to document the fermentation process, but it is highly probable that the nectar of the gods made its appearance even earlier.

Winemaking, or vinification, gradually spread from East to West through centuries of religion, war, exploration and trading. The Romans used it as a sacrament in religious ceremonies, and wine consumption expanded as the Roman Empire spread into Western Europe—particularly, France, Germany, and Austria. When the Empire fell, explorations such as those of Christopher Columbus helped to augment the industry. In 1524, explorer Hernando Cortéz brought vines from Spain to cultivate in Mexico. And with the development of new countries, wine became an international product.

HOW WINE IS MADE

While the process of vinification is similar in many countries, the types of wines differ significantly. Grape cultivation is a finicky process that earns a fine wine rightful prestige. A winemaker may be able to influence viticultural practices such as pruning, irrigation volume and timing, and harvest time, but mother nature governs the climate, soil, and weather—all of which impact a wine's character.

The grapes in finer wines are cultivated at higher elevations on dry rocky slopes, where the climate is cool and the soil allows for superior

> If the identity of the man who made the first wine were known, there would be statues in his honor all over the world.
>
> —Terry Robards, Journalist, Author and Wine Expert

179

drainage. Those grown in flat, warm, and heavily irrigated terrains with a high yield per acre, will usually produce a less elegant beverage.

Too much rain at harvest time may cause mold and affect flavor concentration, so grapes must be harvested before they are drenched. However they must be allowed to grow long enough to get the right sugar content. A good winemaker must understand timing and be a skillful gambler.

Because wine is an art as well as a science, hands-on tasting of the grapes accompanies lab tests to determine sugar content. During the fermentation process, the grape's natural sugar converts to carbon dioxide and alcohol. After fermentation is complete, the wine is normally filtered for clarity. Temperature and length of fermentation are critical; the more complete the process, the less residual sugar and the drier the wine. If fermentation is interrupted, the effect will be a sweeter product. Aging then takes place for varying lengths of time, followed by subsequent aging once the wine is bottled.

WINE STORAGE

The main points to remember about wine storage are (1) avoid extremes in temperature, and (2) never allow the cork to dry out. Bottles should therefore be placed on their sides in a dark, dry, and cool location—preferably 50 to 55°F (10 to 13 degrees Celsius), so that all of a wine's components can blend harmoniously and the cork can remain moist.

If an open bottle is not going to be fully consumed on the day it is opened, its quality can be preserved with a vacuum cork which removes air in the bottle and prevents oxidation. These simple pumplike devices are inexpensive and can be purchased at most stores that sell wines and spirits.

TASTING

Wine tasting is a celebration of subtlely, so the palate should be cleared first by tasting bread. The key components of a wine's character are appearance, bouquet, smell, and taste, and because they are all important to the wine tasting experience, careful attention should be paid to each aspect. When judging appearance, look for color and clarity; setting the wine against a white tablecloth or background will make it easier to "read." As a general rule, white wines gain color with age whereas red wines tend to lose color. To bring out a wine's bouquet, swirl it delicately after pouring it into a glass. Swirling aerates the wine, allowing for the mixing of oxygen. Once the bouquet is brought out, the full aroma ("nose") can be described. Training your senses to pick up the various scents and tastes requires practice. In the end, however, the test of a good wine ultimately comes down to one question: Did you enjoy it?

TYPES OF WINE

With over 4,000 types of grapes, it is easy to see why selecting a wine can be considered an art form. Fortunately, the most "noble" wines, those with great balance and character, come from only a dozen or

> *It is only the first bottle that is expensive.*
> —French proverb

so varietals. And many of the finer wines of the world are identified not by grape, but by region (e.g., Macon, a region of Burgundy which produces an excellent white wine from the Chardonnay grape) or by the name of a domain (e.g., the small Bordeaux chateau).

Whites

White wines are the perfect complement to subtly flavored foods that might otherwise be overwhelmed by a red. The most common white varietals include Chardonnay, Sauvignon Blanc (Fumé Blanc), Johannisberg Riesling, Chenin Blanc, and Gewürztraminer.

The elite Chardonnay grape, rarely blended, is known for its power and complexity. Chardonnay wine can be either fresh, fruity or bitter, depending on the soil and climate, and nearly always has a lingering taste that weighs heavily on the tongue. Usually aged for a short time in oak to smooth out the flavors, Chardonnay is a fully dry wine, with all sugars converted to alcohol. Its alcohol content is generally in the 12.5 to 14 percent range, and the best time for sampling is generally two to five years after vintage.

Less full-bodied is the Sauvignon Blanc, also a fully dry wine, but with an herbal aroma. As a matter of fact, some connoisseurs have described it as "grassy." Sauvignon Blancs are further characterized by an acidic base and medium body, with an alcohol content also in the 12.5 to 14 percent range. Although sometimes vinified sweet to yield dessert wines, at their best they are crisp and dry and serve as wonderful all-purpose dinner companions.

Johannisberg Riesling, the most celebrated grape of Germany, is often vinified with a higher amount of residual sugar, resulting in a sweeter wine. Riesling made in neighboring Alsace (which was a part of Germany before World War I), however, is vinified dry. The best are complex, with both a fruity and flowery bouquet. While most often served as a dessert wine, they can be enjoyed as an aperitif or as a complement to an entree.

Chenin Blanc is not as internationally recognized as the others and is known for its balance and length of flavor. Thought by some to be only a sweet wine, not all Chenin Blancs have a high sugar content. Affordable and quite agreeable in both its sweet and dry form, Chenin Blanc makes an excellent aperitif as well as a fine accompaniment to light meals.

Gewürztraminer is one of the more unusual and less common popular varieties of white wine due to its intense spiciness. Far from a subtle wine, devotees crave its distinctiveness. Among the most treasured of California wines, they tend to be rather expensive.

Reds

More assertive and robust than whites, red wines complement more aggressively flavored foods. Often considered to be more complex because of the differences in fermentation, the varietal reds most often recommended are Cabernet Sauvignon, Pinot Noir, Merlot, and Zinfandel.

Although there are those who would disagree, Cabernet Sauvignon is generally considered the finest red. Aged in oak, Cabernets are immediately identifiable by their strong wood scent. Classic and complex, they have a tannic and astringent quality, and some even contain a hint of green pepper or dried basil flavors or aromas. Although wineries aim to create this varietal with an early maturity, immature Cabernets can be overly acidic so they require proper aging to mellow. Alcohol content of Cabernets is similar to full-bodied white wines: 12.5 to 14 percent.

Pinot Noir is a light ruby-red wine with an intense berry flavor. The basic grape of red Burgundy in France is Pinot Noir. At its best, when combined with the right amount of tannin, it results in a silky finish with a spicy aroma.

Merlot has finally come into its own after spending years in the shadow of Cabernet Sauvignon, and is now competing for the title as the most preferred full-bodied red. Ripening before the Cabernet, Merlot tends to impart a softer and less acidic quality.

The Zinfandel, though of European descent, is grown mostly in California, and has a blackberry flavor and a savory personality. In the past it was often known to be exceedingly heavy, tannic, and high in alcohol. More recently, a lighter Zin has been produced.

Blush Wines

Blush wines are white wines made from red grapes. White Zinfandel, for example, popular since the late 1970s, is produced by filtering out the skins immediately after the grapes are crushed. These tasty wines are medium sweet and make fine aperitifs. In general, they contain a higher residual sugar content than whites, but some tend to be on the drier side. Fresh, fruity and light, they are often best enjoyed within a year or two of vintage. The finer white Zins have the full flavor of the Zinfandel without the tannins or excess acidity.

Dessert Wines: Sherry and Port

Dessert wines generally contain 17 to 21 percent alcohol and are usually enjoyed at the close of a meal. Shakespeare so loved the "sack" (an archaic term for sherry) that he promoted it through characters such as Fal-staff in *Henry IV.* Brought to England from Jerez de la Frontera, Spain, the term *sherry* was derived from the Spanish word *Jerez.* An actual blend of wines, it is combined with brandy to retard the fermentation process.

> *"Salute"*
>
> —Italian Toast

A few sherries still retain their Spanish names: a fino is light and dry, working nicely as an aperitif; an amontillado is nutty but not as dry as a fino and is usually served between meals; and an oloroso is full-bodied with a sweeter hint. Cream sherries are rich and deep golden; brown sherries are nutty, dark, and full-bodied.

"Sleep after toil, port after stormy seas . . ." Many, however, simply enjoy port after dinner. This Portuguese specialty was transformed into a dessert wine by the English, who produced it according to their own country's taste and clime. The result was a seductive blend of Portuguese wine fortified by grape brandy. This process arrests fermentation and provides a unique bouquet. Vintage port is character-ized by a robust yet supple flavor; a ruby port is young and sweet; tawny port is more mature and dry; and white port is similar to the ruby except that it is made solely from white grapes. Another dessert wine, though not as popular today as it was in the past, is Madeira. Madeira is not only believed by many to be the first wine imported into America, but it is also the wine served at the signing of the Dec-laration of Independence.

Champagne / Sparkling Wine

Champagne is a geographical region of France located approximately ninety miles northeast of Paris. Thus, true Champagne comes only from the Champagne region, hence the name "sparkling wine" for the many varieties produced in other parts of the world. The characteristic effervescence of Champagne/sparkling wine is a result of a unique vinification process during which wine is twice fermented. The first fermentation transforms the grape juice into wine. The fermented wine is then stored in casks and chilled to remove bitartrates. After several months the wine is blended with sugar and yeast, the amounts of each depending on the vintner's preference. This wine is then bottled, corked, capped with a metal cap akin to those found on a beer bottle, and stored on its side and gradually inverted. It is at this stage that the wine undergoes its second fermentation. Sediment produced during this stage of fermentation is captured onto the bottom of the cork. Upon completion of this process, the sediment is removed by first freezing the neck of the bottle—which freezes the sediment—and then removing the metal cap. Upon the removal of the cap, the pressure built up inside the bottle causes the cork and frozen sediment to explode. Wine is then added to refill the bottle, which is then recorked. When evaluating a Champagne/sparkling wine, pay close attention to the bubbles, as longer-lasting small bubbles are indicative of a good bottle.

The spectrum of Champagne/sparkling wine varies from brut, the driest, to doux, the sweetest. In between lie the extra dry, sec or dry (which is usually sweet!), and demi-sec. Brut dominates the U.S. market.

Be careful when opening a bottle of Champagne/sparkling wine because the pressure in the bottle is approximately ninety pounds per square inch—almost three times the air pressure of an automobile tire. Because a wayward cork can cause severe injury, be sure to keep one hand on the cork at all times when opening a bottle, especially when removing the wire basket. On another note, avoid trying to chill a bottle in a pinch by placing it in the freezer. The bottle could freeze and explode in less than twenty minutes.

Cool Jazz

1 oz. dry white wine
¾ banana liqueur
½ lime juice
1 slice banana

Shake wine, banana liqueur, and lime juice well with ice. Strain into cocktail glass. Float banana slice on drink.

Empire Punch

3 oz. claret
1 tsp. curaçao
1 tsp. Benedictine
1 tsp. brandy
1 oz. Champagne

In Collins glass, add claret, curaçao, Benedictine, and brandy over ice cubes and top with Champagne. Garnish with fresh fruit.

French Curve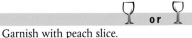

4 oz. chilled dry white wine
1 tsp. Pernod
1 tsp. maraschino liqueur
1 slice lemon
½ slice orange

Pour wine, Pernod, and maraschino liqueur into large wineglass. Add ice cubes. Stir. Add lemon and orange slices.

Little Eva

2 oz. Burgundy
¼ oz. triple sec
1 tsp. lime or lemon juice
4 oz. lemon-lime soda

Pour the wine, triple sec and juice over ice in a glass. Stir. Add the soda and stir gently.

Peach Blush Cooler

3 oz. white zinfandel
1 oz. peach schnapps
2 oz. sweet or dry soda

Garnish with peach slice.

Peach Refresher

1 oz. peach brandy
3 oz. white wine
2 oz. lemon-lime soda

Serve in wineglass over rocks. Garnish with a fresh peach slice and mint.

Peachee Kir

1 oz. peach schnapps
3 oz. Champagne

Garnish with peach slice.

Port Sangaree

3 oz. port wine
1 oz. water
1 tsp. sugar
4–5 oz. seltzer

Mix in bottom of Collins glass, add ice, then fill with seltzer.

Raspberry Kir

1 oz. raspberry schnapps
3 oz. Champagne

Garnish with strawberry.

Strawberry Cooler

1 oz. strawberry liqueur
4 oz. white wine
2 oz. lemon-lime soda

Serve on the rocks in a wineglass. Garnish with a fresh strawberry.

Strawberry Royal

1 oz. strawberry liqueur
3 oz. Champagne

Serve chilled in wineglass. Garnish with a fresh strawberry.

Vesuvio

3 oz. dry white wine
1 tsp. apricot liqueur
1 tsp. amaretto

Stir ingredients well with ice. Strain into wineglass. Garnish with cucumber slice.

Wind Surf

2 oz. Chablis
¼ oz. triple sec
½ oz. bar syrup
2 oz. pineapple juice
3 oz. club soda

Pour wine, triple sec, bar syrup and pineapple juice over ice in a glass. Stir. Add the soda and stir gently.

Wine Collins

4 oz. red wine
juice of ½ lemon
4 oz. sparkling water

Squeeze lemon juice into Collins glass, fill half way with wine. Add ice cubes and fill with sparkling water. Garnish with lemon peel.

FROZEN DRINKS

It's December but the mercury is breaking all records. So what? Summer's just a state of mind, especially when you're holding a frosty cold drink. From the zesty punch of a frozen margarita to the dessert-like appeal of ice cream drinks, frozen beverages conjure up images of white-sand Tahitian beaches and the tropical urbanity of Miami's South Beach.

Cleverly concocted and tagged with exotic monikers, the family of frozen drinks provides a delightful way to sip a cold one, and often substitutes for dessert. In a cold version of the traditionally steaming Italian coffee, the Frozen Cappuccino mixes frothy textures and intense flavors. Or the Frozen Sharkbite offers the tart mingling of tropical rums and citrusy juices.

When you're in the mood for a sweet beverage, there's no shortage of variety. Frosty cold drinks are nostalgic reminders of days gone by. In the mood to celebrate? Try a Banana Popsicle or a Frozen Strawberry Daiquiri.

Perfect for entertaining or simply pampering yourself, ice cream drinks are a welcome companion to an outdoor summer gathering. Mixed in blenders and served with exciting garnishes, these frosty specialties have the punch of decadent sundaes with a spirited touch.

In recent years frozen drinks have become such successful party hits that clever hosts often plan a gathering around a frozen drink theme. Establishments dedicated to serving premixed frozen concoctions have caught on to this craze and are enjoying immense popularity throughout the United States.

Whether summer lasts three months or eleven, when you're holding a frosty cold beverage, summer is *every* day.

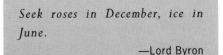

Seek roses in December, ice in June.

—Lord Byron

Amore

¾ oz. amaretto
½ oz. coffee brandy
1 oz. Half-and-Half
2 large scoops vanilla ice
    cream
4 oz. crushed ice.

Blend all ingredients until smooth. Pour into specialty glass. Garnish with a pineapple flag.

Apricot Smoothie

¾ oz. apricot liqueur
¼ oz. anisette
2 oz. orange juice
2 scoops vanilla ice cream

Blend all ingredients until smooth.

April Fool

1¼ oz. apple schnapps
2 oz. cranberry juice
1 scoop vanilla ice cream
1 scoop crushed ice

Blend all ingredients. Pour into a margarita glass. Garnish with fresh mint.

Banana B. Jones

1½ oz. crème de banana
1 oz. cream of coconut
2 scoops vanilla ice cream
½ banana
8 oz. crushed ice
whipped cream

Blend ingredients thoroughly. Pour into specialty glass. Top with whipped cream. Garnish with banana slice and maraschino cherry.

Banana Berry Blender

¾ oz. raspberry schnapps
½ oz. crème de banana
1 scoop vanilla ice cream
1 scoop crushed ice

Blend all ingredients together in a blender. Pour into a margarita glass.

Banana Popsicle

1¼ oz. crème de banana
1 oz. cream of coconut
2 scoops orange sherbet
8 oz. crushed ice

Blend ingredients for five seconds. Pour into specialty glass. Garnish with orange slice and banana slice.

Banana Sandwich

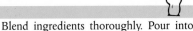

1¼ oz. crème de banana
3 Hydrox or Oreo cookies
2 scoops vanilla ice cream
½ banana
8 oz. crushed ice

Blend ingredients thoroughly. Pour into specialty glass. Garnish with a cookie or whipped cream.

Blue Bayou

¾ oz. Captain Morgan
    Original Spiced Rum
½ oz. blue curaçao
½ oz. heavy cream
1 large scoop vanilla ice
    cream
8 oz. crushed ice

Blend well in blender until smooth and creamy. Serve in a specialty glass. Garnish with a fruit flag.

Blueberry Freeze

1 oz. vodka
¼ oz. wild-berry
    schnapps
1 oz. cream of coconut
2 oz. blueberries
1½ oz. pineapple, crushed
1 scoop vanilla ice cream
8 oz. crushed ice
1 tbsp. whipped cream

Blend ingredients thoroughly. Pour into specialty glass. Top with whipped cream. Garnish with a teaspoon of blueberries.

Brandied Peaches 'n' Cream

¾ oz. peach schnapps
½ oz. peach brandy
1½ oz. cream of coconut
1 scoop vanilla ice cream
8 oz. crushed ice

Mix well in blender until smooth. Serve in specialty glass. Garnish with cinnamon stick or fresh peach wedge.

Brandy Alexander

¾ oz. dark crème de
    cacao
½ oz. brandy
4½ oz. Half-and-Half,
    frozen

Shake and serve in frosted cocktail glass. Garnish with nutmeg.

Captain's Berry Daiquiri

1¼ oz. Captain Morgan Original Spiced Rum
½ cup strawberries or raspberries
1 tsp. lime juice
½ tsp. sugar
½ cup crushed ice

Combine all ingredients in blender. Blend for 10 to 15 seconds. Pour into specialty glass. Garnish with berries.

Captain's Choice

1¼ oz. Captain Morgan Original Spiced Rum
1½ oz. orange juice
½ oz. cream of coconut
3 scoops vanilla ice cream

Blend all ingredients in a blender until smooth.

Captain's Smoothie

1¼ oz. Captain Morgan Original Spiced Rum
1½ oz. chocolate syrup
½ oz. lime juice
1 scoop vanilla ice cream
8 oz. crushed ice

Combine ingredients in a blender. Blend well. Serve in large specialty glass or wine goblet. Garnish with chocolate sprinkles.

Cherry Vanilla

¾ oz. white crème de cacao
½ oz. cherry liqueur
1½ oz. maraschino juice
1 oz. Half-and-Half
6 maraschino cherries
2 scoops vanilla ice cream
4 oz. crushed ice

Blend ingredients thoroughly. Pour into specialty glass. Garnish with a maraschino cherry.

Chocolate Banana

¾ oz. crème de banana
½ oz. dark rum
1 oz. chocolate syrup
2 scoops vanilla ice cream
½ medium banana
8 oz. crushed ice
whipped cream

Blend ingredients thoroughly. Pour into specialty glass. Top with whipped cream. Garnish with banana slices and a maraschino cherry.

Chocolate Tornado

1 oz. amaretto
¼ oz. dark rum
1 oz. Half-and-Half
¾ oz. chocolate syrup
6 drops vanilla extract
2 scoops vanilla ice cream
8 oz. crushed ice
whipped cream

Blend ingredients thoroughly. Pour into specialty glass. Top with whipped cream. Garnish with chocolate sprinkles.

Chuckie's Chuckle

1¼ oz. Captain Morgan
   Original Spiced Rum
½ oz. maple syrup
3 scoops vanilla ice cream

Blend until smooth.

Coco-Mocha Alexander

¾ oz. Captain Morgan
   Original Spiced Rum
½ oz. coffee brandy
1 oz. black coffee, cold
1 oz. cream of coconut
1 oz. heavy cream
8 oz. crushed ice

Mix well in blender until smooth. Serve in specialty glass.

Cool Kiss

1¼ oz. amaretto
2 oz. frozen sweet straw-
   berries, thawed
2 scoops vanilla ice cream

Blend all ingredients until smooth.

Cranberry Apple

1¼ oz. cranberry apple
   schnapps
5 oz. apple juice
1 scoop vanilla ice cream
1 scoop crushed ice

Blend all ingredients. Pour into brandy snifter.

Creamsicle Margarita

1¼ oz. gold tequila
3 oz. orange juice
1 oz. sweet & sour mix or
   margarita mix
1 scoop of vanilla ice cream
6 oz. crushed ice

Blend all ingredients until slushy. Serve in margarita glass.

Eclipse

1¼ oz. amaretto
1 oz. orange juice
½ oz. chocolate syrup
2 scoops vanilla ice cream

Blend all ingredients until smooth.

Fro Joe

¾ oz. Captain Morgan
  Original Spiced Rum
½ oz. coffee brandy
1 oz. cold coffee
1 oz. cream of coconut
1 oz. heavy cream
8 oz. crushed ice.

Mix well in blender until smooth. Serve in specialty glass.

Frozen Cappuccino

1¼ oz. Irish whiskey
3 oz. dark coffee
6 scoops vanilla ice cream
2 dashes cinnamon
whipped cream
biscotti cookie

Blend Irish whiskey, coffee, and ice cream in blender until smooth. Top with whipped cream. Garnish with sprinkle of cinnamon and a biscotti.

Frozen Irish Coffee

1¼ oz. Irish whiskey
1 oz. coffee brandy
3 oz. heavy cream
1 tsp. instant coffee
2 tbsp. bar sugar

Mix ingredients in blender until smooth and creamy. Serve in specialty glass. Garnish with whipped cream and chocolate coffee bean.

Fruit Bang

1 oz. banana-strawberry
  schnapps
¼ oz. Captain Morgan
  Original Spiced Rum
2 oz. pineapple juice
3 oz. fresh berries
1 scoop vanilla ice cream
1 scoop crushed ice

Blend ingredients. Pour into a margarita glass. Garnish with fresh strawberry.

Grasshopper Freeze

¾ oz. green crème de
   menthe
½ oz. white crème de
   cacao
1 oz. Half-and-Half
2 scoops vanilla ice cream
2 Hydrox or Oreo cookies
8 oz. crushed ice

Blend ingredients thoroughly. Pour into specialty glass. Garnish with a fresh mint sprig.

Grizzly Bear

¾ oz. dark rum
½ oz. amaretto
½ oz. chocolate syrup
1 dash vanilla extract
2 scoops vanilla ice cream
8 oz. crushed ice

Blend ingredients thoroughly. Pour into specialty glass. Garnish with chocolate sprinkles and a maraschino cherry.

Honey–Root Beer Float

1¼ oz. root-beer
   schnapps
3 oz. root beer
1 tbsp. honey
1 scoop vanilla ice cream

Blend all ingredients in blender with a scoop of crushed ice. Pour into brandy snifter.

Jamaican Queen

1 oz. Captain Morgan
   Original Spiced Rum
¼ oz. banana liqueur
3 oz. frozen sweetened
   strawberries, thawed
3 scoops vanilla ice cream

Blend all ingredients in a blender until smooth.

Kaleidoswirl

¾ oz. sloe gin
½ oz. peach schnapps
1 oz. sweet & sour mix
1 scoop orange sherbet
8 oz. crushed ice
2 oz. blueberries
2 oz. grape juice
1 oz. cream of coconut
1 oz. sweet & sour mix
8 oz. crushed ice

Blend first five ingredients thoroughly. This is the first part of the swirl. Separately blend balance of ingredients thoroughly. This is the second part of the swirl. Take both sets of ingredients and pour into large specialty glass at the same time. Swiry gently with a spoon or straw to create a different color.

Lavender Sunset

¾ oz. peach schnapps
½ oz. white crème de
  cacao
1 oz. cream of coconut
¾ oz. grape juice
2 scoops lime sherbet
8 oz. crushed ice

Blend ingredients in blender. Pour into a brandy snifter. Garnish with a lime wedge.

Martell Freeze

1¼ oz. Martell VS
½ cup vanilla ice cream
½ cup crushed ice

Combine and blend thoroughly in blender. Serve in a goblet with two soda straws.

Myers's Frozen Sharkbite

1¼ oz. Myers's Original
  Dark Rum
4 oz. orange juice
1 oz. lemon or lime juice
1 oz. simple syrup
1 dash grenadine
12 oz. crushed ice

Blend all until slushy.

Miami Ice

½ oz. melon liqueur
½ oz. strawberry liqueur
¼ oz. crème de banana
2 oz. pineapple juice
1 oz. grenadine
1 oz. cream of coconut
1 scoop orange sherbet
8 oz. crushed ice

Blend ingredients thoroughly. Pour into specialty glass. Garnish with a strawberry and an orange wheel.

Mint Chocolate Chiller

1 oz. green crème de
  menthe
¼ oz. white crème de
  cacao
1 oz. Half-and-Half
2 scoops vanilla ice cream
3 Hydrox or Oreo cookies
8 oz. crushed ice
whipped cream

Blend ingredients thoroughly. Pour into specialty glass. Top with whipped cream. Garnish with chocolate shavings or chocolate chips.

Moonchaser

¾ oz. Myers's Original
    Dark Rum
½ oz. amaretto
3 oz. orange juice
2 oz. cream of coconut
2 oz. orange sherbet
8 oz. crushed ice

Blend ingredients thoroughly. Pour into specialty glass. Garnish with an orange flag.

Mystical Swirl

1¼ oz. peach schnapps
½ oz. grenadine
3 oz. grape juice
1 scoop orange sherbet
8 oz. crushed ice
¾ oz. triple sec
2 oz. pineapple juice
1 oz. sweet & sour mix
2 scoops orange sherbet
8 oz. crushed ice

Blend first five ingredients thoroughly. This is the first part of the swirl. Separately blend balance of ingredients thoroughly. This is the second part of the swirl. Take both sets of ingredients and pour into large specialty glass at the same time. Swirl gently with a spoon or straw to create a different color.

Peaches 'n' Honey

1¼ oz. peach schnapps
¼ cup fresh peaches or
    canned peaches
1 scoop vanilla ice cream
1 tbsp. honey

Blend all ingredients in blender with a scoop of crushed ice. Pour into wineglass. Garnish with fresh mint.

Peanut Butter Shake

1¼ oz. Captain Morgan
    Original Spiced Rum
3 scoops vanilla ice cream
1 tsp. peanut butter

Blend in a blender until smooth.

Rainbow Crush

½ oz. vodka
½ oz. raspberry liqueur
¼ oz. melon liqueur
3 oz. orange juice
1 oz. cream of coconut
2 scoops orange sherbet
4 oz. crushed ice

Blend ingredients thoroughly. Pour into specialty glass. Garnish with orange flag.

Riviera Raspberry

¾ oz. raspberry liqueur
½ oz. coffee brandy
1 oz. cream of coconut
½ oz. chocolate syrup
2 Hydrox or Oreo cookies
2 scoops vanilla ice cream
8 oz. crushed ice

Blend ingredients thoroughly. Pour into specialty glass. Garnish with whipped cream and a raspberry.

Root-Beer Float

1¼ oz. root-beer
   schnapps
3 oz. soda

Fill footed highball glass with schnapps and club soda. Add scoop of ice cream. Stir.

Seagram's Dreamsicle

1 oz. Seagram's 7 Crown
2 oz. orange juice
2 scoops vanilla ice cream

Blend all ingredients in blender until smooth.

Spiced Java Smoothee

1 oz. Captain Morgan
   Original Spiced Rum
⅛ oz. dark crème de
   cacao
⅛ oz. crème de café
3 scoops vanilla ice cream

Blend in blender until smooth.

Strawberry Whip

1¼ oz. banana-strawberry
   schnapps
3 oz. fresh strawberries
1 scoop vanilla ice cream
½ banana
1 scoop ice

Blend ingredients together in blender. Pour into brandy snifter. Garnish with fresh strawberry.

Tequila-Nana Blizzard

¾ oz. tequila
½ oz. crème de banana
1 oz. light cream
¼ banana
1 scoop vanilla ice cream

Blend in blender for 10 to 15 seconds. Pour into large goblet glass. Sprinkle top with nutmeg.

Trinidad

1 oz. Captain Morgan
    Original Spiced Rum
¼ oz. blue curaçao
2 oz. melted vanilla ice
    cream

Blend all ingredients in a blender with a scoop of crushed ice.

Tropical Peach

1¼ oz. peach schnapps
2 oz. cream of coconut
2 oz. orange juice
1 oz. sweet & sour mix
1 scoop orange sherbet
8 oz. crushed ice

Blend ingredients thoroughly. Pour into specialty glass. Garnish with orange flag.

Tutti Frutti Crush

½ oz. melon liqueur
½ oz. crème de banana
1 oz. pineapple juice
½ oz. grenadine
¼ oz. strawberry liqueur
2 scoops orange sherbet
8 oz. crushed ice

Blend ingredients thoroughly. Pour into specialty glass. Garnish with strawberry and orange slice.

SANGRIA, EGGNOG,
& *Other Hot & Cold Punches*

For the entertainer, there is no greater reward than the enthusiastic appreciation of a beautiful, delicious punch. An all-purpose center-piece, the punch bowl is appropriate for functions such as a birthday or a wedding reception. Punches created from light wines can be a tempting delight, entrancing guests with delicate flavors. Make it with brandy or rum and lively compliments will flow your way.

Uncannily versatile, cold punches are appropriate at all times of the year, for just about every occasion imaginable. A Champagne punch, for example, is an excellent way to make a celebration more special. Hot punches, although generally reserved for the winter sea-son, can liven any evening gathering, and are often a great way to round out a late-afternoon sporting event.

The recipes contained in this section can be easily mixed and gen-erally do not take more than an hour to create. Garnished simply with fruit slices and floating blocks of ice, these drinks are irresistible to drinkers of all preferences.

The punch recipes in this section will serve 15 to 20 cups each. Several tasty nonalcohol bowls can be made as well.

Follow your bliss.
　　　　　　　—Joseph Campbell

COLD PUNCHES

Applejack Bowl

12 eggs
½ cup bar sugar
1 qt. applejack
3 qt. milk
1½ cups heavy sweet
  cream
1 tbsp. vanilla extract

Pour eggs and sugar into blender, and blend at low speed 2 minutes. Pour into punch bowl. Gradually add applejack and beat until well blended. Stir in milk, cream, and vanilla. Let mixture ripen in refrigerator for 1 hour. Stir well before serving. Serve in punch cups. Sprinkle with cinnamon.

Archer's Punch

1 quart bourbon
9 oz. light rum
4 oz. dark rum
6 oz. apricot-flavored
  brandy
1 qt. strong black tea
24 oz. orange juice
12 oz. lemon juice
¼ cup bar sugar

Pour all ingredients over a large block of ice in punch bowl. Stir well to dissolve sugar. Let mixture ripen 1 hour in refrigerator before serving.

Banana Bowl

8 medium bananas
1 cup lime juice
1 cup bar sugar
1 fifth light rum
8 oz. dark rum
28 oz. pineapple juice
12 oz. mango nectar
2 limes

Chill all ingredients except bananas. Cut six bananas into thin slices and place in blender with lime juice and sugar. Blend until smooth. Pour over block of ice in punch bowl. Add both kinds of rum, pineapple juice and mango nectar. Stir well. Let mixture ripen in refrigerator 1 hour before serving. Cut remaining bananas into thin slices. Float banana and lime slices on punch.

Black Cherry Punch

1 fifth light rum
8 oz. Cherry Heering
8 oz. crème de chassis
4 oz. rum
4 oz. dark rum
8 oz. fresh lemon juice
4 oz. fresh orange juice
4 oz. fresh lime juice
2 limes, thinly sliced
34 oz. pitted black
   cherries in heavy syrup
1 qt. club soda

Put all ingredients except soda into punch bowl. Add block of ice. Stir Well. Refrigerate 1 hour. Add soda. Stir.

Blue Moon Punch

1 fifth blue curaçao
8 oz. lemon juice
4 fifths dry Champagne
peel of 2 lemons

Chill all ingredients. Cut lemon peel into 2" x 2" strips. Pour curaçao and lemon juice into punch bowl. Stir. Add Champagne and stir. Float lemon peel.

Bombay Punch

½ cup bar sugar
juice of 12 lemons
juice of 6 limes
4 bottles chilled
   Champagne
1 liter brandy
1 liter dry sherry
4 oz. triple sec
4 oz. maraschino liqueur
2 oz. kirschwasser
2 liters sparkling water

Stir the fruit juices and sugar in a large punch bowl until sugar is dissolved. Add remaining ingredients and one large block of ice. Garnish with seasonal fruit.

Brandy Eggnog Punch

12 eggs
½ cup bar sugar
1 fifth Cognac
4 oz. dark rum
3 qt. milk
8 oz. heavy cream

Separate egg yolks from whites. Combine yolks and sugar in punch bowl. Beat well with a wire whisk. Add Cognac, rum, milk, and cream. Beat well. Add more sugar if desired. Place bowl in refrigerator for 2 hours. Before serving, beat egg whites until stiff. Fold whites into punch until thoroughly blended. Sprinkle with nutmeg.

Champagne Punch 🍵

8 oz. Cognac
8 oz. cherry liqueur
8 oz. triple sec
4 oz. fresh lemon juice
4 oz. simple syrup
2 bottles Champagne

Pour all chilled ingredients except Champagne into a large punch bowl with a block of ice. Stir. Add Champagne.

Champagne Sherbet Punch 🍵

2 qt. lemon sherbet
5 fifths iced brut
    Champagne
1½ tsp. Angostura bitters

Place lemon sherbet in prechilled punch bowl. Pour Champagne over sherbet. Add bitters. Stir. Refrigerate for 15–20 minutes.

Champagne Sorbet Punch 🍵

2 bottles Champagne
1 bottle white dessert
    wine
1 qt. pineapple sorbet

Combine Champagne and wine in a punch bowl with a block of ice. Stir. Scoop in sorbet.

Bordeaux Punch 🍵

3 bottles Bordeaux
16 oz. brandy
8 oz. Cointreau
24 oz. fresh lemon juice
½ cup bar sugar

Stir all ingredients in large punch bowl. Add block of ice. Stir. Top with sliced fruit.

Eggnog 🍵

1 cup bar sugar
1 dozen eggs
1½ qt. milk
1 pt. whipped heavy
    cream
1 bottle brandy

Separate eggs and beat the yolks with sugar in a large punch bowl. Stir in milk and whipped cream. Add brandy and refrigerate for an hour. Before serving, whip egg whites and fold into eggnog. Garnish with fresh nutmeg.

Fancy Sparkling Punch

1 qt. sparkling water
1 cup cubed sugar
1 bottle Burgundy wine
4 oz. brandy
2 bottle Champagne

Dissolve sugar in a cup of sparkling water and pour into a punch bowl. Add Burgundy and brandy, stirring well. Place a block of ice in the punch bowl adding Champagne and the rest of sparkling water. Garnish top of ice block with berries or other fruit in season.

Irish Apple Bowl

20 oz. applejack
20 oz. Irish whiskey
10 oz. lime juice
4 limes, sliced thin
2 large red apples
80 oz. ginger ale

All ingredients should be prechilled. Pour applejack, whiskey, and lime juice over ice block in punch bowl. Add lime slices and apples diced into ½" pieces. Stir. Refrigerate 1 hour. Pour cold ginger ale into bowl. Stir.

Louisiana Planter's Punch

16 oz. gold rum
8 oz. Bourbon
8 oz. Cognac
¼ cup Pernod
2 tbsp. bitters
8 oz. fresh lemon juice
8 oz. sparkling water
4 oz. simple syrup

Combine all ingredients in an ice–filled punch bowl. Garnish with lemon slices.

Mountain Red Punch

3 qt. chilled red wine
½ cup amaretto
½ cup brandy
½ cup cherry-flavored
  brandy
1 pt. ginger ale
2 oz. toasted almonds

Pour wine, amaretto, and brandies over block of ice in punch bowl. Refrigerate 1 hour. Stir. Add ginger ale. Stir. Float almonds on top.

Out-of-This-World Punch

1 fifth light rum
4 oz. dark rum
12 oz. peppermint
  schnapps
1 qt. mango nectar
12 oz. heavy cream
1 qt. orange juice
8 large sprigs mint
1 fresh mango, sliced
6 thin slices orange

Prechill all ingredients. Place block of ice in punch bowl. Add both rums, schnapps, mango nectar, cream, and orange juice. Stir. Float mint sprigs, fresh mango slices, and orange slices.

Polynesian Punch Bowl

1 fifth light rum
8 oz. sloe gin
5 oz. peppermint
  schnapps
40 oz. pineapple juice
6 oz. cream of coconut
3 cups orange juice
1 cup lemon juice
12 thin slices pineapple
12 thin slices orange
1 pt. club soda

Pour all ingredients except fruit and soda into punch bowl. Stir well until all ingredients, particularly cream of coconut, are well blended. Add a large block of ice, pineapple and orange slices. Refrigerate 1 hour. Add soda and stir before serving.

Rum Cup with White Wine

20 oz. light rum
10 oz. dry white wine
2 oz. Falernum
2 oz. triple sec
1 cup orange juice
½ cup lime juice
2 oz. almond syrup
6 slices lime
6 sprigs mint

Pour all ingredients except lime slices and mint into large pitcher. Chill 2 hours. Top pitcher to rim with ice cubes. Stir. Garnish individual drinks with the lime and mint.

1964 World's Fair Sangria � or ♖

1 bottle red Spanish wine
2 tbsp. bar sugar
1 lemon, cut into slices
½ orange, cut into slices
1 oz. Spanish Brandy
1 oz. Cointreau
2 cups ice cubes
1 cup cold club soda

Pour the wine into a large pitcher at least an hour before serving. Add sugar and mix well. Stir in lemon and orange slices, brandy, and Cointreau. Chill until ready to serve. Just before serving, add the ice cubes and club soda, stirring just enough to chill very well. Pour sangria only— leave fruit and ice in the pitcher. Serves 4.

White Sangria ♖ or ♖

1 bottle dry white wine
2 slices lemon
2 slices lime
1 oz. cognac
2 tbsp. bar sugar
1 cinnamon stick
8 large strawberries, halved
1 whole orange
6 oz. club soda

Pour wine into glass pitcher. Add lemon, lime, cognac, sugar, cinnamon, and strawberries. Stir to dissolve sugar. Cut entire peel of orange in a single strip, leaving bottom attached to fruit. Carefully place orange in pitcher, fastening top end of peel over rim. Refrigerate 1 hour. Add soda and tray of ice cubes. Stir.

HOT PUNCHES

Brandy Punch ♖

8 cups brandy
1 cup amaretto
peel of four lemons
nutmeg
cinnamon

Simmer ingredients over low heat. Serve warm in brandy snifters.

Christmas Cheer ♖

1 gallon apple cider
8 cinnamon sticks
1½ cups rum
1 cup applejack
¾ cup apple schnapps

Bring cider and cinnamon to a boil. Reduce heat and add liquor, stirring until heated. Serve in pousse-cafe glasses. Garnish with cinnamon sticks.

Grog

2 bottles dry red wine
1 bottle brandy
25 whole cloves
20 crushed cardamom
  seeds
4 cinnamon sticks
2 cups currants
2 cups blanched almonds
2 oz. dried orange peel
1 pink aquavit
16 oz. sugar cubes

Put all ingredients except sugar and aquavit in a large pan and bring to a boil. Simmer for 15 minutes, stirring occasionally. Place a strain over pan and spread sugar cubes over it. Pour the aquavit over sugar. Ignite in pan and let sugar melt into mixture. Stir. Serve in heated mugs.

Hot Buttered Rum Punch

1 cup brown sugar
1 cup boiling water
3 qt. sweet cider
1 qt. dark rum
⅛ cup butter

Dissolve sugar in water, add cider and heat to boiling. Add rum and butter. Serve in punch bowl, topped with cinnamon.

Hot Milk Punch

1 liter whiskey
1 qt. milk
½ cup bar sugar
cinnamon sticks

Heat all ingredients except cinnamon over low heat in a sauce pan. Stir until mixture is very hot. Pour into warmed mugs. Garnish with cinnamon stick and sprinkle with nutmeg.

NO ALCOHOL PUNCHES

Cupid's Arrow

1 qt. cold milk
2 cups frozen strawberries, thawed and crushed
1 cup orange juice
⅓ cup lemon juice

Blend at medium speed for 1 minute. Pour into pitcher, cover, and refrigerate for 1 hour.

Eskimo Kiss

1 qt. orange juice
1 qt. lemon-lime soda
1 qt. ginger ale
3 cups apricot nectar
3 cups pineapple juice

Combine all the juices in a punch bowl. Stir. Add ice cubes and mix in ginger ale. Garnish with lemon slices.

Lime Love

2 qt. pineapple juice
1 cup simple syrup
1 qt. lemon-lime soda
1 qt. lime sherbet

Add pineapple juice and simple syrup to an ice block–filled punch bowl. Stir. Add soda and sherbet. Stir to blend well. Garnish with lime slices and maraschino cherries.

Reindeer Punch

6 oz. frozen lemonade
　　concentrate, undiluted
6 oz. frozen orange juice
　　concentrate, undiluted
6 cups water
½ cup grenadine
1 qt. ginger ale, chilled

Combine first four ingredients in a punch bowl. Add ice cubes and mix in ginger ale. Garnish with lemon slices.

LIQUORED COFFEES, TEAS,

& *Other "Hot Toddies"*

When hot drinks were reserved for cold weather, people would pray for a roaring storm and a crackling fire. Although those were lovely Currier and Ives moments, any breezy eve is reason enough to enjoy brimming mugs of cappuccino and grogs—and not just by the fireplace. A warm liqueur or brandy in the evening is a popular celebration of another full day and anticipation of a good night's sleep.

The relaxing qualities of hot drinks have long been understood. At the turn-of-the-century, the "hot toddy"—a designation for any warm drink enhanced by a distilled spirit—was used medicinally for nervous disorders and insomnia. Today, hot coffee drinks are popular alternatives to after-dinner liqueurs.

A good portion of hot beverages begins with coffee. It's no wonder, since western civilization taps a direct artery to the heart of the coffee empire. In recent years the success of bohemian-style coffeehouses and cafés has seen a resurgence in the simple enjoyment of coffee. Add your favorite spirit, and the cup seems a little lighter on the tongue.

Hot drinks should be just warm enough so that the flavors melt and spread across the taste buds, warming the throat—but not so hot that they burn the lips. Here is a tip for achieving the right temperature: Heat the mixture in a saucepan just short of boiling, turn off the flame, and let it cool a bit before pouring. Drinks can also be heated in the microwave oven, but beware of scalding your guests since microwaves heat from the inside out and can be deceptively hot.

Take your first sip. Enjoy the aroma that the marriage of warmth and liquors provides. Take another sip and savor the experience. After all, you've got all the time in the world.

Almond Chocolata

1¼ oz. amaretto
5 oz. hot chocolate
whipped cream

Combine in a mug or cup. Top with whipped cream.

Almond Coffee

1¼ oz. amaretto
5 oz. hot coffee
whipped cream

Add amaretto and coffee into a heated mug. Top with whipped cream. Garnish with a maraschino cherry.

Anisette Coffee

½ oz. gin
¾ oz. anisette
5 oz. hot coffee

Add ingredients to heated mug. Garnish with lemon twist and add cream or sugar if desired.

Bananas Barbados

¾ oz. dark rum or
    Captain Morgan
    Original Spiced Rum
½ oz. crème de banana
5 oz. hot chocolate
1 tbsp. whipped cream

Combine rum, liqueur, and hot chocolate in a heated mug. Top with whipped cream. Sprinkle with cinnamon.

Black Honey

¾ oz. coffee brandy
½ oz. Drambuie
5 oz. hot coffee
1 tbsp. whipped cream

Combine in a heated mug or tempered glass. Top with whipped cream. Garnish with orange slice.

Café Amaretto

1¼ oz. amaretto
5 oz. hot coffee, strong

Combine in a mug or cup.

Café Amour

¾ oz. Cognac
½ oz. amaretto
5 oz. hot coffee
1 dollop unsweetened
    whipped cream

Pour liquids into a heated mug. Top with whipped cream. Sprinkle with nutmeg.

Café aux Cognac

1¼ oz. Cognac
5 oz. hot coffee
superfine sugar
lemon

Rim heavy goblet with lemon, dip in sugar. Fill glass with cognac and coffee. Add cream, if desired.

Café Barbados

¾ oz. dark rum
½ oz. Tia Maria
6 oz. hot coffee

Rim glass with sugar and cinnamon. Serve in pousse-café glass.

Cafe-Cello

1¼ oz. Capucello
6 oz. hot coffee

Pour coffee into mug and add the Capucello.

Café Michelle

½ oz. amaretto
½ oz. coffee brandy
¼ oz. Irish cream
5 oz. hot coffee
1 tbsp. whipped cream

Combine liqueurs and coffee in a heated mug or sugar-rimmed tempered glass. Top with whipped cream. Garnish with maraschino cherry.

Café Royale

1¼ oz. Cognac
6 oz. hot black coffee
1 lump sugar
cream (optional)

Combine in a heated mug or tempered glass. Stir to dissolve sugar.

Canadian Coffee

1¼ oz. Canadian whisky
6 oz. hot coffee
1 tbsp. maple syrup
1 dollop whipped cream

Pour coffee and whisky into a heated mug. Stir in maple syrup until dissolved. Top with whipped cream.

Canadian Tea

1¼ oz. Canadian whisky
5 oz. hot tea
1 tbsp. maple syrup
1 cinnamon stick
1 orange slice

Combine whisky and tea in a heated mug, stir in maple syrup. Add orange slice and cinnamon stick.

Captain Morgan Cinnamon Toast   ♈ or ♈

1¼ oz. Captain Morgan
    Original Spiced Rum
1 pack instant hot spiced
    cider
5 oz. hot water

Rim glass with sugar and cinnamon. Stemmed glass is recommended.

Captain's Coconut Brownie   🍺

1 package hot chocolate
    mix
6 oz. hot water
½ oz. cream of coconut
1¼ oz. Captain Morgan
    Original Spiced Rum
whipped cream

Empty hot chocolate into mug. Stir in hot water. Add cream of coconut and stir until well mixed. Stir in the rum. Top with whipped cream. Garnish with finely chopped walnuts.

Chocolate Banana   🍺

½ oz. dark rum
½ oz. crème de banana
¼ oz. dark crème de
    cacao
5 oz. hot chocolate
1 tbsp. whipped cream

Combine rum, liqueurs and hot chocolate in a heated mug. Top with whipped cream. Sprinkle with nutmeg.

Chocolate Coffee   🍺

¾ oz. Cognac
½ oz. dark crème de
    cacao
½ oz. chocolate syrup
4 oz. hot coffee
1 oz. milk
whipped cream

Heat ingredients and serve in a heated mug. Top with whipped cream. Sprinkle with cocoa.

Chocolate Kiss   🍺

¾ oz. Cognac
½ oz. raspberry schnapps
6 oz. hot chocolate
1 tbsp. whipped cream

Combine liquids in a heated mug. Top with whipped cream. Sprinkle with powdered cocoa.

Chocolate Mint

¾ oz. gin
¼ oz. peppermint schnapps
¼ oz. green crème de menthe
6 oz. hot chocolate
whipped cream

Combine liquids in a heated mug. Top with whipped cream. Sprinkle with powdered cocoa.

Chocolate Sin

1¼ oz. peppermint schnapps
5 oz. hot chocolate
1 tbsp. whipped cream

Combine schnapps and chocolate in a heated mug or sugar-rimmed tempered glass. Top with whipped cream.

Cinnaccino

¾ oz. Captain Morgan Original Spiced Rum
½ oz. cinnamon schnapps
3½ oz. espresso coffee
2½ oz. steamed whipped milk

Add rum and schnapps to espresso in heated mug. Top with steamed milk. Sprinkle with cinnamon.

Cobana Coffee

1¼ oz. banana-strawberry schnapps
6 oz. sweetened coffee

Mix ingredients into mug. Garnish with sweetened whipped cream.

Coco Java

1¼ oz. coffee brandy
1 oz. cream of coconut
5 oz. hot chocolate
1 tbsp. whipped cream

Combine brandy and hot chocolate in a heated mug or tempered glass. Add cream of coconut. Top with whipped cream. Garnish with chocolate jimmies, sprinkled cocoa, or a maraschino cherry.

Coffee Float

¾ oz. whiskey
½ oz. crème de noya
5 oz. hot coffee
2 oz. scoop vanilla ice cream

Mix whiskey, liqueur, and hot coffee in a large mug. Add vanilla ice cream and nutmeg.

Cognac and Cream

¾ oz. Cognac
½ oz. light crème de cacao
5 oz. steamed milk or hot milk

Serve in a stemmed glass. Garnish with nutmeg.

Cranapple Toddy

6 oz. hot cranberry juice
sugar cube
1¼ oz. cranberry-apple schnapps
1 splash lemon juice

Pour hot cranberry juice into mug. Add sugar cube then remaining ingredients. Garnish with lemon twist.

Cupid's Cocoa

1¼ oz. amaretto
2 tsp. instant cocoa
5 oz. hot strong coffee

In a mug, mix amaretto with cocoa and fill with coffee.

Godiva Cafe

6 oz. hot coffee
1¼ oz. Godiva Liqueur
whipped cream

Pour coffee into mug. Add liqueur. Stir. Top with whipped cream.

Godiva Chocolate-Covered Berry

1 packet hot cocoa mix
1 oz. Godiva Liqueur
¼ oz. Chambord

Empty cocoa packet into mug, add hot water, liqueur, and Chambord and stir until dissolved. Garnish with a dollop of whipped cream. Note: This drink may be served frozen, substituting 1 cup of ice for half the hot water, and blending until smooth.

Grog

1¼ oz. dark rum
1 sugar cube
juice of ½ lemon
1 cinnamon stick
4 oz. boiling water

Combine rum, sugar, lemon juice and cinnamon in a mug. Fill with boiling water. Stir. Garnish with lemon twist.

Hot Apple Pie

6 oz. hot apple juice
1¼ oz. amaretto
whipped cream

Combine hot apple juice and amaretto in mug. Top with whipped cream. Sprinkle of cinnamon and a cinnamon stick, if desired.

Hot Apple Pie II

1 oz. Captain Morgan
   Original Spiced Rum
¼ oz. cinnamon schnapps
5 oz. hot apple juice

Combine ingredients in a mug. Garnish with cinnamon stick and apple wedge.

Hot Brown Cow

1¼ oz. dark rum or
   Captain Morgan
   Original Spiced Rum
3 oz. hot milk
3 oz. hot coffee

Pour rum, milk and coffee into heated mug. Top with nutmeg.

Hot Buttered Rum

1¼ oz. dark rum
1 dash bitters
1 sugar cube
1 tsp. butter
2 cloves
4 oz. boiling water

Add all ingredients except water to a mug. Fill with boiling water. Stir.

Hot Buttered Rum II

1¼ oz. dark rum or
   Captain Morgan
   Original Spiced Rum
1 tsp. lemon juice
4 oz. water
1 tbsp. sugar
1 tsp. sweet butter

Heat rum, juice, water, and sugar. Pour into a heated mug. Add butter. Garnish with a lemon slice and sprinkling of nutmeg.

Hot Caribbean

1¼ oz. Captain Morgan
   Original Spiced Rum
3 oz. pineapple juice
3 oz. orange juice
½ oz. coconut cream

Heat all ingredients. Garnish with cinnamon stick and orange slice.

Hot Irish & Port

½ oz. Irish whiskey
¾ oz. port
3 oz. hot water

Combine in a heated mug. Garnish with cinnamon stick and orange slice.

Hot Scotch

¾ oz. Scotch
½ oz. Drambuie
1 oz. lemon juice
5 oz. hot water
1 tsp. sugar

Combine in a tempered old-fashioned glass.

Hot Toddy

1¼ oz. dark rum
3 oz. boiling water
1 oz. sugar cube

Combine in an old-fashioned glass and stir to dissolve sugar. Garnish with lemon slice and sprinkle with cinnamon.

Hot Toddy 7

1¼ oz. Seagram's Crown whiskey
5 oz. boiling water
1 tbsp. sugar
3 whole cloves
cinnamon stick

Combine in heated mug. Garnish with a lemon slice and sprinkle with nutmeg.

Irish Coffee

1¼ oz. Irish whiskey
6 oz. hot coffee
whipped cream

Pour whiskey into a stemmed glass rimmed with sugar. Add coffee. Top with mound of whipped cream.

Irish Coffee II

1¼ tsp. brown sugar
6 oz. hot coffee
1¼ oz. Irish whiskey
1 dash cinnamon

In a mug or heat proof glass, dissolve the sugar in the coffee. Stir in the whiskey. Add a dash of cinnamon and float lime slice on the drink.

Irish Coffee III

1¼ oz. Irish whiskey
6 oz. hot coffee
1 tsp. sugar
sweetened whipped cream
1 dash green crème de
menthe

Pour whiskey, coffee and sugar into Irish coffee glass. Top with whipped cream and a dash of crème de menthe.

Irish Tea

1¼ oz. Irish whiskey
6 oz. hot Irish breakfast
tea
1 tbsp. sugar
1 clove
cinnamon stick

Place ingredients in a heated mug. Garnish with lemon slice or mint sprig.

Island Cocoa

1 pkg. hot chocolate mix
6 oz. hot water
½ oz. cream of coconut
1¼ oz. Captain Morgan
Original Spiced Rum

Empty the package of hot chocolate mix into a mug and stir in the water. Add the cream of coconut and stir until completely mixed in. Stir in the rum.

Mexican Coffee

½ oz. tequila
¾ oz. coffee liqueur
6 oz. hot coffee

Pour tequila and coffee liqueur into coffee cup. Add coffee. Top with mound of whipped cream.

Mexican Coffee II

¾ oz. tequila
6 oz. hot coffee
½ oz. coffee brandy
1 dollop sweetened
whipped cream

Pour tequila, coffee, and liqueur into a heated mug. Top with whipped cream. Sprinkle with cinnamon.

Myers's Original Hot Buttered Rum

1¼ oz. Myers's Original
   Dark Rum
1 bar spoon Trader Vic's
   or comparable hot rum
   batter
6 oz. hot water

Serve in large mug. Top with pat of butter and cinnamon.

Night Flight

1¼ oz. banana-strawberry
   schnapps
6 oz. hot chocolate

Mix ingredients into a mug. Garnish with sweetened whipped cream.

Operetta

¾ oz. Cognac
½ oz. orange curaçao
5 oz. hot tea
1 tbsp. honey
1 lemon slice
cinnamon stick

Combine Cognac, curaçao, tea and honey in a heated mug, stir. Add lemon slice and cinnamon stick.

Orange Mocha

1 pkg. hot chocolate mix
6 oz. hot coffee
1 oz. Captain Morgan
   Original Spiced Rum
¼ oz. orange curaçao

Empty the package of chocolate mix into a mug and stir in the coffee. Add the rum and curaçao. Stir.

Peanut Butter Cup

1¼ oz. Captain Morgan
   Original Spiced Rum
1 bar spoon creamy style
   peanut butter
1 packet of instant cocoa
5 oz. hot water

Mix and dissolve cocoa and peanut butter. Add rum. Top with fresh whipped cream and crushed peanuts.

Pirate's Spiced Rum Tea

1¼ oz. Captain Morgan
   Original Spiced Rum
6 oz. hot tea
1 cinnamon stick
1 tbsp. honey

Combine rum, tea, and cinnamon in a heated mug. Stir in honey. Garnish with an orange slice.

Raspberry Warm-up

¾ oz. raspberry schnapps
½ oz. Cognac
6 oz. hot tea
1 tsp. sugar

Combine schnapps, Cognac, tea, and sugar in a heated mug. Garnish with an orange slice.

Snowberry

¾ oz. Captain Morgan
  Original Spiced Rum
½ oz. strawberry
  schnapps
5 oz. water
½ oz. simple syrup
½ oz. lemon juice
1 tsp. grenadine

Heat liquids and serve in a heated mug. Garnish with a cinnamon stick.

Spirited Coconut Coffee

1 oz. Irish whiskey
¼ oz. cream of coconut
6 oz. hot coffee
whipped cream

Combine in a heated mug or tempered coffee glass. Stir. Top with dollop of whipped cream.

Tea-Liscious

1¼ oz. amaretto
5 oz. hot black tea
whipped cream

Combine amaretto and tea in a heated mug. Top with whipped cream. Sprinkle with nutmeg.

DRINKS FOR EVERY OCCASION,

Holiday, and Season

This chapter is an essential party-planning source for stress-free, fool-proof entertaining. In this section we've listed many of the drinks introduced in the first part of the book to offer you suggestions for holiday and seasonal gatherings. Although you're certainly not limited to the following classifications, we're certain that they will encourage you to plan many innovative and exciting parties.

Whether you enjoy a large gathering of friends for cocktails, a smaller buffet, open house, or intimate dinners, you'll find many options here, ranging from dressed-up to down-home and relaxed. To make it simpler for you to choose the type of party you want to throw, this section has been divided into special occasions, holidays, and seasons. For holidays and special occasions, the recipes feature festive, adventurous concoctions that are meant to be enjoyed by partyers. The spring and summer party recipes make the most of the season, using plenty of fresh fruits and frosty ice creams. Fall and winter drinks are delicious and warming, and can be enjoyed alone or at a sparking holiday meal.

The following ideas will keep last-minute party jitters to a minimum, from the planning stages to the last departing guest's farewell.

Before deciding what type of party to throw, you should ask yourself, who am I going to invite? Will it be a few good friends, or colleagues from the office? Once you determine the "who," you'll be better able to select the "where" and the "when."

Themed gatherings are always great fun for party guests—and a clever theme enhances the likelihood that your party will be a rousing success. So to that end, be imaginative and don't be afraid to jump feet first into your planning. A New Year's Eve fete, for example, doesn't have to be all party hats and noisemakers. An elegant jazz party, replete with dimmed lights and Champagne cocktails, formal attire, and a live band is a thrilling way to ring in a new era.

To encourage guests to mingle and stimulate new conversations, create "islands" of food and drink through the party. If you've set up a bartending station, you may want to place a punch bowl at the other side of the room. By doing so, you prevent your guests from "hanging out in the kitchen," or just standing around the one food table.

If you're throwing an outdoor party in the evening or expect your afternoon gathering to linger into the evening, be sure to prepare for adequate lighting. Candles, torchieres, or simple outdoor lighting such as white Christmas lights make a lovely impression throughout the yard. Make sure, however, to have a grounded, outdoor extension cord to prevent wiring shorts. Candles are a beautiful accent to tables, but make sure to place them where they can't tip over.

Remember, any party or gathering you give should have your special touch. The guests aren't coming just to be served, they're coming to see and enjoy you. So make sure you've made adequate preparations so that you, too, can enjoy the party.

No matter what occasion you're celebrating, or season you're ringing in—or even if you're just saluting good friendships—guests will appreciate the thought that you've given to their enjoyment and will undoubtedly raise a glass to you. Cheers!

HOLIDAYS

Bastille Day (France)—July 14
Café de Paris Cocktail—68
Foreign Affair—40
French Rose—73
French 75—40
Mon Cherie—42
Montmartre—82
Normandy Cocktail—83
Parisian—84

Canada Day—July 19
Canadian and Bitters—160
Canadian Blackberry Fizz—160
Canadian Cocktail—160

Canadian Old-Fashioned—161
V.O. Canadian Cooler—170

Christmas—December 25
Angel's Tip—47

Cinco de Mayo—May 5
Acapulco Apple Margarita—128
Adios Mother—64
Baja Banana Boat Margarita—129
Cactus Margarita—131
Cha-Cha-Cha Cherry Margarita—131
Margarita 43—132
Margarita—133
Pineapple Cancun Margarita—135
South of the Border—169

Halloween—October 31
Black Cat—48
Black Widow—97
Witches Tail—61

Independence Day—July 4
All-American Fizz—65
Betsy Ross Cocktail—37
Liberty Cocktail—55
Union Jack—114

Labor Day—First Monday in September
Planter's Punch—110
7 Seas—168

Memorial Day—Last Monday in May
Beachcomber—97
Myers's Heatwave—107

Mardi Gras—February/March
Absolut Peppar Ragin' Cajun—142
Blue Bayou—191
Cajun Martini—145
Dixie Cocktail—71
Hurricane—104
Hurricane II—104
Lafayette—29
Muddy River—42
New Orleans Buck—108
New Orleans Cocktail—29
New Orleans Fizz—83
New Orleans Night—150

May Day—May 1
Black Russian—144
Russian Rose—153
White Russian—155

St. Patrick's Day—March 17
Everybody's Irish Cocktail—162
Godiva Irish Freeze—53
Irish Angel—162
Irish Cooler—163
Irish Delight—163

Irish Eyes—163
Irish Horseman—163
Irish Kiss—163
Irish Knight—163
Irish Magic—163
Irish Prince—163
Irish Summer Coffee—163

Thanksgiving—Fourth Thursday in November
Homestead Cocktail—78
Wrath of Grapes—115

Valentine's Day—February 14
Ambrosia—95
Amorous Duo—47
Cupid's Cocoa—216

SEASONS

Spring
Absolut Citron Blue Lemonade—142
Apricocious—35
Apricot Sweetie—37
April Fool—190
Banana Scream—159
Blue Moon Cocktail—67
Cajun Martini—145
Cherry Blossom—38
Cherry Snap—39
Crisp Apple Cocktail—39
Deep Sea—70
Eclipse—194
Golden Daze—76
Golden Glow—28
Hearts—40
Hurricane Cocktail—162
Hurricane III—162
Jellybean—41

Kentucky Orange Blossom—28
Ladybug—41
Leap-Year Cocktail—80
New Orleans Night 150
North Star—150
Opera—83
Orange Blossom—83
Paisley Martini—84
Rainbow—57
Red Snapper—152
Seagram's High Tea—87
Yellow Parrot Cocktail—43
Wedding Belle Cocktail—90

Summer
Angler's Cocktail—65
Captain's Tropical Spiced Tea—99
Irish Summer Coffee—163
Myers's Frozen Sharkbite—196
Myers's Heatwave—107

Piñata—135
Root Beer—42
7 Seas—168
Seagram's Sunburn—87
Summer Lemonade—153
Summer Sailor—154
Valencia II—43

Fall
Chocolate Tornado—193
Falling Star—102
Fare Thee Well—72
Hot Irish & Port—218
Hot Scotch—218
Hurricane—104
Hurricane II—104
Ice Breaker—104
Lavender Sunset—196
Moonchaser—197
Mudslide—150
Night Flight—220
Operetta—220
Orange Mocha—220
Patrón Silver Sunrise—134
Pirate's Spiced Rum Tea—220
Sunset—43

Winter
Almond Frost—35
Anisette Coffee—212
Café Amaretto—212
Café Amour—212
Chocolate Coffee—214
Cinnaccino—215
Cognac and Cream—216
Frostbite—132
Godiva Cafe—216
Hot Buttered Rum—217
Hot Toddy—218
Myers's Original Hot Buttered Rum—220
Scotch Holiday Sour—122

Snowball—89
Snowberry—221
Winter Solstice/Zero Mint Julep—171

MISCELLANEOUS CELEBRATIONS

Aloha Week (Hawaii)—November 7
Aloha—95
Blue Hawaiian—97
Gin Aloha—73
Hula-Hula—78
Lei Lani—105

April Fools—April 1
April Fool—190

Cherry Blossom Festival—March/April
Cherry Blossom—38

Kentucky Derby—1st Saturday in May
Belmont Stakes—144
Frozen Mint Julep—27
Jolly Julep—28
Kentucky Colonel Cocktail—28
Kentucky Orange Blossom—28
Mint Julep—29
Zero Mint Julep—171

Repeal of Prohibition—December 5
7 Highball—168
Whiskey Cocktail—170
Whisky Sour—170
Whisky Fizz—170
Whisky Rickey—170

Super Bowl—January
Aggravation—118
All-American Fizz—65
Grand Finale—54

Tax Day—April 15
Aggravation—118
Copper Penny—52
Greenback—77
Income Tax Cocktail—79
Write-Off—61

LOW- AND NONALCOHOL DRINKS

Some of your guests may prefer low-alcohol or non-alcohol beverages. Just like your guests who prefer beverage alcohol, your non-drinking guests will appreciate a tasty drink, so be prepared to offer them more than just sodas and juices. Develop a repertoire of delicious drinks and serve them with as much style as you bring to your spirited concoctions. Your guests' happy smiles will be quite gratifying.

Because your guests may also prefer low-alcohol drinks for after-work get-togethers or late-night soireés, this section also contains recipes that have been formulated with this type of drinker in mind. Although many of the drinks throughout this guide can be prepared with less alcohol—not compromising taste—these drinks are delicious, creative combinations, full of tasty juices and spirits.

LOW ALCOHOL

Aurora

½ oz. amaretto
½ oz. triple sec
2 oz. pineapple juice
1 oz. cream of coconut

Blend all ingredients with a scoop of crushed ice.

Bahama Breeze

¾ oz. melon liqueur
½ oz. crème de banana
2 oz. pineapple juice
2 oz. cream of coconut
1 oz. orange juice
2–8 oz. crushed ice

Blend ingredients thoroughly. Pour into specialty glass. Garnish with a pineapple flag.

Berry Berry

¾ oz. raspberry schnapps
½ cup fresh raspberries
6 oz. cream soda
1 scoop crushed ice

Blend all ingredients together in a blender. Pour into a margarita glass.

California Swirl

¾ oz. blue curaçao
½ oz. peach schnapps
1¼ oz. cream of coconut
1 oz. sweet & sour mix
8 oz. crushed ice
3 oz. pineapple juice
1 oz. sweet & sour mix
8 oz. crushed ice

Blend first five ingredients thoroughly. This is the first part of the swirl. Separately blend the next three ingredients thoroughly. This is the second part of the swirl. Take both sets of ingredients and pour into one glass at the same time. Swirl gently with a straw or spoon to create a different color. Garnish with a pineapple flag.

Chartbuster

1¼ oz. strawberry schnapps
1 oz. pineapple juice
1 oz. cream of coconut
½ cup strawberries

Blend all ingredients with scoop of crushed ice.

Cherry Rummer

¾ oz. dark rum
½ oz. black-cherry schnapps
4 oz. chocolate milk

Place into blender. Blend well. Serve in specialty glass. Garnish with fresh or maraschino cherry.

Coco Tropical

1 oz. crème de banana
1 oz. cream of coconut
2 scoops lemon sherbet
8 oz. crushed ice

Blend ingredients for 5 seconds. Pour into specialty glass. Garnish with lemon slice.

Cordial Colada

1 oz. strawberry liqueur
2 oz. pineapple juice
1 oz. cream of coconut

Blend all ingredients with a scoop of crushed ice.

Cranapple Cheer

1¼ oz. apple schnapps
2 oz. cranberry juice
4 oz. heavy cream
1 scoop crushed ice

Blend all ingredients. Pour into a margarita glass. Garnish with fresh mint.

Honey, Honey?

1 oz. amaretto
4 oz. Half-and-Half
1 tbsp. honey

Blend in blender until smooth. Serve in frosted old-fashioned glass.

Koala Kolada

¾ oz. peach schnapps
½ oz. melon liqueur
1½ oz. cream of coconut
1 oz. orange juice
1 oz. pineapple juice
2 oz. crushed pineapple
½ fresh kiwi, peeled
8 oz. crushed ice

Blend ingredients thoroughly. Pour into specialty glass. Garnish with a kiwi wheel.

Nutty Buddy

1 oz. coffee brandy
4 oz. chocolate milk
1 oz. Half-and-Half
6 oz. crushed ice

Blend ingredients thoroughly. Pour into specialty glass. Garnish with small marshmallows and pecans.

Paradise Lost

1¼ oz. piña colada
  schnapps
1 oz. pineapple juice
1 oz. cream of coconut
1 oz. Half-and-Half
1 scoop crushed ice

Blend all ingredients. Pour into tulip wineglass. Garnish with pineapple wedge.

Peachy Keen

½ oz. dark rum
1 oz. heavy cream
2 peach halves
½ tsp. cinnamon
8 oz. crushed ice

Combine ingredients until smooth and creamy in blender. Serve in specialty glass. Garnish with fresh peach slice.

Piña Banana

1½ oz. crème de banana
¼ cup pineapple juice
1 oz. cream of coconut
1 scoop pineapple sherbet
8 oz. crushed ice

Blend ingredients thoroughly. Pour into specialty glass. Top with whipped cream. Garnish with pineapple wedge and maraschino cherry.

Rich Smooch

½ oz. amaretto
2 oz. frozen raspberries
1 oz. milk

Blend all ingredients until smooth.

Straw Honey

1¼ oz. strawberry
    schnapps
½ cup milk
1 tbsp. honey
¼ cup strawberries, sliced

Blend all ingredients with a scoop of crushed ice. Pour into footed highball glass. Garnish with a strawberry.

Sunset Boulevard

¾ oz. melon liqueur
2 oz. orange juice
½ oz. pink grapefruit juice
1 oz. grenadine
2 scoops lemon sherbet
8 oz. crushed ice

Blend ingredients thoroughly. Pour into specialty glass. Garnish with orange slice.

NO ALCOHOL

Apricoco Smoothie

6 oz. apricot nectar
3 oz. coconut milk
1 small banana, sliced

Blend all until smooth. Serve in frosty mugs. Garnish with shredded coconut.

Banana Nana

2 oz. cream of coconut
¼ oz. lemon juice
¼ oz. lime juice
1 medium banana
8 oz. crushed ice

Mix well in blender until smooth. Serve in frosted specialty glass.

Cherry-Cherry Boom

2 oz. ginger ale
½ oz. cherry nectar
½ oz. sweet & sour mix
½ oz. grapefruit juice
1 tsp. bar sugar
8 oz. shaved ice

Shake vigorously with shaved ice. Pour contents into large cocktail glass. Garnish with a citrus wheel and a maraschino cherry.

Chocolate Dragon

1 cup cold milk
½ cup chocolate syrup
1 tsp. sugar
2 scoops vanilla ice cream

Blend until smooth. Pour into tall glass and garnish with chocolate shavings or sprinkles.

Chocolate Malted

or

¾ cup cold milk
½ cup chocolate syrup
2 oz. malted milk powder
1 scoop chocolate ice cream

Combine all in blender until smooth. Pour into large wine glass or specialty glass.

Cider Cipher

1 oz. apple cider
1 oz. orange juice

Pour into ice cube–filled highball glass. Garnish with orange slice and maraschino cherry.

Cooler-than-Cool

2 oz. orange juice
1 oz. peach nectar
1 oz. grenadine
1 oz. lime juice
2 oz. lemon-lime soda

Shake well. Pour into ice cube–filled Collins or specialty glass. Top with lemon-line soda. Garnish with an orange flag.

Frozen Cappuccino

⅓ cup espresso or very strong coffee, chilled
⅓ cup milk, chilled
⅓ cup crushed ice
1 tsp sugar

Combine espresso, milk, ice, and sugar in blender. Blend at high speed until smooth. Pour into large goblet. Garnish with a dollop of whipped cream and a dusting of cinnamon.

Grapefruit Granita

1 oz. pink grapefruit juice
2 tsp. powdered sugar
6–8 oz. ginger ale

Muddle juice and sugar in Collins glass. Fill with ice. Add ginger ale and stir. Garnish with maraschino cherry.

Great Grape

3 oz. purple grape juice
1 tsp. grenadine
3–4 oz. club soda

Pour juice and grenadine into ice-filled highball glass. Top with club soda. Garnish with maraschino cherry or three grapes on a pick.

Groovy Guava

3 oz. guava nectar
2 oz. Half-and-Half
1 oz. cream of coconut
8 oz. crushed ice

Mix well in blender until smooth. Serve in specialty glass. Garnish with shredded coconut.

Hula Shake

2 oz. fresh coconut milk
2 oz. pineapple juice
1 tsp. chocolate syrup
½ tsp. coconut syrup
1 scoop vanilla ice cream

Blend all ingredients until smooth. Pour into frosted Collins glasses. Garnish with pineapple wheel and maraschino cherry.

Kentucky Mock Julep

½ cup sugar
1 cup cold water
½ cup lemon juice
4–5 fresh mint leaves
¾ qt. ginger ale

Mix sugar, water, and lemon juice in a bowl. Add washed mint leaves. Let stand for 45 minutes. Pour into a large pitcher with ice cubes. Add ginger ale and thin lemon slices. Serves 4.

Lemon Cafe

¼ cup strong coffee
2 oz. lemon sherbet
½ tsp. lemon juice
1 tsp. grated lemon rind
1 tsp. sugar

Blend until smooth. Serve in frosted Collins glass. Garnish with maraschino cherry.

Luscious Limeade

1 tbsp. fresh lime juice
2 oz. cold water
1 tsp. sugar

Pour into ice cube–filled Collins glass. Stir well. Garnish with mint sprig.

Mango Madness

2 oz. mango nectar
2 oz. cream of coconut
2 oz. Half-and-Half
1 oz. orange juice
1 tbsp. of grenadine
8 oz. crushed ice

Shake well with crushed ice. Pour into highball glass. Garnish with shredded coconut.

Mint Condition

juice of 1 lime
8 oz. ginger ale

Squeeze fresh lime juice into a frosted Collins glass. Add ice cubes and fill with ginger ale. Stir. Garnish with a mint sprig.

Minty Chocolate Smoothie

1 oz. cream of coconut
1 oz. chocolate syrup
1 oz. chocolate milk
1 oz. heavy cream
1 tsp. peppermint extract
8 oz. crushed ice

Mix ingredients in blender until smooth and creamy. Serve in specialty glass. Garnish with whipped cream and maraschino cherry.

Mom Collins

juice of ½ lemon
1 tsp. powdered sugar
6–8 oz. club soda

Shake lemon and sugar with ice and strain into Collins glass. Add several ice cubes, fill with club soda. Stir. Garnish with citrus fruits and maraschino cherry. Serve with straw.

Nectarine Nirvana

1 oz. orange juice
1 tsp. lemon juice
1 medium nectarine
1 tsp. sugar
¼ oz. crushed ice

Blend all ingredients until smooth. Pour into specialty glass.

Orange Twizzle

4 oz. ginger ale
2 oz. orange juice

Pour into crushed ice–filled Collins glasses. Garnish with orange slice and maraschino cherry.

Peanut Butter Coffee

1 cup cold coffee
1 cup milk
1 tbsp. smooth peanut butter
1 tbsp. sugar

Blend all ingredients until smooth.

Piña Carrot Cocktail

1 cup pineapple juice,
  unsweetened
1 medium carrot, sliced
1 dash lemon juice

Blend all until smooth. Add a handful of crushed ice and blend again. Serve in old-fashioned glass. Garnish with carrot slice.

Pink Elephant

1 tsp. lime juice
1 tsp. grenadine
1 tsp. sugar
½ cup bitter lemon
½ cup pink grapefruit
  juice

Mix lime juice, grenadine, and sugar together in a brandy snifter. Add ice cubes, bitter lemon, and grapefruit juice. Stir.

Pleasant Piña Colada

1½ oz. cream of coconut
1½ oz. pineapple juice
2 tsp. lime juice
1 tsp. lemon juice
1 cup crushed ice

Mix all ingredients in blender. Pour into Collins glass. Garnish with pineapple slice and maraschino cherry.

Raspberry Delight

2 oz. club soda
½ oz. raspberry syrup
½ oz. chocolate syrup
½ oz. grenadine
8 oz. crushed ice

Blend until slushy.

Shirley Temple

1 dash grenadine
6–8 oz. ginger ale

Pour grenadine in Collins glass filled with ice. Top with ginger ale. Garnish with maraschino cherry and orange slice.

Strawberry Spritzer

4 oz. strawberry nectar
4–6 oz. club soda

Pour nectar into crushed ice–filled wine-glass. Top with club soda. Garnish with fresh strawberry.

Sour Passion

4 oz. passion-fruit nectar
1 tsp. lemon juice
4–6 oz. ginger ale

Combine juice and nectar in highball glass. Add ice. Top with ginger ale. Garnish with lemon slice.

Sun Shine

6 oz. apple juice
3 oz. orange juice
1 scoop strawberry sherbet

Pour juices into frosted ice-filled Collins glass. Top with sherbet and garnish with orange peel.

Tall Guy

4 oz. orange juice
¼ cup heavy cream
½ banana

Mix all ingredients in blender until smooth. Pour into specialty glass and garnish with orange slice.

Vanilla Cola

1 tbsp. vanilla extract
6–8 oz. cola

Add vanilla to ice-filled Collins glass. Fill with cola. Stir. Add two straws.

Very Berry

3 oz. strawberry nectar
2 oz. heavy cream
2 tbsp. raspberries or strawberries in syrup
8 oz. crushed ice

Combine ingredients until smooth and creamy in blender. Serve in specialty glass. Combine with strawberry.

Virgin Mary

4 oz. tomato juice
1 tsp. lemon juice
½ tsp. Worcestershire sauce
2 dashes Tabasco sauce
salt to taste
pepper to taste

Pour tomato juice into a large wineglass filled with ice. Add remainder of ingredients. Stir and garnish with lime wedge.

Virgin Strawberry Margarita

6 ripe strawberries
5 oz. sweet & sour mix
12 oz. crushed ice

Blend all ingredients until slusy. Serve in a chilled margarita glass.

Watermelon Cooler

2 cups watermelon, cubed
    and seeded
½ cup lemon sherbet
1 tsp. raspberry syrup
½ cup ice cubes

Combine all ingredients in blender. Blend until smooth and thick.

Ye Olde Egg Cream

3 tsp. cold milk
3 tsp. chocolate syrup
4 oz. seltzer or club soda

Pour milk and syrup into tall glass. Fill with seltzer or club soda.

RECIPES FOR THE CHEF

Spirits have long been an integral part of the culinary arts. They bring out the subtle flavors of food, provide an exotic flair to a dish, or flambé a fancy dessert.

Since everyone enjoys good food, the following section celebrates the exciting, sheer delight of eating. Favorite spirits and wines are used in simple-to-prepare recipes for everything from hors d'oeuvres to desserts—and all are guaranteed to win rave reviews from appreciative family members and guests.

Bon Appetit!

HORS D'OEUVRES

Calypso Grilled Shrimp

2 lb. raw shrimp, large
1 cup olive oil
¼ cup Captain Morgan
    Original Spiced Rum
½ cup chili sauce
½ tsp. Tabasco
1 tsp. salt
2 cloves garlic, mashed

Shell and devein shrimp, leaving tail shell attached. Mix with remaining ingredients and marinate 1 hour. Thread onto skewers. Place on grill six inches above gray coals. Grill 2–3 minutes each side, basting often with marinade. Makes 8 appetizer servings.

Fresh Anisette Vegetable Dip

2 pt. sour cream
1 cup anisette
2 pkg. onion soup mix
1 cup walnuts, thinly
    sliced

Blend all ingredients well and pour into a covered serving dish. Chill for a couple of hours. Serve with sliced vegetables.

Stuffed Ginger-Gin Mushrooms

2 lb. large white
    mushrooms
1 small clove garlic
¾ lb. freshly ground pork
¼ lb. freshly ground lean
    beef
½ cup dry bread crumbs
1 egg
5 scallions
¼ cup soy sauce
⅛ tsp. ground cloves
¼ cup grated ginger
¼ tsp. salt
¼ tsp. white pepper
½ cup drained water
    chestnuts
¾ cup gin

Clean mushrooms, removing stems. Peel garlic and rub sides of mixing bowl with it. Crumble meat into bowl. Mix in bread crumbs and egg. Mix well. Chop the scallions. Add to mixture. Add soy sauce, cloves, ginger, salt, and pepper. Mix again. Chop up mushroom stems and water chestnuts. Add to mixture. Pour gin and mix well.

Place mushroom caps on greased pan. Fill each cap with the meat mixture. Bake at 350° for 35 minutes. Serves 10.

SOUPS

Gin Cioppino

1 lb. fresh fish fillets
1 small green pepper,
    diced
2 tbsp. chopped onion
1 clove garlic, minced
1 tbsp. cooking oil
½ tsp. basil
1 16-oz. can tomato sauce
3 tbsp. parsley, chopped
¼ tsp. dried oregano,
    crushed
½ tsp. salt and pepper to
    taste
9 oz. fresh shrimp
1 6½-oz. can minced
    clams
1½ oz. gin
1½ oz. anisette
garlic croutons

A unique twist on an Italian favorite.

Cut fish into 1-inch pieces. Cook green pepper, onion, and garlic with oil in a large saucepan until fish is tender. Add tomato sauce, parsley, oregano, and basil, ½ tsp. salt, and dash pepper. Cover and simmer 20 minutes. Add shrimp, and undrained clams. Cover and simmer 5–7 minutes. Add gin and anisette and top with croutons. Serves 6.

Lobster and Spring Vegetable Soup

2 cups Chardonnay
1 carrot, peeled and
    thinly sliced
1 small onion
1 tbsp. sea salt
10 black peppercorns
1 lobster (2 lb.)
1 cup creme fraiche
juice of 1 lemon
salt and black pepper to
    taste
1 bunch baby carrots
¼ cup small peas
8 green beans
8 asparagus tips
1 bunch scallions
1 small zucchini, cut into
    tiny slices
1 tbsp. chopped chervil

Put first six ingredients in a large stock-pot with 2 cups of water. Bring to a boil, reduce heat, and continue to cook lobster for 6 minutes. Remove from heat and allow lobster to cool in the liquid. When cool, remove meat from the tail and claws, as well as the coral.

In a bowl, combine creme fraiche, lemon juice, coral, salt, and pepper. Whisk until well mixed; strain and refrigerate.

Cook all of the vegetables separately in boiling salted water; refresh with ice water.

Dice lobster; add soup, vegetables, lobster and chervil to a soup tureen. Serves 4.

Scotch Leek Soup

4 lb. chicken
2 qt. cold water
2 medium yellow onions
2 medium white onions
3 stalks celery
½ tsp. fresh thyme
½ tsp. fresh basil
½ tsp. salt
½ tsp. pepper
2 bay leaves
6 leeks
4 medium yellow
    potatoes
3 tbsp. barley
1 cup Scotch
½ cup chopped fresh
    parsley

Wash and clean chicken. Heat cold water in large kettle. Peel and quarter onions and cut celery into small pieces, including leaves. Put vegetables in water with the chicken. Add thyme, basil, salt, pepper, and bay leaves. Bring to a boil. Boil for 2 minutes, then reduce heat and simmer 1½ to 2 hours or until chicken is tender.

Wash leeks several times to remove all soil. Trim ends and cut into 1-inch pieces. Peel and chop potatoes. Remove the chicken from pot, skim off excess fat from broth. Add leeks and potatoes to the pot and simmer for several minutes. Add barley and simmer for 20 minutes, until barley is cooked.

Bone, skin, and cut chicken into small chunks and put back in kettle. Simmer 5 to 10 minutes more. Remove bay leaves. Add Scotch. Simmer 3 to 5 minutes. Pour into soup bowls and sprinkle with parsley. Serves 4–6.

Vodka Gazpacho

6 large tomatoes
2 cups tomato juice
1 medium cucumber, seeded and chopped
1 medium onion, finely chopped
1 small green pepper, finely chopped
1 small clove garlic, minced
¼ cup olive oil
2 tbsp. vinegar
1 dash hot pepper sauce
1 tsp. salt
⅛ tsp. pepper

3 oz. vodka
croutons
1 tbsp. scallions, sliced

Plunge tomatoes in boiling water for 30 seconds to loosen skins, then immerse in cold water. Slip skins off, core, and coarsely chop tomatoes. In a large mixing bowl combine tomatoes, juice, cucumber, onion, green pepper, garlic, oil, vinegar, hot pepper sauce, salt, and pepper. Cover and chill. Add vodka and stir. Garnish with croutons and sliced scallions. Serves 6–8.

Creamy Cannelini Bean and Chestnut Soup with Morels

1 lb. Cannelini beans or red kidney beans
¼ lb. dried chestnuts*
2 tsp. vegetable oil
1 large onion, coarsely chopped
½ lb. mushrooms, coarsely chopped
1 qt. defatted chicken stock
½ cup white wine
½ tsp. dried thyme
1 tbsp. salt
Fresh ground black pepper
½ oz. dried morels or 1 oz. other dried mushrooms or ¼ lb. fresh mushrooms
½ cup Founder's Reserve Port
¼ cup chopped parsley
2 tbsp. lemon juice
2 cups low-fat (1%) milk

chopped parsley or chives for garnish

*Be certain to purchase the European chestnut, not Oriental water chestnuts.

Soak beans overnight in ample water. Drain and rinse beans. Soak chestnuts overnight in water to cover.

In a large heavy casserole heat oil and saute onion over medium high heat about 10 minutes until well browned. Add drained beans, chestnuts and their soaking water, chopped fresh mushrooms, stock, white wine, thyme, salt (decrease if stock is salty) and several grindings of black pepper. Bring to a boil, cover and simmer slowly for 1½ hours or until beans and chestnuts are tender. Meanwhile soak morels or other dried mushrooms in water to cover. When soft, remove and slice thinly. Strain soaking water through a fine sieve or carefully pour off, leaving any sand or grit. Reserve. Slice fresh mushrooms if using in place of dried mushrooms.

Process the soup in a blender or food processor until it is a somewhat chunky puree, return to casserole, and add morels or other mushrooms, Port, parsley, lemon juice, several grindings of pepper and the mushroom water. Bring to a boil, cover and simmer about 10 minutes. Stir in milk, season with additional salt and pepper to taste and serve garnished with a light sprinkle of chopped parsley or chives.

Serves 8 as a main dish, 12–16 as a first course.

VEGETABLES

Half-Baked Rum Sweet Potatoes

4 firm large sweet
  potatoes
1 tsp. salt
3 tbsp. butter
1 orange
¼ cup dark rum
1 tbsp. brown sugar
1 tsp. freshly ground
  nutmeg

Peel and cut sweet potatoes into quarters. Bring potatoes and ½ tsp. salt to boil. Cook until tender. Drain. Mash until coarse and scoop into large oven pan. Stir in butter.

Grate orange peel into the potatoes. Cut orange in half, squeezing the juice into a bowl. Stir the rum into orange juice.

Dissolve the brown sugar into the rum mixture. Stir in remaining salt. Blend well and stir into the potatoes. Smooth top and sprinkle nutmeg. Bake at 350° for 20 to 25 minutes. Serves 8.

Zucchini Martini

1 lb. fresh zucchini
1 stalk celery
2 tbsp. butter
¼ tsp. salt
¼ tsp. white pepper
¾ tsp. dried basil
3½ oz. gin
½ oz. vermouth

Wash and trim the ends from zucchini, slicing in even ¼-inch rounds. Dice celery finely.

Melt butter in large skillet. Add salt, pepper, and basil. Mix well. Add gin and vermouth. Cook covered for 3 to 5 minutes. Uncover and add zucchini and saute for several minutes. Serve in warmed serving dish. Serves 4.

Roasted Beets with Dill and Port Glaze

2 bunches small-medium–size beets (approximately 1½ lb.)
½ cup Founder's Reserve Port
1 tbsp. wine vinegar
¼ cup white wine
¼ cup defatted chicken stock
¼ tsp. salt
1 tbsp. fresh chopped dill or 1 tsp. dried dill and 2 tsp. fresh parsley or chives
fresh ground black pepper

Trim beets leaving 1 inch of stem. Do not remove "tails." Scrub beets and place in a covered baking dish or roasting pan covered tightly with aluminum foil. Bake in a 350° oven for about 1½ hours or until beets are tender (test with a toothpick). Baking time will vary according to size and age of beets.

Allow beets to cool. Cut off stems and "tails" and slip off skins. Either slice beets thickly or cut into wedges; if small, cut into halves or quarters. Can be done up to several days in advance and refrigerated until needed.

Shortly before serving, combine Port, vinegar, white wine, stock and salt in a saucepan or skillet. Reduce over high heat by ½. Lower heat and add beets. Simmer, tossing occasionally until beets are hot and liquid reduced to a glaze. Add dill (and other herbs), a grinding of black pepper and additional salt to taste. Serves 6–8.

Port Glazed Carrots with Mint

1½ lb. carrots
½ cup white wine
¼ cup Founder's Reserve Port
1 tbsp. Balsamic vinegar
½ tsp. salt
1 tbsp. chopped fresh mint
fresh ground black pepper
for garnish: fresh chopped parsley

If possible select small, young carrots 2–3 inches long. Trim off stem and tail, but peeling is unnecessary. Regular, large carrots should be peeled and cut into 2–3 -inch lengths. Thick pieces should be halved lengthwise.

In a large skillet or casserole that will hold the carrots in a single layer, combine all ingredients. Add sufficient water to cover carrots half-way. Bring to a boil, cover and keep at a moderate simmer, stirring or tossing the carrots occasionally, for about 30 minutes or until carrots are fully tender. Cooking time will vary according to size and type of carrots.

Liquid should be reduced to a thick glaze; if necessary uncover pan and reduce over high heat. Should the pan dry out before carrots are done, add water as necessary. Can be prepared in advance and rewarmed before serving. Season with additional salt and fresh black pepper to taste. If desired, sprinkle with chopped fresh parsley when serving. Serves 6–8.

ENTREES

Lemon & Sage Roasted Chicken Breasts Mushroom Port Sauce

12 fresh sage leaves plus additional leaves or sprigs
2 cloves garlic, slivered
6 chicken half-breasts approximately 8 oz. each (with bone and skin)
12 thin slices lemon
½ tsp. fresh ground black pepper

for sauce:
¼ lb. mushrooms
2 cups chicken stock
½ cup white wine
½ cup Founder's Reserve Port
2 tbsp. cornstarch dissolved in ¼ cup cold water
salt
fresh ground black pepper
lemon juice

Slip a sage leaf and some garlic slivers between the muscle separations of each chicken breast. Slip another leaf, a lemon slice, garlic slivers and pepper under the skin. Top each breast with a lemon slice. Cover with plastic wrap and refrigerate for at least 8 hours or overnight for flavors to penetrate meat.

Slice mushrooms and spread in a roasting pan. Broil directly under the flame of a preheated broiler until mushrooms are browned—watch carefully—set aside.

Arrange chicken breasts in a shallow roasting pan and strew with additional leaves or sprigs of sage. Roast in a preheated 450° oven for 30 minutes or until nicely browned and cooked through—DO NOT OVERCOOK.

While chicken is roasting combine mushrooms and stock in a saucepan and simmer for 5 minutes. When chicken breasts are done, remove from pan and set aside in a warm place. Add white wine and Port to roasting pan, set over high heat and deglaze pan, scraping up brownings. Strain through a sieve and degrease carefully. Add deglazing to stock and mushrooms and bring to a boil. Slowly add dissolved cornstarch, stirring rapidly, using just enough to thicken sauce lightly. Add salt, pepper and drops of lemon juice to taste.

Remove skin from chicken breasts and serve with sauce.

For a more elegant presentation, roast the chicken breasts in advance. When cool, remove skin and carefully remove meat in one piece from bone. Slice breasts crosswise on the diagonal. Heat sauce in a large skillet. Carefully place each sliced breast in the sauce and heat gently just until warmed, taking care not to overcook the meat. Remove each breast carefully with a spatula, arranging the slices on individual plates or a platter. Top with remaining sauce. Serves 6.

Red Snapper Courtbouillon

1 cup chopped onion
½ cup green onion, chopped
2 cups tomato, seeded and chopped
½ cup Pinot Noir or Merlot
2 cloves garlic, minced
¼ tsp. thyme
¼ tsp. marjoram
¼ tsp. allspice
¼ tsp. freshly ground black pepper
1 bay leaf
pinch of cayenne pepper
1 lb. whole red snapper, drawn and scaled

Heat a skillet large enough to hold the fish. Dry-cook onion and green onion, stirring, until they start to color.

Add all remaining ingredients except the fish. Cover the skillet and simmer for 2 minutes.

Lay fish in the sauce, cover the skillet, and cook at a simmer for 8 minutes. With two spatulas, carefully turn fish over in the sauce, re-cover the pan, and cook for 10 minutes more, or until the fish flakes apart at the touch of a fork. Serves 2.

Dijon Lamb Chops

4 small double-ribbed lamb chops, of medium thickness
3 tbsp. Dijon-style mustard
½ cup fine dry bread crumbs
1 cup Chardonnay or Sauvignon Blanc
1 cup beef broth
½ tsp. dried rosemary
3 tbsp. minced shallots
2 tbsp. unsalted butter, chopped into bits

Sprinkle lamb chops with salt and pepper, coat them with mustard and bread crumbs and set aside. In a saucepan combine wine, broth, rosemary, and shallots, bringing liquid to a boil until it is reduced to about ⅓ cup. Broil chops on a broiler rack pan about 4 inches away from the heat for about 5 minutes. Turn chops and broil them for 5 additional minutes for medium-rare chops. Place chops on a platter and let them sit for about 5 minutes before serving.

Add butter to the sauce, swirling the pan until the butter mixes in. Serve sauce with the chops. Serves 2 or 4.

London Broil à la Russe

1 thick-cut top round London Broil steak approximately 1¾ lb. or any size desired

8 or more grindings black pepper

8 dashes Angostura bitters

1 tbsp. chopped shallots

½ cup Founder's Reserve Port

For sauce:

½ lb. fresh shiitake mushrooms or other specialty mushrooms

2 tbsp. chopped shallots

2 cups defatted beef stock

½ cup white wine

2 tsp. dijon mustard

1 tsp. tomato paste

¼ cup Founder's Reserve Port

¼ cup chopped fresh dill or 2 tablespoons dried dill

¼ cup finely chopped sour dill pickle or cornichon

2 tbsp. cornstarch dissolved in 4 tbsp. cold water

salt

fresh ground black pepper

¼ cup low-fat sour cream

For garnish:

Chopped fresh dill parsley or chives

Trim the steak of all visible fat and poke it all over with a fork. Place in a baking dish and rub with pepper; add bitters, shallots and port. Cover and marinate, refrigerated, at least 8 hours or overnight.

Meanwhile clean shiitake mushrooms. Slice caps and chop stems finely (shiitake stems are very tough). Spread out in a roasting pan with shallots and broil close to flame until browned, stirring frequently and watching carefully. Combine with stock and white wine in a saucepan and whisk in mustard and tomato paste. Simmer 15 minutes, covered. When steak is removed from marinade, add marinade, ¼ cup port, dill and pickles. Simmer 5 minutes. Stir in dissolved cornstarch, using just enough to thicken sauce lightly, simmer a few minutes more and correct seasoning with salt and pepper to taste. Reheat sauce when ready to serve and whisk in sour cream without letting it boil.

Remove steak from refrigerator an hour or two before cooking. Drain and add marinade to sauce. Pat dry before cooking and lightly oil a broiler pan or baking pan. Broil near full flame on each side until nicely browned, then lower and continue cooking to desired degree of doneness (medium-rare suggested). Remove and let rest 5 minutes in a warm place. Sprinkle lightly with salt. Slice on the diagonal, across the grain, making slices as thin as possible. Add any rendered juices to the sauce.

For an elegant presentation arrange steak slices on a pool of sauce and drizzle a ribbon of sauce across the center and garnish. Serves 4.

PASTA & RICE

Linguine with Red Mussel Sauce

3 lb. mussels
¾ cup Chianti or
    Cabernet Sauvignon
½ cup bottled clam juice
1 tbsp. garlic, minced
3 tbsp. olive oil
1 28-oz. can of Italian
    plum tomatoes,
    drained
½ cup celery, chopped
1 tsp. dried oregano
1 tsp. dried thyme
½ tsp. dried hot peppers
1 tsp. fennel seeds
¼ cup minced parsley
    leaves
1 lb. dried linguine

Scrub mussels thoroughly, scraping off the beards and rinsing in several changes of water. Steam mussels in wine in a large kettle, covered, over high heat for 3 to 5 minutes or until mussels open up. Discard any unopened shells. Remove mussels from shells, and transfer the mussels to a small bowl. Chill them, covered.

Strain cooking liquid through a fine sieve set over a large measuring cup. To measure two full cups, add clam juice if necessary. In the cleaned kettle cook garlic in oil over low heat, stirring, until it is golden. Add tomatoes, chopping them fine with a spoon. Stir in cooking liquid and clam juice mixture, celery, oregano, thyme, red pepper, fennel seeds, and salt and pepper to taste. Bring liquid to a boil, and simmer, stirring occasionally for 20 minutes or until it thickens slightly. Stir in parsley and mussels and keep warm over low heat. In a separate kettle of boiling water, cook linguine for 8 to 10 minutes or until it is al dente. Drain well and transfer to a large bowl. Spoon sauce over the linguine. Serves 4.

Pasta with Vino Marinara Sauce

1 large onion, chopped
2 medium carrots,
    chopped
2 cloves garlic, minced
2 tbsp. cooking oil
2 28-oz. cans tomatoes,
    cut up
¾ cup Bordeaux
1 tsp. sugar
1 tsp. salt
1 tsp. dried oregano,
    crushed
dash pepper

dash crushed red pepper
8 oz. spaghetti, linguine, or
    capellini pasta

In a large saucepan, cook onion, carrots, and garlic in hot oil until tender. Add tomatoes, wine, sugar, salt, oregano, pepper, and red pepper. Bring to boiling, reduce heat. Simmer uncovered for 45 minutes or until desired thickness is reached.

Cook pasta in large amount of boiling water until tender or al dente. Drain well. Spoon sauce over pasta. Serves 4.

2 cups whole rye berries
1 cup wild rice
2 tsp. vegetable oil
½ tsp. dried thyme
1 cup white wine
1 cup water
2 cups defatted chicken
 stock
2 tsp. salt

1 orange
3 scallions
1 tbsp. finely chopped
 parsley
2 tbsp. Founder's Reserve
 Port
fresh ground black pepper

Clean rye berries in cold water, then cover with 3 cups boiling water and soak 3 to 4 hours. (Preliminary soaking allows rye to cook in same time as wild rice.) Drain well. Clean wild rice in cold water and drain well.

In a large saucepan or casserole heat oil and add rye and wild rice. Saute over medium-high heat, stirring frequently, for about 10 minutes or until grains are lightly browned and have a nutty fragrance. Add thyme, white wine, water, stock and salt. When boiling, reduce heat, cover and simmer slowly for about 1¼ hours until the rye is tender (but still chewy) and the wild rice has opened. Uncover and reduce any liquid that may remain.

Meanwhile, remove two strips of orange zest about 3 inches long, using a vegetable peeler to remove only the orange skin, not the white pith. Cut the strips in half crosswise and with a very sharp knife cut into very fine slivers. Alternately, use a fine zester to remove fine threads of zest from about half the orange—or about 2 tsp. Chop the scallion, including the tender green.

When grains are cooked taste carefully and add salt if indicated. Add orange zest, parsley, scallions, port and several grindings of pepper. Toss lightly with a large fork to combine. Cover pan and let sit on turned-off stove for 10 minutes to perfume before serving. Transfer to a covered serving dish or bring covered casserole to table so everyone can enjoy the exquisite fragrance when the cover is removed. Serves 4.

DESSERTS

Brandy Hard Sauce

1 cup sweet butter
2½ cups confectioner's
   sugar
½ cup brandy

Cream butter into mixing bowl. Add sugar, a bit at a time. Blend well and drizzle in brandy, continuing the creaming. Transfer into smaller bowl and refrigerate for 2 hours before serving over ice cream, bread pudding, or coffee cake. Enough for 6–8 servings.

Captain's Banana Bread

½ cup butter, softened
1 cup sugar
2 eggs, beaten
3–4 bananas
½ cup Captain Morgan
   Original Spiced Rum
2 cups flour
1 tsp. baking soda
1 tsp. baking powder
½ tsp. salt
½ cup chopped nuts,
   optional

Preheat oven to 350°. In a large mixing bowl, cream butter and sugar, then add eggs. In a separate bowl, combine bananas and rum. Sift dry ingredients together, except nuts. Gradually beat banana and flour mixtures into egg mixture. Stir in chopped nuts, if desired. Turn into well-greased 8½″x4½″x2½″ loaf pan. Bake 1 hour. Serves 6–8.

Captain's Ginger Cookies

1 cup sweet butter,
   softened
1 cup confectioner's sugar
2½ cups flour
pinch salt
3 tbsp. crystallized ginger,
   minced
1 tsp. ground ginger
½ cup Captain Morgan
   Original Spiced Rum

In a large bowl, first cream the butter and sugar. Then mix with the remaining ingredients into a soft dough. Shape the dough into a cylinder approximately 2 inches in diameter and wrap in plastic. Refrigerate 2 hours or freeze 45 minutes.

Slice dough into ¼-inch-thick cookies. Bake at 400° on a greased cookie sheet for 12 minutes or until edges are lightly brown. Cool. Makes about 6 dozen.

Godiva Brownies

5 oz. unsweetened
    chocolate
5⅓ oz. (⅔ cup) butter
1 tbsp. instant coffee
5 eggs
½ tsp. salt
2 cups sugar
1 tsp. vanilla extract
½ cup Godiva Liqueur
½ cup sifted all-purpose
    flour
10 oz. (2½ cups) chopped
    walnuts

In double boiler, melt chocolate and butter; when smooth, add instant coffee and set aside to cool. Beat eggs and salt together until slightly fluffy, add sugar gradually and beat until mixture is ribbony (about 10 minutes.). Add vanilla extract, Godiva and cooled chocolate to eggs while beating on low speed. Fold in sifted flour until just incorporated, then fold in nuts.

Pour batter onto greased, floured and parchment-lined 11″x17″ baking pan. Place in preheated 450° oven, lowering temperature to 400°; bake 20 to 22 minutes or until toothpick inserted into center comes out clean. Makes 20 3″x3″ brownies.

Godiva Chocolate Covered Banana

2 oz. Godiva Liqueur
½ oz. Myers's Rum
½ banana, sliced
½ cup vanilla ice cream

Pour Godiva into blender. Add rum, banana, and ice cream. Blend until smooth. Pour into serving glass. Garnish with banana slice. Makes 2 drinks.

Godiva Strawberry Torte

2 envelopes unflavored
    gelatin
½ cup cold water
3 egg yolks
½ cup sugar
¼ tsp. salt
½ cup milk, scalded
1 tsp. vanilla extract
1 10-oz. pkg. frozen
    unsweetened straw-
    berries, pureed
2 cups Godiva Liqueur,
    divided
1 cup heavy cream
1 9-inch sponge cake
1 qt. fresh strawberries,
    hulled
whipped cream

Soften gelatin in water, set aside. In double boiler, cook egg yolks, sugar, salt, and milk until slightly thickened, stirring constantly. Remove from heat, add gelatin and stir until dissolved. Add vanilla, strawberry puree, and 1½ cups Godiva; chill until slightly thickened and mixture mounds on a spoon

Whip cream until stiff, fold into strawberry mixture, and set aside.

To assemble the torte, place sponge cake in 9-inch greased springform pan, sprinkle with Godiva, cover with strawberries, hulled side down, and top with strawberry mousse. Refrigerate several hours before serving. Garnish with whipped cream and fresh strawberries. Serves 12.

Godiva Tiramisu

5 oz. Godiva Liqueur,
  divided
½ cup strong coffee or
  espresso
16–20 ladyfingers
1 lb. Mascarpone cheese
2 eggs, separated
⅓ cup confectioner's
  sugar
3–4 oz. dark chocolate,
  grated

Mix 3 ounces of Godiva with coffee and set aside.

For each serving trim 4 ladyfingers to fit along the sides and bottom of a 1-cup soufflé dish. Pour 1 ounce of the reserved coffee into each soufflé dish and set aside.

Beat together the Mascarpone cheese, egg yolks, sugar, and remaining 2 ounces of Godiva until smooth. Whip the egg whites until stiff and fold into the cheese. Divide the filling evenly among the soufflé dishes. Sprinkle with chocolate and refrigerate overnight. Serves 4.

Scotch-Espresso Ice Cream

1 oz. Scotch
⅛ cup ground espresso
  beans
vanilla ice cream

Add Scotch to the freshly ground espresso beans and pour over 1 or 2 scoops of ice cream. Serves 1.

TRADEMARKS

Seagram's and Seagram Crest Design are trademarks of The Seagram Group of Companies, used under license.

The following trademarks appearing in this book are owned by The Seagram Group of Companies:

Captain Morgan	Passport
Capucello	Seagram
Chivas Regal	Seagram's
Coyote	Seagram's Canadian Hunter
Crown Royal	Seagram's Extra Dry Gin
Mariachi	Seagram's 7 Crown
Martell	Seagram's V.O.
Myers's	The Glenlivet
Myers's Sharkbite	

Godiva is a trademark of Godiva Chocolatier, Inc., or N.V. Godiva Belgium S.A., used under license.

Absolut Country of Sweden Vodka & logo, Absolut, Absolut Bottle Design and Absolut Calligraphy are trademarks owned by V&S Vin & Spirit AB. Imported by The House of Seagram, New York, New York.

Patrón is a trademark of St. Maarten Spirits.

Many of the brands mentioned in this book are owned by companies other than The Seagram Group of Companies.

INDEX

Abbey Cocktail, 64
Absinthe Cocktail, 46
Absolut Citron Blue
  Lemonade, 142
Absolut Kurant Collins,
  142
Absolut Kurant Kir,
  142
Absolut Kurant
  Margarita, 142
Absolut Kurant Sunrise,
  142
Absolut Peppar Bloody
  Mary, 142
Absolut Peppar Ragin'
  Cajun, 142
Absolut Peppar Salty
  Dog, 142
Acapulco, 94
Acapulco Apple
  Margarita, 128
Acapulco Blue, 128
Acapulco Clam Digger,
  129
Adam & Eve, 46
Adios Mother, 64
Affinity Cocktail, 118
Aggravation, 118
Alabama Fizz, 64
A la Mode, 46
Alaska Cocktail, 65
Alexander, 65
Alexander Martell, 35
Alexander's Sister, 35
Alfonso Special, 65
Algonquin, 159
Algonquin Bloody Mary,
  143
All-American Fizz, 65
Allegheny Cocktail, 159
Almond Chocolate, 212
Almond Coffee, 212
Almond Delight, 47
Almond Frost, 35
Aloha, 95
Amaretto Sour, 47
Amaretto Spritzer, 47
Amaretto Supreme, 47
Ambrosia, 95

American Beauty
  Cocktail, 35
Amore, 190
Amorous Duo, 47
Añejo Banger, 129
Añejo Pacifico, 129
Angel Face, 47
Angel's Tip, 47
Angler's Cocktail, 65
Anisette Coffee, 212
Anna's Banana, 143
Anna's Wish, 95
Antoine's Lullaby, 95
Apple Calabash, 48
Applecar, 35
Applejack Bowl, 202
Apple Pie à la Mode,
  95
Apple Pie Cocktail, 95
Apple Smile, 48
Apricocious, 35
Apricoco Smoothie, 237
Apricot Anise Collins,
  65
Apricot Blush, 36
Apricot Cocktail, 36
Apricot Colada, 36
Apricot Cooler, 36
Apricot Fizz, 36
Apricot Jerk, 36
Apricot Smoothie, 190
Apricot Stone Sour, 37
Apricot Sour, 159
Apricot Sweetie, 37
April Fool, 190
Aqueduct, 143
Archer's Punch, 202
Aruba, 65
Aurora, 233

Bahama Breeze, 234
Bahama Mama, 96
Bahia Cooler, 96
Bairn, 118
Baja Banana-Boat
  Margarita, 129
Ballet Russe, 143
Balmoral Cocktail, 119
Banana Barbados, 212

Banana Berry Blender,
  190
Banana B. Jones, 190
Banana Bowl, 202
Banana Chi Chi, 143
Banana Crown, 159
Banana Mamba, 48
Banana Colada, 96
Banana Daiquiri, 96
Banana Daiquiri II, 96
Banana Nana, 237
Banana Popsicle, 190
Banana Sandwich, 191
Banana Scream, 159
Banana Slushee, 96
Barbados Punch, 97
Barnum, 66
Bat Bite, 97
Bayard Fizz, 66
Bay Breeze, 143
Beach Berry, 48
Beachcomber, 97
Beadlestone, 119
Belmont, 66
Belmont Stakes, 144
Bennett Cocktail, 66
Bermuda Highball, 66
Bermuda Rose Cocktail,
  66
Berries 'n' Cream, 97
Berrissimmio, 48
Berry Berry, 234
Berta's Special, 129
Betsy Ross Cocktail, 37
Bijou Cocktail, 66
Bird of Paradise Cooler,
  67
Black Cat, 48
Blackberries & Cream,
  49
Blackberry Sip, 144
Black Cherry Margarita,
  49
Black Cherry Punch,
  203
Black Devil, 97
Black Honey, 212
Black Russian, 144
Blackthorn, 49, 159

Blackthorn Cocktail, 159
Black Widow, 97
Blended Comfort, 26
Blood & Sand Cocktail, 67
Bloody Bull, 144
Bloody Caesar, 144
Bloody Maria, 130
Bloody Mary, 144
Bloody 7, 160
Blue Bayou, 144, 191
Blueberry Freeze, 191
Blue Devil, 67
Blue Hawaiian, 97
Blue Lady, 49
Blue Lagoon, 49
Blue Lemonade, 145
Blue Meanie, 130
Blue Monday, 49
Blue Moon Cocktail, 67
Blue Moon Punch, 203
Blue Passion, 98
Blue Shark, 145
Bobby Burns Cocktail, 119
Boilermaker, 160
Bolero Cocktail, 98
Bombay Cocktail, 37
Bombay Punch, 203
Boomerang, 67
Bordeaux Punch, 204
Border Passion Margarita, 130
Bossa Nova, 37, 98
Bourbon and Branch, 26
Bourbon Cobbler, 27
Bourbon Collins, 27
Bourbon Sidecar, 27
Bourbon Sloe Gin Fizz, 27
Bourbon Sour, 27
Boxcar, 67
Brandied Peaches 'n' Cream, 191
Brandy Alexander, 191
Brandy Branch, 38
Brandy Eggnog Punch, 203
Brandy Fizz, 38
Brandy Punch, 207
Brandy Rim, 38
Brandy Sour, 38
Brave Bull, 130
Breeze Punch, 98
Brittany, 67

Bronx Cocktail, 68
Bronx River, 68
Brown Bear, 38
Brown Derby, 98
Bucking Irish, 160
Bullfrog, 145
Bullshot, 145
Bunny Bonanza, 130
Burnt Almond, 49
Buttoned Lip, 50

Cabaret Cocktail, 68
Cactus Colada, 130
Cactus Margarita, 131
Café Amaretto, 212
Café Amour, 212
Café aux Cognac, 213
Café Barbados, 213
Café-Cello, 213
Café de Paris Cocktail, 68
Café Michelle, 213
Café Royale, 213
Cajun Martini, 145
Californian, 145
California Swirl, 234
Calypso Cooler, 98
Campari, Gin, and Soda, 68
Canadian and Bitters, 160
Canadian Blackberry Fizz, 160
Canadian Cocktail, 160
Canadian Coffee, 213
Canadian Old-Fashioned, 161
Canadian Tea, 213
Cape Codder, 145
Cape Colada, 146
Captain Morgan Cinnamon Toast, 214
Captain Morgan's Daiquiri, 98
Captain's Berry Daiquiri, 192
Captain's Cap, 50
Captain's Choice, 192
Captain's Coconut Brownie, 214
Captain's Margarita, 99
Captain's Peach Daiquiri, 99
Captain's Smoothie, 192

Captain's Tropical Spiced Tea, 99
Capucello Cream Soda, 50
Capucello Dreamsicle, 50
Capucello Raspberry Creme, 50
Capucello Solo, 50
Capucello Tropico, 50
Caribbean Chat, 100
Caribbean Cooler, 99
Caribbean Grasshopper, 51
Caribbean Shooter, 38
Caribbean Smuggler, 99
Caribe Cocktail, 99
Caruso, 68
Casino, 68
Cha-Cha-Cha Cherry Margarita, 131
Champagne Punch, 204
Champagne Sherbet Punch, 204
Champagne Sorbet Punch, 204
Changuirongo, 131
Chapala, 131
Chanticleer, 69
Charmer, 119
Chartbuster, 234
Cheap Sunglasses, 51
Chelsea Sidecar, 69
Cherry Blossom, 38
Cherry-Cherry Boom, 237
Cherry Cobbler, 69
Cherry Hound, 51
Cherry Rummer, 234
Cherry Snap, 39
Cherry Sour, 161
Cherry Vanilla, 192
Chi-Chi, 146
Chilly Chocolate Mint, 100
Chocolate Almond, 51
Chocolate Banana, 192, 214
Chocolate Coffee, 214
Chocolate Dragon, 238
Chocolate Kiss, 214
Chocolate Malted, 238
Chocolate Mint, 215
Chocolate Sin, 215
Chocolate Tornado, 193
Christmas Cheer, 207

261

Chuckie's Chuckle, 193
Chuck Razzberry, 51
Ciao Baby, 100
Cider Cipher, 238
Cinnaccino, 215
Cinnamon Toast, 100
Citrus Cooler, 100
Clover Club Cocktail, 69
Cobana Coffee, 215
Co-Co Cow, 100
Coco Java, 215
Coco-Mocha Alexander, 193
Coconut Bon-Bon, 147
Coconut Cap, 51
Coconut Climber, 101
Coconut Daiquiri, 101
Coco Tropical, 235
Coffee Float, 215
Cognac and Cream, 216
Colada Fizz, 51
Colonial Cocktail, 69
Colony Club, 69
Cookie-Cello, 52
Cooler-than-Cool, 238
Cool Jazz, 184
Cool Kiss, 193
Cooperstown Cocktail, 69
Copperhead, 147
Copper Penny, 52
Cordial Colada, 235
Coronado, 70
Cosmopolitan, 147
Cossack, 147
Country & Western, 101
Count Stroganoff, 147
Cranapple Cheer, 235
Cranapple Toddy, 216
Cranberry Apple, 193
Cranberry Cooler, 52
Creamsicle Margarita, 193
Creamy Screwdriver, 147
Crème de Cacao Nightcap, 39
Crimson, 70
Crisp Apple Cocktail, 39
Crown and Cola, 161
Crownberry Royal, 161
Crowning Glory 161

Crown Jewels, 161
Cuba Libre, 101
Cupid's Arrow, 208
Cupid's Cocoa, 216
Daiquiri, 101
Danish Gin Fizz, 70
Deauville Cocktail, 39
Deep Sea, 70
Déjà Vu, 52
Delmonico Cocktail, 70
Derby, 70
Derby Fizz, 119
Diamond Fizz, 70
Diamond Head, 71
Diana Cocktail, 52
Dixie Cocktail, 71
Dixie Whiskey, 162
Dream Cocktail, 39
Dry Manhattan, 162
Dry Martini, 71
Dry Rob Roy, 119
Dubarry Cocktail, 71

East India Cocktail, 39
Eclipse, 194
Eggnog, 204
El Diablo, 131
Electric Banana, 52
Emerald Cooler, 71
Emerald Isle Cocktail, 71
Empire Punch, 184
Eskimo Kiss, 208
España Cocktail, 40
Everybody's Irish Cocktail, 162
Eve's Apple Daiquiri, 101

Fallen Angel Cocktail, 71
Falling Star, 102
Fancy Sparkling Punch, 205
Fare Thee Well, 72
Farmer's Cocktail, 72
Fashion Passion, 147
Fifty-Fifty, 72
Fino Martini, 72
Flamingo Cocktail, 72
Florida Banana, 148
Florida Daiquiri, 102
Florida Freeze, 102
Florida Punch, 102
Floridita Daiquiri, 102
Flying Grasshopper, 148

Foreign Affair, 40
Fort Lauderdale, 102
14-Carat Rock, 72
Fox Trot, 103
Frazzled Strawberry, 52
Free Silver, 72
French Collection, 40
French Curve, 186
French Rose, 73
French 75, 40
Frostbite, 132
Flying Horse, 40
Fro Jo, 194
Frozen Cactus Colada, 132
Frozen Cappuccino, 194, 238
Frozen Daiquiri, 103
Frozen Irish Coffee, 194
Frozen Matador, 132
Frozen Mint Julep, 27
Fruit Bang, 194
Fuzzy Charlie, 103
Fuzzy Charlie II, 103
Fuzzy Navel, 53

Genoa, 73
Georgia Peach, 148
Gibson Martini, 73
Gilroy, 73
Gimlet, 73
Gin Aloha, 73
Gin and Berries, 73
Gin and Bitters (Pink Gin), 74
Gin and Ginger, 74
Gin and Tonic, 74
Gin Buck, 74
Gin Cobbler, 74
Gin Cooler, 74
Gin Daisy, 74
Gin Fix, 75
Gin Fizz, 75
Gin Frozen Margarita, 75
Ginger Colada, 103
Ginger Snap, 103
Gin Margarita, 75
Gin Rickey, 75
Gin Sangaree, 75
Gin Sidecar, 75
Gin Sling, 76
Gin Sour, 76
Gin Swizzle, 76
Ginza Mary, 148
Glasgow, 119

Godfather, 119
Godiva Cafe, 216
Godiva Chocolate-
  Covered Berry, 216
Godiva Cocoa Latte, 53
Godiva Cream Soda, 53
Godiva Ice Cream Soda,
  53
Godiva Irish Coffee, 53
Godiva Irish Freeze, 53
Godiva Italiano, 53
Godiva Martini Noir, 53
Godiva Mocha Almond,
  53
Godiva Originale, 54
Godiva Peppermint Kiss,
  54
Godiva Whisper, 54
Godiva White Russian,
  54
Golden Daze, 76
Golden Fizz, 76
Golden Glow, 28
Golf Cocktail, 76
Gorky Park, 148
Grand Finale, 54
Grand Matador, 132
Grand Passion, 76
Grand Royal Fizz, 77
Grapefruit Cocktail, 77
Grapefruit Granita, 238
Grasshopper, 54
Grasshopper II, 55
Grasshopper Freeze,
  195
Great Dane, 77
Great Grape, 238
Great Secret, 77
Greenback, 77
Green Dragon, 77
Greyhound, 148
Grizzly Bear, 195
Grog, 208, 216
Groovy Guava, 239

Harvey Wallbanger, 149
Hasty Cocktail, 78
Havana Beach Cocktail,
  104
Hawaiian Cocktail, 78
Hawaiian Lemonade,
  149
Hazel Nut, 55
Hearts, 40
Hibiscus Holiday
  Margarita, 132

Highland Cooler, 120
Hole-in-One Cocktail,
  120
Homestead Cocktail, 78
Honey, Honey?, 236
Honey-Root Beer Float,
  195
Honolulu Cocktail, 78
Hoot Mon, 120
Hop Scotch, 120
Hot Apple Pie, 217
Hot Apple Pie II, 217
Hot Brown Cow, 217
Hot Buttered Rum, 217
Hot Buttered Rum II,
  217
Hot Buttered Rum
  Punch, 208
Hot Caribbean, 217
Hot Irish & Port, 218
Hot Milk Punch, 208
Hot Scotch, 218
Hot Toddy, 218
Hot Toddy 7, 218
Hula-Hula, 78
Hula Shake, 239
Hurricane, 104
Hurricane II, 104
Hurricane III, 162
Hurricane Cocktail,
  162

Ice Breaker, 40, 104
Ice Pick, 149
Ideal Cocktail, 78
Imperial Cocktail, 78
Income Tax Cocktail,
  79
Irish Angel, 162
Irish Apple Bowl, 205
Irish Coffee, 218
Irish Coffee II, 218
Irish Coffee III, 219
Irish Cooler, 163
Irish Delight, 163
Irish Eyes, 163
Irish Horseman, 163
Irish Kiss, 163
Irish Knight, 163
Irish Magic, 163
Irish Prince, 164
Irish Summer Coffee,
  164
Irish Tea, 219
Island Cocoa, 219
Italian Stinger, 40

Jamaican Blues, 104
Jamaican Queen, 195
Jamaican Shakin', 28
Jellybean, 41
Jolly Julep, 28
Journalist, 79
Judgette Cocktail, 79
Jujube, 55
Jupiter Cocktail, 79

Kaleidoswirl, 195
Kamikaze, 149
Kentucky Colonel
  Cocktail, 28
Kentucky Mock Julep,
  239
Kentucky Orange
  Blossom, 28
Key Club Cocktail, 79
Key Lime Quencher,
  104
Key West Song, 105
Kingston, 105
Kir Gin Cocktail, 79
Knickerbocker, 79
Koala Kolada, 236
Kremlin Kernel, 149
Kretchma Cocktail, 149
Kyoto Cocktail, 80

Ladies' Cocktail, 164
Lady Be Good, 41
Ladybug, 41
Lady Finger, 80
Lady Luck, 55
Lafayette, 29
Lavender Sunset, 196
Leap Frog Highball,
  80
Leap Year Cocktail,
  80
Lei Lani, 105
Lemon Cafe, 239
Liberty Cocktail, 55
Lichee Nut Cocktail,
  105
Licorice Slush, 149
Lime Love, 209
Little Eva, 186
Loch Lomond, 120
Loch Ness Mystery, 120
London Cocktail, 80
Long Beach Iced Tea,
  80
Long Island Iced Tea,
  80

Louisiana Planter's Punch, 205
Lounge Lizard, 105
Lounge Lizard II, 105
Lovebird, 55
Luscious Limeade, 239

Mad Hatter, 149
Madras, 106
Maiden's Blush Cocktail, 81
Mai Tai, 106
Mai Tai II, 106
Mai Tai Mai, 106
Mamie Taylor, 120
Mango Daiquiri, 106
Mango Madness, 239
Manhasset, 164
Manhattan, 164
Man o' War, 29
Margarita, 133
Margarita 43, 132
Mariachi Melon Margarita, 133
Martell Chanteloupe, 41
Martell Chic, 41
Martell Daisy, 41
Martell Emeraude, 41
Martell Freeze, 196
Martell Highball, 41
Martell President, 42
Martell Shake, 42
Martell Swing, 42
Martini, 81
Mary Pickford, 107
Matador, 133
Matinee, 81
Maurice, 81
Melonball, 150
Melon Cocktail, 81
Melon Spritz, 107
Melon Vodka Margarita, 150
Merry Widow, 81
Metro Cocktail, 42
Mexicana, 133
Mexican Berry, 133
Mexican Coffee, 219
Mexican Coffee II, 219
Miami Ice, 196
Million Dollar Cocktail, 81
Mint Chocolate Chiller, 196
Mint Collins, 82
Mint Condition, 240

Mint Julep, 29
Mint Sunrise, 121
Mint Whisper, 55
Minty Chocolate Smoothie, 240
Mississippi Mule, 82
Modern Cocktail, 121
Mojito, 107
Moldau, 82
Mom Collins, 240
Mon Cherie, 42
Monk's Secret, 56
Montmartre, 82
Moonchaser, 197
Moonshot, 82
Morgan Madras, 107
Morro, 82
Moscow Mule, 150
Mountain Red Punch, 205
Muddy River, 42
Mudslide, 150
Muscle Beach, 56
Multiple Orgasm, 150
Myers's Frozen Sharkbite, 196
Myers's Heatwave, 107
Myers's Original Hot Buttered Rum, 220
The Myers's Sharkbite, 107
Myrtle Bank Punch, 108
Mystical Swirl, 197

Napoleon, 82
Narragansett, 29
Nectarine Nirvana, 240
Newbury, 83
New Old-Fashioned, 164
New Orleans Buck, 108
New Orleans Cocktail, 29
New Orleans Fizz, 83
New Orleans Night, 150
Newport Cooler, 83
The New Wave, 56
New Yorker Cocktail, 164
Night Cap, 56
Night Flight, 220
1964 World's Fair Sangria, 207
Normandy Cocktail, 83

Northside Special, 108
North Star, 150
Nuclear Meltdown, 133
Nutty Banana, 56
Nutty Buddy, 236
Nutty Tropic, 56

Old Fashioned, 165
Olé, 134
Opera, 83
Operetta, 220
Orange Blossom, 83
Orange Crusher, 151
Orange Mocha, 220
Orange Oasis, 83
Orange Twizzle, 240
Out-of-This-World Punch, 206

Paisley Martini, 84
Palm Beacher, 108
Paradise Lost, 236
Park Avenue, 84
Parisian, 84
Passion Colada, 108
Patrón Blue Boss, 134
Patrón Cruiser, 134
Patrón Inferno, 134
Patrón Matador, 134
Patrón Silver Sunrise, 134
Patty's Pride, 165
Peach Blush Cooler, 186
Peach Daiquiri, 108
Peachee Keen, 57
Peachee Kir, 186
Peaches 'n' Honey, 197
Peach Fuzz, 56
Peachie Keen, 57
Peach Margarita, 135
Peach Melba, 109
Peach Punch, 109
Peach Refresher, 186
Peach Schnapps Splash, 56
Peachy Colada, 109
Peachy Keen, 236
Peanut Butter Coffee, 240
Peanut Butter Cup, 220
Peanut Butter Shake, 197
Pegu Club Cocktail, 84
Peppermint Treat, 57
Perfect Manhattan, 165

Perfect Martini, 84
Perfect Rob Roy, 121
Piccadilly Cocktail, 84
Piña Banana, 236
Piña Carrot Cocktail, 241
Piña Colada, 109
Piñata, 135
Pineapple Cancun Margarita, 135
Pineapple Lemonade, 151
Pink Baby, 151
Pink Elephant, 241
Pink Flamingo, 57
Pink Lady, 84
Pink Lemonade, 109
Pink Orchid, 109
Pink Panther, 151
Pink Pussycat, 84
Pink Rose, 85
Pink Squirrel, 57
Pinky & the Captain, 110
Pirate's Spiced Rum Tea, 220
Planter's Punch, 110
Pleasant Piña Colada, 241
Polar Ice Cap, 151
Polo Dream, 29
Polynesian Cocktail, 151
Polynesian Pepper Pot, 152
Polynesian Punch Bowl, 206
Port Sangaree, 186
Prairie Oyster, 152
Prince's Smile, 85
Princess Morgan, 110
Purple Passion, 152

Queen's Park Swizzle, 110

Racquet Club Cocktail, 85
Rainbow, 57, 152
Rainbow Crush, 197
Ramos Fizz, 85
R & B, 112
Raspberry Delight, 241
Raspberry Kir, 186
Raspberry Reef, 57

Raspberry Warm-up, 221
Razzaretto, 58
Razzle Dazzle, 58
Red Cloud, 85
Red Lion, 85
Red Ruby, 58
Red Snapper, 152
Reindeer Punch, 209
Remsen Cooler, 121
Renaissance, 86
Rendezvous, 86
Resolute Cocktail, 86
Rich Smooch, 237
Riviera Raspberry, 198
Rob Roy, 122
Rock and Rye Cooler, 153
Rocky Green Dragon, 86
Roman Cooler, 86
Roman Punch, 110
Rosita, 135
Rootarama Bananarama, 58
Root Beer, 42
Root-Beer Float, 198
Rootie Frootie, 58
Royal Chill, 165
Royal Family, 165
Royal Gin Fizz, 86
Royal L.A., 165
Royal Majic, 165
Royal Milk Punch, 166
Royal Peach, 166
Royal Regalia, 166
Royal Schnapreme, 166
Royal Splash, 166
Royal Stinger, 166
Royal Ward 8, 166
Ruby Tuesday, 58
Ruby Tuesday II, 58
Rum and Cola, 111
Rum and Ginger, 111
Rum Collins, 111
Rum Cup with White Wine, 206
Rum Fizz, 111
Rum Julep, 111
Rum Rickey, 111
Rum Runner, 111
Rum Sour, 112
Rummy Sour, 112
Russian Rose, 153
Rusty Aggravation, 121
Rusty Nail, 121

Sadie Song, 30
Saketini, 86
Salt Lick, 153
Salty Dog, 153
Salty John, 166
Scandinavian Martini, 153
Scepter, 167
Schnappin' Strawberries, 59
Schnappy Dresser, 59
Scorpion, 112
Scotch Buck, 121
Scotch Cobbler, 122
Scotch Holiday Sour, 122
Scotch Mist, 122
Scotch Old-Fashioned, 123
Scotch Orange Fix, 123
Scotch Rickey, 123
Scotch Smash, 124
Scotch Solace, 124
Scotch Sour, 124
Scotch Swizzle, 124
Screwdriver, 153
Screwy 7 Fizz, 167
Seabreeze, 153
Seagram's Dreamsicle, 198
Seagram's Gin Frisco Collins, 87
Seagram's Gin Gimlet, 87
Seagram's Gin Lemonade, 87
Seagram's Gin Salty Dog, 87
Seagram's High Tea, 87
Seagram's Pink Lemonade, 87
Seagram's 7 Sidecar, 167
Seagram's Sunburn, 87
Secret, 124
7 & 7, 168
7 Crown Collins, 168
7 Crown Julep, 168
7 Crown Rickey, 168
7 Highball, 168
7 'n' Bitters, 168
7 Seas, 168
7th Heaven, 169
7th Sunset, 169
Seville, 88
Sex on the Beach, 59
Shirley Temple, 241

Sidecar, 59
Silver Fizz, 88
Silver Fox, 59
Silver King Cocktail, 89
Silver Shell, 88
Singapore Sling, 89
Singapore Sling II, 89
Singing Orchard, 112
Sloe Gin Fizz, 59
Snake Bite, 169
Sneaky Peach, 59
Snowball, 89
Snowberry, 221
Soul Kiss, 30
Sour Passion, 242
Southern Ginger, 30
South of the Border, 169
Spiced Banana Daiquiri, 112
Spiced Java Smoothie, 198
Spirited Coconut Coffee, 221
Star Daisy, 89
Stinger, 42
Stone Fence, 125
Strawberry Banana Colada, 112
Strawberry Cooler, 186
Strawberry Daiquiri, 113
Strawberry Daiquiri II, 113
Strawberry Royal, 187
Strawberry 7, 169
Strawberry Spritzer, 241
Strawberry Whip, 198
Straw Honey, 237
Summer Lemonade, 153
Summer Sailor, 154
Summer Sunrise, 60
Sunnier Sour, 113
Sunniest Sour, 113
Sunny Sour, 113
Sunset, 43
Sunset Boulevard, 237
Sun Shine, 242
Super Sidecar, 43
Super Tart, 60
Sweet & Sour Bourbon, 30
Sweetheart Sip, 60
Sweet Martini, 89

Tall Guy, 242
Tango Cocktail, 89
Tea-Liscious, 221
Tequila Colada, 136
Tequila Collins, 136
Tequila Fizz, 136
Tequila Martini, 136
Tequilia-Nana Blizzard, 198
Tequila Rickey, 136
Tequila Sour, 137
Tequila Sunburst, 137
Tequila Sunrise, 137
Tequila Sunset Margarita, 138
Tequila Tango, 138
Tequini, 138
Tijuana Bulldog, 138
Tijuana Blues Margarita, 138
Tipperary, 169
T.L.C. (Tequila, Lime, Campari), 135
T.L.C. (Tequila, Lime, Cognac), 135
T.L.C. (Tequila, Lime, Cola), 136
Toasted Almond, 60
Tom Collins, 90
Top Ten, 113
Trilby Cocktail, 30
Trinidad, 199
Tropical Paradise, 114
Tropical Peach, 199
Tropical Treasure, 60
Tropic Colada, 60
Tropic Freeze, 114
T.T.T. (Tequila, Triple Sec, Tonic), 136
Tucson Tumbler, 139
Turtledove, 114
Tutti Frutti Crush, 199
Twin Six Cocktail, 90

Union Jack, 114

Valencia II, 43
Vanderbilt Cocktail, 43
Vanilla Cola, 242
Very Berry, 242
Very Berry Colada, 114

Vesuvio, 187
Virgin Mary, 242

Virgin Strawberry Margarita, 242
V.O. Canadian Cooler, 170
Vodka Collins, 154
Vodka Cooler, 154
Vodka Fizz, 154
Vodka Gimlet, 154
Vodka Grasshopper, 154
Vodka Martini, 154
Vodka Rickey, 154
Vodka Sling, 155
Vodka Sour, 155
Vodka Stinger, 155
Vodka Tonic, 155
V.O. Manhattan, 170
Voyager, 114

Waikiki Tiki, 115
Waldorf Cocktail, 31
Watermelon Cooler, 243
Wedding Belle Cocktail, 90
Wedding Cake I, 60
Wedding Cake II, 61
Western Rose, 90
Whiskey Cocktail, 170
Whiskey Sour, 170
Whisky Fizz, 170
Whisky Rickey, 170
Whisky Sling, 170
White Alexander, 90
White Elephant, 155
White Rose Cocktail, 90
White Russian, 155
White Sangria, 207
White Spider, 155
Wind Surf, 187
Wine Collins, 187
Witches Tail, 61
Wrath of Grapes, 115
Write-Off, 61

Xanthia Cocktail, 90

Yellow Parrot Cocktail, 43
Yellow Bird, 115
Yellow Bird II, 115
Ye Olde Egg Cream, 243

Zero Mint Julep, 171
ZuZu's Petals, 91